Religious Tolerance, E(
the Curriculum

Religious Tolerance, Education and the Curriculum

Edited by

Elizabeth Burns Coleman
Monash University

Kevin White
Australian National University

SENSE PUBLISHERS
ROTTERDAM/BOSTON/TAIPEI

A C.I.P. record for this book is available from the Library of Congress.

ISBN: 978-94-6091-410-2 (paperback)
ISBN: 978-94-6091-411-9 (hardback)
ISBN: 978-94-6091-412-6 (e-book)

Published by: Sense Publishers,
P.O. Box 21858,
3001 AW Rotterdam,
The Netherlands
https://www.sensepublishers.com

Printed on acid-free paper

TABLE OF CONTENTS

ACKNOWLEDGEMENTS

We would like to express our thanks to the Australian National University Research School for the Humanities, the Freilich Foundation, GovNet (an Australian Research Council Research Network) and the Centre for Applied Philosophy and Public Ethics (an Australian Research Council funded Special Research Centre) for their support of the conference, Tolerance, Education and the Curriculum, which formed the basis for this collection. This is the fourth volume based on a series of conferences under the umbrella 'Negotiating the Sacred' that were supported, technically and intellectually, by the then Centre for Cross Cultural Studies at the Australian National University. We are extremely gratefully to Professor Howard Morphy and his staff for this support. We also are extremely grateful, yet again, for the support and commitment of Maria-Suzette Fernandes Dias.

ELIZABETH BURNS COLEMAN AND KEVIN WHITE

INTRODUCTION

Education may be considered central to the development of a tolerant society. In *Intolerance, the Ecoli of the Mind*, Donald Akenson argues that the education system was one of the main institutional structures that maintained sectarian intolerance within Ireland.[1] According to Akenson, the creation of a secular education system was one of the great social experiments designed to break down these social divisions. One of the elements was administrative, involving non-denominational or mixed schools, and the other involved a centralised curriculum that had been approved by major religious groups and promoted civic virtue. With increasing tensions based on religious belief in many multicultural societies, it is an appropriate time to revisit the assumptions and practice of secular education, and the contemporary issues that have arisen in attempting to meet these ideals. Is a secular, non-denominational education system the only means of breaking down intolerance? Does secular education necessarily involve the provision of an environment that is free from all religious symbolism and doctrine? State education systems centralise curriculum in order to ensure that all children receive an adequate education, but may it be equally considered an imposition of a specific form of materialism?

This volume of collected papers arose from a small, interdisciplinary conference on the theme of 'Toleration, Education and the Curriculum' held at the Australian National University's Research School of the Humanities over 1–2 September 2007. This conference brought together sociologists, lawyers, philosophers and education-alists to discuss the issue of the role of education in promoting tolerance within multicultural societies. Many of the chapters in this volume were presented at the conference, although some have changed quite dramatically in their final form as a result of the discussions and disagreements that took place, while other papers were commissioned to provide a point of comparison or to explore an issue in greater depth.

Four major themes arose in the discussion. The first was the ways in which different models of liberalism and the secular state may have very different outcomes in relation to the education system. The second and third themes that arose concerned the whether the state education system had a role in teaching values, such as tolerance, and if so, how was this best achieved. The fourth theme challenged the manner in which liberalism constructs or frames religion, but also the manner in which the ideal of a 'value free' education masks the values that the secular state teaches. We have not, however, attempted to force the various papers into discrete sections on these ideas but have allowed them to refer back and forwards as the result of these conversations.

Our first chapter, by Susan Mendus, explores the question of why issues such as the wearing of headscarves in state-run schools have such different administrative and public reactions in different liberal democracies. Whereas the wearing of head-scarves is not an issue in the UK, it has become a major issue in France. Mendus traces the source of these reactions to different models of liberalism: 'perfect' or comprehensive liberalism, and political liberalism. Comprehensive liberalism involves encouraging citizens to adopt liberal values, whereas political liberalism asks simply that they be good citizens. Initially, political liberalism appears the more liberal as it does not assume that citizens will hold specific values. However, it seems that comprehensive liberalism is better able to negotiate difference in multicultural societies.

Chapters two and three explore some of the major political issues over state funding for religious schools in the USA and Australia, and the role of religion within those schools. In chapter two, Janice R. Russell and James T. Richardson trace the history of funding for religious schools from the early 1600s, when the public education system was established with the purpose of ensuring children had the education necessary to obtain salvation and reflected Protestant values, and argue that public education system has significantly evolved in purpose, and in relation to the tolerance with which religious ideas and values may be taught or expressed. These changes are especially evident after 1947, when a decision of the Supreme Court found that state law must comply with the Constitution. The First Amendment of the Constitution guarantees individual freedom of religion and precludes the establishment of a state religion. Since 1947, challenges to religious instruction in public schools in the Supreme Court have led to the reduction of certain religious activities in public schools in line with the ideal of separation of church and state. In contrast, in Australia religious schools have been funded by the state, and the High Court rejected the idea that the funding for religious schools contravened the requirement for a separation between church and state in the Constitution. Financially, religious schools have benefited not only from direct grants, but also from generous taxation provisions for gifts to schools. However, state governments require that religious schools are registered, and a condition of this is that they teach the same syllabus as a public school, although this may be modified upon application. There is freedom about what else may be taught, and, except in relation to whether corporal punishment is acceptable, religious schools have autonomy, and religious instruction in public education has not become a flash point for legal challenge as found in the United States.

It does not follow from the relative legal quietude of the Australian legal system, however, that the same the questions about values in the school curriculum do not arise. Indeed, the teaching of children leads inevitably to the question of 'which' values should be taught within an education system, what holding those values really means, and how they are best taught.

Peter Balint presents two different interpretations on the concept of tolerance, a thick, rich conception of tolerance as respect for and appreciation of difference, and a thin model of tolerance as forbearance. He argues that the thin conception of tolerance not only makes the most sense, and against the approaches of other contributors in this volume (Windle, who thinks we should confront specific pre-judices with information, and Laura and Chapman, and de Silva, who suggest that students should be taught to practice empathy) that the fundamental means by which public education systems should teach tolerance is through ensuring that students are aware that respect for the rights of different people is non-negotiable. Balint's approach may be considered a form of political liberalism: he suggests that within a liberal society, not all the views of citizens need to be to be liberal; what matters is that they respect the liberal position of the state. Most of the contributors to this volume would disagree, however, and argue that tolerance, and the values and dispositions that promote it, should be a fundamental concern of the education system. The question then arises - how should it be taught?

Philip Cam (chapter 5), also a liberal philosopher, interprets tolerance not as not 'forbearance', but as the 'limits of variation within which a system can function without significantly affecting its performance'. However, the significant difference between Balint and Cam is in the resources Cam finds in liberalism for promoting a concern with the attitudes and values of individuals. For instance, he argues that according to John Locke, religious tolerance requires both an attitude to be expressed towards others, 'the common offices of humanity and friendship', and that we should overcome our ignorance by engaging 'in all the gentle and fair ways of information'. In John Stuart Mill, Cam finds the promotion of intellectual virtues, in particular the love of truth and evidence, offered as a means of combating prejudice and intolerance in out societies. Cam suggests that these virtues are required in order to develop the dispositions of tolerance.

In chapter 6, Joel Windle, an education theorist, argues that the state education system has a major role in promoting tolerance and actively combating contemporary prejudices through the provision of information about the groups that are most likely to suffer from the intolerance of others. In Australia, this involves educating children about Islam. Muslims represent a mere one per cent of the population, and yet are perceived as a threat. Windle's analysis of the root of prejudice, like Locke's and Mill's, perceives misinformation and ignorance as the foundation of prejudice and intolerance. Accordingly, he argues that the provision of information about the Islamic faith should be provided within the curriculum. The link between receipt of information and attitude change is not secure, as is shown by the empirical research into whether the provision of information change attitudes, and when it is most likely to be effective. As Windle points out, it may occasionally be the case that the provision of information does not change intolerance of certain things or towards certain groups, however, if this were the case, the intolerance could no longer be considered a 'prejudice', as the term prejudice implies a lack of information or some kind of want of reasoning. Finally, Windle concerns himself with where in the curriculum such material should be introduced, and how, arguing that this should be included in all aspects of the curriculum, as has been the case for combating ignorance of, and prejudices towards, Australian indigenous peoples.

In chapter 7, Winifred Lamb argues that how one understands 'truth' is important for understanding fundamentalism and questions of intolerance. Today's teenagers, she points out, often assume that relativism about truth is necessary for tolerance of others. From such a perspective, the bold truth claim of the believer is seen as an impediment to engagement with others. Similarly, many political philosophers have assumed that religion and 'metaphysical thinking' leads to closed minded intolerance. An example of this is JJ Rousseau's assertion that theological intolerance must necessarily lead to social intolerance. Lamb argues against the position that faith is necessarily intolerant from a theological perspective concerned with the epistemology of faith. While acknowledging that in fact there may be some religious believers who are intolerant of others, Lamb traces the source of such disagreement to conceptions of truth that are held by the people disagreeing. Rather than address 'intolerance' directly, which raises complex issues such as 'To whom should we be tolerant?' 'What are the limits of tolerance?' 'Is tolerance always a virtue?', Lamb focuses on the concept of dialogue and our ability to understand and to engage with others. Lamb suggests that a concern for truth in our exchanges with others necessarily involves not only questions of epistemology, but also a concern with our accountability for our beliefs.

Padmasiri de Silva (a Buddhist counsellor and philosopher, chapter 8) argues that schools should promote tolerance through the development of a skill in empathetic listening. According to de Silva, tolerance and empathy are 'natural allies' and a pedagogy and a curriculum that fosters empathy would also foster tolerance. He argues that in western academic culture, most listening is critical listening: we pay attention long enough to develop a counter argument. In responding to the speaker this way, we fail to engage with them as a person, and when we critique the student's or the colleague's writings, we mentally grade them. Secondly, he argues, we have developed a whole culture of techniques focused on speed, accuracy, rigour and certainty, extending its hegemony not only to education and work but also the way we spend our leisure and even our kids at play. But we also need a less deliberative and a slower and intuitive approach to deal with situations more intricate, shadowy and at times seeming paradoxes. Quoting Jon Kabat-Zinn, a pioneer in contemplative education, de Silva argues that 'When you are grounded in calmness and moment-moment awareness, you are most likely to be creative and to see new options, new solutions to problems'.

The final two chapters of the collection deal with the place of values in the education sector. Continuing this epistemological theme, Ronald S. Laura and Amy K. Chapman argue that, according to what might be termed 'the dominant paradigm of educational epistemology', the objectivity of scientific knowledge ensures that what we know is value-free, as is the technology which derives from it. The assumption behind this dominant paradigm of epistemology is that what we come to know is neither good nor bad, but rather value-neutral. It is how people use knowledge and the technological innovations to which it gives rise which determines its moral status. Laura and Chapman argue that most education is a form of 'transformative subjugation'. According to Laura and Chapman, 'what we claim to know, implicitly, is defined by the capacity of what is "known" to provide us a power advantage over the world in which we live'. Laura and Chapman argue that within the educational curriculum, there is a conceptually endogenous bias in favour of an epistemology, not only of control, but of subjugation. Given that the primary form of knowledge which underpins the curriculum is driven an obsession with power and dominance, much of the technology which follows from it will be designed and deployed in ways that allow us to restructure the world so that it suits our interests, which aggrandizes the freedom human kind has to desacralise and denigrate the earth and other peoples as a resource for our own ends.

In the final chapter, Anthony Manseuto takes up the opportunity of a debate at Harvard University on whether a unit in comparative religion should be taught as a core unit in a liberal arts education to reflect on the role of religion in the creation of what we now recognise as a liberal arts education. Manseuto sets out his reasons for considering the study of religion fundamental to the capacity of students to question social value, and to understand their societies. Finally, he sets out an agenda for how religion should be taught within universities and argues that instead of a 'core unit', religious issues should be addressed across the curriculum. In his essay, Manseuto observes that there is a difference between the establishment a 'secular state', and a state that has disestablished its connection with a particular religion. This distinction, although not identical with the distinction Mendus draws between comprehensive and political liberalism in our introduction, complements this idea to develop new ways of considering how we articulate the dynamics of religious pluralism in contemporary societies, and the assumptions that are made in political debates about the meaning of liberalism, as well as the place of religion in our societies.

This is the fourth volume resulting from the series of conferences on the theme 'Negotiating the Sacred', which cumulatively explored questions of multiculturalism, tolerance and religious beliefs and practices. The other titles are: *Medicine, Religion and the Body* (Leiden: Brill, 2009); *Negotiating the Sacred II: Blasphemy and Sacrilege in the Arts* (Canberra: ANU E-press, 2008); *Negotiating the Sacred: Blasphemy and Sacrilege in a Multicultural Society* (Canberra: ANU E-press, 2006).

NOTES

[1] Donald Akenson, *Intolerance, the Ecoli of the Mind*, Canberra: Humanities Research Centre, Australian National University, 2004.

SUSAN MENDUS

1. RELIGION AND EDUCATION

More on God v John Rawls[1]

On the morning of 2 October 1989, three teenage girls—Samira Saidani, Leila
Achaboun and her sister Fatima—set off for the Gabriel-Havez secondary school in
the small industrial town of Creil in northern France. The three girls were Muslims
who had decided to wear headscarves to cover their hair in public at all times. They
must have known that their decision would immediately bring them into conflict
with the school authorities because they had been involved in disputes over this
issue in the previous school year and in fact just three days earlier, a teacher had
excluded Samira from a lesson, writing on her report card that this was because she
refused to remove her headscarf in class.

Earlier in the year, the principal of Gabriel-Havez school, M. Ernest Chenière,
had made a ruling about headscarves, which established a policy that they must be
dropped to the shoulders during lessons but could be worn during private study
in the library. His decision represented a compromise which had been reached after
a long-running dispute about the wearing of scarves in class. As one commentator
put it: 'The principal feared that if he allowed the three girls to wear their headscarves, he next would have thirty wearing them, and then twenty Jewish students
again refusing to attend school on Fridays and Saturdays, and then community chaos.
So he prohibited the wearing of headscarves in class, and Leila, Fatima and Samira
refused to attend class without them, other students became radicalized, the national
press began to cover the story, and then there was community chaos nonetheless'.[2]

What happened next put Creil at the eye of an increasingly violent political storm.
The then Education Minister, Lionel Jospin, over-ruled the suspension and ordered
that the girls be re-admitted to classes even if they continued to wear their headscarves. M. Chenière, the principal, refused to follow this instruction and he was
backed by his teaching staff. It was not *illegal* in France to wear the headscarf in
class and other students at other schools continued to do so, but M. Chenière was
not prepared to allow it at Gabriel-Havez. Thus, the *affaire du foulard* was born
and it escalated because the school authorities interpreted the girls' actions as a
deliberate challenge to a secular tradition of public education which they were
determined to defend.

Fifteen years passed, but the *affaire* did not go away. From time to time, it fell
quiet and from time to time, it flared up again. Finally, in 2004, a law was passed
that prohibited the wearing of conspicuous religious apparel in public schools in
France. This includes large crucifixes and Jewish skull caps, but the real 'mischief'
against which the law is aimed is the wearing of the headscarf and indeed, since

E.B. Coleman and K. White (eds.), Religious Tolerance, Education and the Curriculum, 1–9.

2004, other countries have also sought to ban the headscarf in schools and, more recently, some have sought to ban the wearing of the burqa in all public places.[3]

CRISIS? WHAT CRISIS?

I have chosen to make the *affaire du foulard* central to this paper for two reasons: the first is that it is a practical case and therefore may be a useful way of testing more abstract principles, whether educational principles in particular, or principles of political philosophy in general. Just to anticipate a little—if we think that one of the main values of a liberal society is individual autonomy, and if we think that one of the main purposes of education is to instil or promote autonomy in pupils, then we might wonder what an understanding of education as autonomy-promoting would imply for policies which ban the wearing of headscarves in schools. Is such a ban neglectful of the autonomous decisions made by Muslim girls, or is the headscarf a manifestation of the oppression, rather than the autonomy of women? How does moral and political principle translate into public policy?

However, the second reason for choosing this example is that although it is often useful to test principles against practical cases, the *affaire du foulard* seems to be a case in which it is not entirely clear which principles are at stake. I say this partly because although, in France, the *affaire* was hugely divisive, similar cases have prompted very little controversy in the United Kingdom where there was (and remains) widespread bewilderment as to what the French were making a fuss about. It is of course true that there have been controversial cases in the U.K. (the case of Shabina Begum, for instance[4]), and it is also true that some British politicians have recently objected to the wearing of the burqa, but there has been no general proposal to ban the wearing of headscarves in schools and the issue is, in general, much less controversial in Britain than in France.

Just to underscore the differences between France and the U.K, it is worth noting that in 1990 (less than a year after the incident at Creil), two girls were sent home from Altrincham Grammar School for Girls because they were wearing headscarves but, within a week, the head teacher's decision had been overturned, the girls had returned to school, and very little more was heard of the matter.[5] I hasten to add that I don't draw this contrast in an attempt to try to show that the U.K. is more tolerant than France. Rather, I raise it in order to emphasise that teachers, politicians, and ordinary citizens in the U.K. were at a loss to know what principle was being invoked by those who wished to ban the headscarf. 'If people want to wear scarves to school, that's up to them'—was roughly the thinking in Britain. By contrast, in France, the debate ran for years, it was a national debate, and it was conducted at the very highest political level. It also prompted large demonstrations of public opinion in favour of the ban and, indeed, by the end of 1989 (just three months after the initial exclusion of the three girls from their secondary school), opinion polls showed that the vast majority of non-Muslims in France supported the ban, and indeed that most Muslims were also against wearing headscarves in school.

This stark difference in public opinion between two sister countries of the European Union—between France, on the one hand, and the U.K. on the other—is intriguing: both are liberal societies, both are societies with significant Muslim minorities, and (regrettably) both are societies which suffer from racial and religious intolerance. Moreover, it isn't simply that the two countries differ in their answers to the problem of 'veiling' as it is often called; it is rather that in the U.K. veiling is a very small problem, if a problem at all, whereas in France veiling is the source of enormous controversy.

Why are there these differences and what are the implications of them for liberal societies and for liberal political philosophy? These are the questions I want to address here and, just to anticipate, I want to suggest that the answer lies in the different 'flavours' of liberalism adopted by France, on the one hand, and the U.K. on the other. I will say more about that and about its implications towards the end of the paper. For now, however, I will focus on the question of why these two liberal democracies have such dramatically different approaches to veiling and, especially, to veiling in an educational context.

My answer comes in three parts: first I will say something about why, as a matter of fact and as a matter of history, 'veiling' is a particularly contentious issue in France; then I will say something about the principles that underpin different kinds of liberalism and about the ways in which these different kinds of liberalism imply different educational practices. Finally, I will make some rather speculative remarks about the relationship between liberalism and problems of cultural and religious diversity.

First, however, a few words about the overall 'shape' of the problem. In 'The Idea of an Overlapping Consensus' John Rawls famously remarks that 'the aims of political philosophy depend on the society it addresses' and he goes on to note that modern, democratic societies are characterised by the fact of pluralism.[6] They are societies that contain people with vastly different conceptions of the good, and vastly different understandings of the best way to lead one's life morally speaking. The pressing question, therefore, for modern democratic societies, is how all these different kinds of people (people with different preferences, different moral beliefs, and different religious beliefs) might nonetheless live together in conditions of peace and stability.

Moreover, and crucially for Rawls, the fact of pluralism is permanent. It is not going to go away, indeed it is increasing and we should not regret the fact that it is increasing because this plurality (diversity of opinion and belief about the best way to lead one's life) is the natural outcome of the operation of reason under conditions of freedom. Unlike science, where we expect that, over time, people will come to converge on a single right answer to problems, morality and religion are areas where we must expect divergence, not convergence. The only societies where there is convergence and unanimity about the right way to lead one's life are societies where there is an enforced orthodoxy.

So pluralism is the natural outcome when human beings are able to use their reason freely about matters of morality, and the aims of political philosophy in modern societies reflect this fact: in conditions of modernity, our central question is not Plato's question: 'What is the best way to live?'; our central question is 'How should we live together given that we cannot agree about the best way to live?'

In other words, our question is 'How can people of very different and conflicting moral and religious conviction live together harmoniously in a single society?' With that preliminary stated, then, I will now move on to my first theme—the veiling case and the question: 'why was it (and is it) so contentious in France?'

VEILING: SOME PRACTICAL CONSIDERATIONS

There are three, inter-connected, considerations that help to explain why veiling was (and is) so very problematic in France: the first concerns state policies for handling cultural (including religious) diversity; the second concerns the relationship between church and state; the third concerns the purposes of education. I will discuss them in that order.

Cultural Diversity: Assimilation or Plurality

Given that pluralism is permanent, how should we deal with it? There are, broadly speaking, two kinds of response to this question: assimilation and diversity. France officially adopts the former response; the U.K. officially adopts the latter. So, consider the different responses of the two countries in their reports to the United Nations Human Rights Council. The U.K. report reads:

> Although it is hoped that minority groups will ultimately be fully integrated into British society, integration is not seen as a flattening process of assimilation, but as equality of opportunity accompanied by cultural diversity in an atmosphere of mutual toleration.[7]

By contrast, the French report reads:

> …indivisible, secular, democratic and social. It shall ensure the equality of all citizens before the law, without distinction…of origin, race or religion. It shall respect all beliefs, since the basic principles of public law prohibit distinction between citizens on grounds of origin, race, or religion. France is a country in which there are no minorities…[8]

The distinction is, I think, pretty clear: in France, the aspiration is that of assimilation: in the end, members of minorities will come to think of themselves as French citizens and not as members of a minority group. Self-identification as a member of a minority bespeaks political failure. By contrast, the aspiration in Britain is to retain minorities with their different cultural practices and religious convictions, and to aspire to a society in which those differences do not cause antagonism or mutual hostility. So, in France, the response to minorities is to aim for their assimilation into the wider citizenry; in Britain the response is to nurture diversity but without antagonism or animosity. Why do the different countries have these different responses to diversity and, in particular, why is France so enthusiastically assimilationist? The answer to that question lies in the history of France and, in particular, in the vexed history of the relationship between church and state. This, then, is the second consideration.

Church and State

Here, the crucial point to bear in mind is that the Revolution of 1789 which overthrew the King and established the first French Republic also attacked the position of the church, which had been closely associated with the defence of the monarchy. The association of republicanism and secularism was, therefore, a legacy of the French Revolution and a legacy which made the role of the church in French society a deeply divisive one throughout the nineteenth century.

After the final defeat of Napoleon and the restoration of the monarchy in 1815, the Catholic Church became a bastion of the political right and opposition between republicanism and the church (the Catholic Church) became a persistent feature of French politics. In short, then, in the revolutionary and post-revolutionary period religion was deeply political and deeply divisive. It was precisely in order to 'keep the lid' on those differences—precisely in order to handle religious difference and to ensure equal rights for all under the law and independent of religious conviction or affiliation—that the French republic became, and remains, self-consciously and determinedly secular. In the French republican tradition, people may have whatever religious beliefs they want, but those beliefs must not be introduced into the public world or the political arena. Moreover, if religious differences are to be rendered politically and legally irrelevant by confining them to a private sphere, then education will be an important means for bringing about this objective. This brings me to the final consideration—education.

Purposes of Education

In a world that had been riven by religious discord, and where religious differences had historically hardened into political ones (in the nineteenth century, the Catholic Church was closely associated with the political right), it was thought that the proper strategy for managing pluralism and ensuing peaceful coexistence lay in keeping religion out of the public sphere. The French republic would therefore be strictly neutral between religious faiths, and it would gain that neutrality by determinedly separating religious belief from public life.

One way—one very important way—of ensuring that religion and politics did not occupy the same 'space' (that religion did not occupy the public square, as it is sometimes expressed) was through state education. Religious influence in schools was therefore constructed so as to prioritise the universal values of the republic which guaranteed the equality of all French citizens, and secularism thus became a crucial part of an education system which strongly emphasised the benefits that everyone derives from that French citizenship. In other words, French schools had and have a very active role in promoting the linked values of secularism, republicanism, and French national identity. They had—and should have—no role in supporting religious belief and indeed they should keep reference to religious conviction (which was both irrelevant and politically divisive) out of the school room.[9]

Sum
↑

In short, then, the secularism of the French state and of French education initially, and perhaps ironically, arose in an attempt to defuse extensive, and bloody, religious and political conflict. From the outside, it is easy to see the banning of headscarves as simply a manifestation of racism, or of bigotry, and those elements were indeed present to an alarming degree. But sympathy for the ban extended also to the political left and, especially, to some feminists who, in an open letter to *Le Nouvel Observateur* (November 1989), accused Jospin (who had overruled the headscarves ban) of 'selling out' the French national tradition of secular education.[10] And one leading feminist, Elisabeth Badinter, who was a signatory to the open letter, wrote: 'people must be reminded that the secular state school means neutrality imposed on everybody…it is the only way to cement our national community'.[11] So, it was not only the extreme right who favoured an insistence on secularism and the banning of the headscarves; this position also found favour amongst the political left and indeed amongst feminists many of whom saw the headscarves as symbols of female oppression.

how many
of those
were Muslim
women?

These, then, are some of the main practical factors contributing to and explaining the policy of *laïcité* (secularism) in France generally and in the French education system in particular. What are its philosophical and educational underpinnings? In the next section, I will turn to that question, and in the final, very brief, section I will make some rather speculative remarks about liberal political theory more generally.

PHILOSOPHICAL AND EDUCATIONAL PRINCIPLES

If, as Rawls and others insist, the fact of pluralism is permanent, then the question arises 'on what grounds, and to what degree, should we tolerate diversity?' There are two main ways of responding to this question: the first defends toleration on grounds of neutrality—the state should accommodate diversity by being strictly neutral between competing conceptions of the good. The second defends toleration on grounds of individual autonomy: the state should ensure that people are able to lead the kind of life they want to lead. They should be (as we might say) 'authors of their own lives'. The former claim is often associated with what is called political liberalism; the latter with comprehensive (or perfectionist) liberalism.

The differences between these two forms of liberalism are (or can be) stark in the area of education. Political liberals emphasise neutrality and urge that state education is, above all, education for citizenship: pupils should be equipped with the knowledge and skills necessary to be fully functioning and participating citizens of the society. Their education should not aim to instil liberal virtues, such as individuality or autonomy, and the reason for this is that since pluralism about the good is permanent, it would be wrong to use education to instil just one set of virtues—liberal virtues.

political
liberals

By contrast, comprehensive liberals believe that it is an important purpose of education in a liberal society to instil liberal virtues and, in particular, to educate for that quintessential liberal virtue—autonomy. To dramatise the difference between the two kinds of liberalism, and the two kinds of education they dictate, here are

6 *comprehensive*
liberals

two quotations—the first comes from John Rawls, and exemplifies the understanding of education implicit in political liberalism; the second comes from Joseph Raz and exemplifies the understanding of education implicit in comprehensive (perfectionist) liberalism. Rawls writes:

> Political liberalism does not seek to cultivate the distinctive virtues and values of…autonomy and individuality. We try to answer the question of children's education entirely within the political conception. Society's concern with their education lies in their role as future citizens.[12]

By contrast, Raz writes: 'For those who live in an autonomy-supporting environment, there is no choice but to be autonomous: there is no other way to prosper in such a society'.[13] So, for Rawls, education for autonomy is to be avoided because autonomy is a distinctively liberal virtue, and the purpose of education is simply to equip people with the skills needed for citizenship. It is not to make them into liberals. By contrast, and for Raz, education is a matter of ensuring that people have the ability to flourish in the society in which they find themselves, and in societies like ours (western liberal democracies) that means that education must encourage and enable pupils to become autonomous—to be authors of their own lives and to decide, independent of their background, culture, or religion, how they want their lives to be.

It is often thought that political liberalism makes room for greater diversity than does comprehensive liberalism: to educate for autonomy is, it is said, to attempt to instil in pupils the qualities of character that will make them liberals, not simply citizens of a liberal society. However, if we map this claim on to the *affaire du foulard* it delivers (I think) a rather odd conclusion. The explicit aim of French public education is to educate for citizenship. In that sense, the French system is explicitly political and, as has been indicated already, its *raison d'être* is precisely to avoid the encouragement of values associated with any religious conviction at all. Whether it succeeds in this aim is, of course, a separate matter, but that is its aim. What is also true, however, is that this aim—this explicitly political aim—is conspicuously intolerant of diversity. It is because everyone must first and foremost think of themselves as citizens that the French education system finds veiling much more problematic than it is in societies such as the U.K. where (traditionally) there has been very little concern to educate for citizenship. So the *affaire du foulard* seems to me to cast doubt on the claim that political liberalism is more tolerant and accommodating of diversity than comprehensive liberalism. To put the point rather bluntly, education for citizenship can be non-sectarian only on the assumption that the skills and qualities needed for citizenship are themselves non-sectarian. But those skills are not necessarily non-sectarian. They may, as the French case suggests, be rather forthrightly secular and, to that extent, quite inhospitable to religious diversity.

What, then, of the alternative account—the comprehensive or perfectionist form of liberalism according to which education is a matter of enabling students to develop autonomy? If we map that on to the *affaire du foulard*, what are the results? Here, there are deep difficulties, not least because the argument from autonomy can appear to cut both ways: on the one hand, it might be said, the girls themselves wanted to wear the headscarf and therefore respect for their autonomy seems to require that they be allowed to do so. On the other hand, however, there are those (for instance, feminists such as Elisabeth Badinter) who wonder whether the desire to wear a scarf is itself a sign of heteronomy rather than autonomy: a symbol of oppression and a sign that the girls are not autonomous, but are 'led' by the senior members of their community. And of course, this concern is especially pressing in educational contexts where, by definition, we are dealing with young people who may not yet have a clear idea of what they themselves want as distinct from what their parents want, or what their religious leaders want, or what other girls in their group want.

some adults still don't differen- tiate

Just to summarise, then, I began with a puzzle: 'why is it that "veiling" has been such a controversial issue in France, but has been largely unproblematic in the U.K?' These are both liberal societies and what is odd is not simply that the two societies offer different solutions to the problem; what is odd is that in one society there seems not to be much of a problem at all, whereas in the other the problem is urgent and divisive. Having noted this difference, I then tried to explain how and why the question of veiling came to be problematic in France and, in particular, I noted that it is problematic in some part because the secularism of French education is a deliberate attempt to ensure cultural harmony and to avoid cultural and religious divisiveness. However, as things have turned out, what is officially a 'thinner' and more accommodating form of liberalism (political liberalism) with its emphasis on education for citizenship only, has emerged, in this context, as no more—and possibly less—accommodating than the 'thicker' form of liberalism (comprehensive liberalism) which emphasises the need to inculcate liberal virtues and values. This is an odd turn of events and one which, I believe, raises important questions about liberal political philosophy itself. I will end by saying just a few words about these questions.

LIBERAL POLITICAL PHILOSOPHY

There are just two points that I want to make in conclusion. The first is that liberal political philosophy is (to my mind) strangely insensitive to the historical and cultural background against which its own problems arise. It is, of course, often noted that Holocaust denial is properly an offence in Austria, but not in the United Kingdom, and the reason for that difference is properly traced to the different histories of the two countries. Beyond that, however, there is very little discussion of whether, and why, different histories might make different approaches to toleration appropriate. This strikes me as a mistake.

The second point I want to make is connected, and it is that, in political philosophy, discussion of religious diversity and educational policy is dominated by writers in the Anglo-American tradition and indeed is largely dominated by Americans. But the history of cultural and religious diversity in the United States is very distinctive. It is quite different from that history in France, or the U.K, or indeed in Australia. If, as Rawls insists, the aims of political philosophy depend on the society it addresses, then perhaps liberal writers would do well to look more closely at the differences that divide actual liberal societies, and at the different strategies that we may therefore need to adopt in order to attain the same, liberal, aspirations.

NOTES

[1] My subtitle is a reference to Stephen Macedo's justly famous article from 1995, 'Liberal Civic Education and Religious Fundamentalism: The Case of God v John Rawls?' in *Ethics*, 105 (3), pp. 468–496.

[2] NC Moruzzi (1994), 'A problem with headscarves: Contemporary complexities of political and social identity', *Political Theory*, 22(4), pp. 653–672.

[3] Spain, France and Belgium have all initiated burqa bans and, at the time of writing (13th July 2010), the French National Assembly voted 335-1 in favour of a ban on the burqa in public places. Unlike the foulard, the burqa covers the face and body completely.

[4] Regina (Begum) v. Governors of Denbigh High School (2006) UKHL 15.

[5] See Sebastian Poulter (1997), 'Muslim Headscarves in Schools: Contrasting Legal Approaches in England and France', *Oxford Journal of Legal Studies*, 17(1), pp. 43–74.

[6] John Rawls (1999), 'The Idea of an Overlapping Consensus' in Samuel Freeman (ed.) *John Rawls: Collected Papers*. Harvard University Press, pp. 421–448.

[7] Cited in Pouler, 'Muslim Headscarves in Schools', p. 53.

[8] Ibid.

[9] Pouler's article provides an account of the legal history concerning religion and education in France.

[10] Mouruzzi, 'A problem with headscarves', p. 659.

[11] Maxim Silverman (1992) *Deconstructing the nation: Immigration, racism and citizenship in modern France*. London: Routledge, p. 114.

[12] John Rawls (1993), *Political Liberalism*. Columbia: University Press, pp. 199–200.

[13] Joseph Raz (1986), *The Morality of Freedom*. Oxford: Clarendon Press, pp. 390–395.

Susan Mendus
Department of Politics
University of York, UK

JANICE R. RUSSELL AND JAMES T. RICHARDSON

2. RELIGIOUS VALUES AND PUBLIC EDUCATION IN THE UNITED STATES

Religion and public education have been intertwined since the inception of public education in colonial America.[1] However, this intersection has not always been problematic. In the early 1600s, the predominantly Protestant citizenry of the United States founded the public education system in the New England Colonies.[2] Horace Mann, one of the prominent forces behind the founding of common schools, based the curriculum of the common school on his own liberal protestant beliefs.[3] It was *Horace Mann* Mann's view that because of the liberal nature of his religious beliefs, those beliefs could be considered secular, and serve as a philosophical underpinning for a system of public schools.

Early education systems in the states of the new nation were developed according to a Protestant view that all individuals are responsible for their own salvation.[4] In line with Protestant beliefs, individuals needed to learn to read and write in order to read the Bible, thus the public education system initially was focused on this eventual outcome.[5] Schools across the United States adopted curriculum that included implicitly if not explicitly, Protestant morality.[6] The ideology behind the common and public school systems was that the curriculum, including some religious content, was representative of and accepted by the majority of the population of the United States, therefore individuals with differing beliefs and concerns about religion in the public schools could be ignored.[7] This approach was not an issue in American society until the mid 1800s, when the demographic make-up of the population changed dramatically with the arrival of millions of immigrants who were not of northern European Protestant origin. This trend can be seen quite clearly in the development of the public school system in New York State.

In 1805, an organisation was founded in New York State to ensure that free education was available for all children. The Free School Society (FSS), whose board contained predominantly Protestant men, was instrumental in building many schools in the state of New York.[8] The FSS had full support of the New York State Legislature, which contributed thousands of dollars to the building and maintaining of the schools.[9] The State of New York chose not to support public schools; rather, they chose to fund private schools such as those opened by FSS. As the majority of the schools in the state were opened and run by the FSS, financial support from the state was tolerated by the citizenry. However, this changed as the population of New York State became more diverse.

In the early 1800s, the Catholic population was quite small, vastly outnumbered by the Protestant population.[10] In 1800, New York had only 1300 Catholics, but that number increased to between 60,000 and 80,000 by 1840. In the early 1800s, *Catholics*

E.B. Coleman and K. White (eds.), Religious Tolerance, Education and the Curriculum, 11–26.

two Catholic schools were opened in New York City. Both applied for and received state funds for schools. The Catholic schools functioned well alongside Protestant oriented schools which also received their share of state funds.[11]

However, in 1924, the FSS was able to change the state law regarding disbursement of educational funds. The FSS changed its name to Public School Society and lobbied the New York Legislature to pass a law to direct state funds only to their schools.[12] This legislation put an end to all state support for sectarian schools in New York. Although public support to the private schools in New York was ended, the success was primarily due to local political pressure and not to existing laws or statutes that prohibited such funding.[13] Laws and statutes were yet to be written and challenged.

THE FIRST AND FOURTEENTH AMENDMENTS

The First Amendment of the United States Constitution, adopted in 1791, guarantees individual freedom of religion and precludes the establishment of a state religion. The first clause, 'Congress shall make no law respecting an establishment of religion...' is referred to as the Establishment Clause, while the second clause, '...or prohibiting the free exercise thereof' is referred to as the Free Exercise Clause.[14] These two clauses had originally been applicable only on the federal level, and indeed the Establishment Clause was initially apparently meant to preclude federal interference with the state churches that had been officially sanctioned by seven of the original colonies.

The Establishment Clause and the Free Exercise Clause have posed many challenges with respect to public education in the United States. Initially these two clauses were applicable only to the Federal Government; thus there was little activity in the federal courts concerning these provisions for decades as such matters were left to the individual states. However, in 1947, a very important development occurred in *Everson v. the Board of Education of the Township of Ewington*, when the U.S. Supreme Court made it clear that the Fourteenth Amendment made First Amendment protections pertaining to the Establishment Clause in the area of religion applicable to local and state law.[15] (This case, having to do with aid to parochial schools, will be detailed below.)

Since the end of WWII, several challenges to Bible reading and prayer in schools, and the inclusion of religious teaching in public schools, have come before the Supreme Court of the United States.[16] Many of these challenges have led to the reduction of certain religious activities in public schools; this move toward more secular public schools comports well with a strict separationist view of the United States Constitution and the ideal of separation of church and state. However, controversy and argument continue to exist over what should be taught in the public schools. Should morals and values be taught, and, if so, then who decides which morals and values are appropriate?

THE *LEMON* TEST

In 1971, the U.S. Supreme Court established the famous but much-maligned '*Lemon* test' in order to determine when a statute was violative of the Establishment Clause of the First Amendment.[17] The *Lemon* test contains three criteria that should be met in order for a statute to pass the challenge. First, a statute must have a secular legislative purpose; second, the goal of the statute must not advance or inhibit any religion; third, the statute must not lead to excessive entanglement between church and state.

The Court's use of the *Lemon* test has been inconsistent, however. There are cases in which the Court examines only the first two criteria in deciding a case. For example, in the case of state support for private schools, the Court has chosen to overlook possible entanglement issues by employing a 'child benefit' theory which states that some aid can be considered a benefit to all children of a state rather than a benefit to a non-public school per se.[18]

More recently, as justification for lowering the bar against state support for private and parochial schools, other more lenient tests have been developed, including the so-called 'coercion' test, which means that funding can be delivered to parochial schools if there are no overt kinds of coercion involved that would cause citizens to think that a state approved church was being permitted.[19] This is clearly a reflection of the large number of students enrolled in Catholic schools—numbers had reached 5.5 million by the early 1960s—supporting the claim that the Catholic school system was carrying a major burden of educating students, particularly in some states.

The Free Exercise Clause has also seen considerable reinterpretation over the years, with it no longer justifying impressing Protestant values on all students in public schools, but still functioning as an underpinning for cases that disallowed forced actions such as saluting the flag. In more recent times, Free Exercise interpretations have allowed more religious activities to occur on school campuses.[20]

PRAYER, BIBLE READING, AND RELEASED TIME PROGRAMS IN PUBLIC SCHOOLS

The practice of opening the school day with prayer and Bible reading was common in American public schools.[21] Many cases challenging this practice were heard before state courts before any cases were heard by the U.S. Supreme Court.[22] Rulings by state courts generally indicated that Bible reading in public schools was acceptable as long as two criteria were met. The first condition was that Bible passages be read without comment; this was to ensure that no indoctrination took place. The second condition was that an 'opt out' be provided for students whose parents did not want them to participate.[23] Other issues related to concerns about prayer and Bible reading involved release time for religious instruction, and whether moments of silence might pass muster even if prayer was itself ruled unconstitutional.

Released Time Programs

The Week Day Religious Education (WDRE) program was introduced by William Wirt, superintendent of schools in Gary, Indiana in 1914.[24] This program included moving students from one area to another for diversified activity including library time and playground time. One of the activities included in this program was religious education. Children were released to separate areas of the school in order to study the religion that their parents wished them to study. The program was a failure in the Gary school system, but other schools in the country adopted the Religious Education piece of Wirt's program.[25]

Programs similar to WDRE continued through the 1950s with approximately five per cent of public schools in the U.S. adopting the practice of teaching religion during school time using public school facilities.[26] The teaching generally included one or two sessions per week. Students gathered in separate classrooms depending on their denomination to learn religion. Students whose parents did not want them to participate were excused to a study hall to continue their secular studies.[27]

In 1940, the city of Champaign, Illinois adopted a WDRE system in which Catholic, Jewish, and Protestant clergy taught. Those students who did not wish to participate were excused to a study hall. The instruction was held in school class-rooms. This practice was challenged in 1948 by a parent, Ms. McCollum, with a child in the Champaign Illinois public school system.[28] Ms. McCollum's child had been enrolled in Protestant instruction, but Ms. McCollum was not happy with the instruction given and withdrew her son from the program. He was subsequently harassed by students and teachers for not participating.[29] Due in part to the harass-ment experienced by her son, Ms. McCollum sought to end the practice of religious instruction in public classrooms in Champaign.[30]

The case moved through the court system with the Illinois Circuit Court finding that the 'released time' program was not in violation of the First Amendment. The Supreme Court of Illinois affirmed the ruling. However, the case was appealed to the U.S. Supreme Court which reversed the finding, stating that the 'released time' arrangements were not correctly established (*McCollum, Illinois ex Rel v. Board of Education*, 1948). The use of public school time and property was problematic because it led to excessive entanglement of church and state.[31]

This case was timely in that the ruling in Everson in 1948 made it clear that the protection of the First Amendment also applied to states and local governments. This was the first of many cases in which the U.S. Supreme Court began to delineate which religious behaviours and actions were appropriate in the public school system.

Many Christian groups were very displeased with *McCollum*, and made it well known after the decision. Subsequently, the U.S. Supreme Court chose to hear a similar case from New York State in which they decided that 'released time' arrangements were, in some cases, acceptable (*Zorach et al. v. Clausen et al.*, 1952). New York instituted a program in which students were released from class in order to leave school property for religious instruction. Students who did not have parental permission for release were kept at school. New York courts found that the program was not in violation of the First Amendment.[32] The U.S. Supreme Court affirmed stating that allowing the children to leave school property and offering an 'opt out' for students not interested in religious instruction was adequate. The Court explained the different rulings in the *McCollum* and *Zorach* cases by stating that each represented a different degree of separation of church and state.[33] The removal of religious teaching from the public school setting was enough to ensure no excessive entanglement.

Prayer

Engel et al. v. Vitale et al., (1962) and *School District of Abington Township, Pennsylvania et al. v. Schempp et al. [heard with Murray et al. v. Curlett et al.],* (1963) were very controversial cases for the U.S. Supreme Court. The 'roots of the dominant conservative religious organisations of the 1970s and 1980s, the Moral Majority and the Christian Coalition, lie in the public responses to these two unprecedented decisions'.[34] These decisions marked the end of the Protestant Americanisation that had dominated since the beginning of the pubic school movement in America.[35]

In 1958, the New York State Board of Regents recommended that the school day begin with prayer.[36] A specific prayer written by the Board of Regents was to be recited in every classroom at the beginning of every school day. The prayer recited was 'Almighty God, we acknowledge our dependence upon Thee, and we beg Thy blessings upon us, our parents, our teachers and our country. Amen'.[37] The prayer was purported to be secular in nature and children whose parents objected were given the option of leaving classrooms during the prayer.

A group of parents brought suit to end the recitation of the prayer. *Engel v. Vitale* (1962) was brought by Mr. Roth, the Jewish father of two boys, and other parents. The two boys were asked by their father to leave the classroom during prayer and were harassed by classmates and experienced hostility from teachers.[38] The parents objected to the recitation of the prayer because it 'was contrary to the beliefs, religions, or religious practices of both themselves and their children'.[39] The New York courts found that having the children pray at the beginning of the school day was not in violation of either the New York State Constitution or the First Amendment of the United States Constitution.

On appeal, the U.S. Supreme Court reversed the decision of the lower courts stating that the practice of prayer during the school day was 'wholly inconsistent' with the Establishment Clause of the First Amendment. The Court also stated that it was not the business of any government agency to institute official prayers to be recited by any group of Americans.

The second controversial case also concerned prayer in the schools, but in this case it was the recitation of the Lord's Prayer as well as the reading of verses from the Bible.[40] The initial suit brought by Schempp was to challenge the policy of the Abington Township in the State of Pennsylvania. Schempp won the first case with a ruling by the U.S. District Court for the Eastern District of Pennsylvania, and the recitation of the Lord's Prayer and reading of Bible verses was halted.[41] However, the state of Pennsylvania rewrote the law to include an 'opt out' for students whose parents did not wish for them to participate. Students were allowed to leave the room during the opening day ritual.

A second suit was brought by Schempp and eventually was heard by the U.S. Supreme Court in conjunction with another case (*School District of Abington Township, Pennsylvania et al. v. Schempp et al. [heard with Murray et al. v. Curlett et al.],* 1963). *Murray et al. v. Curlett et al.* was a similar case that challenged the Baltimore City Board of Commission requirement that all school days open with the reading of verses from the Bible and the recitation of the Lord's Prayer.

Madeline Murray sued to stop the practice. Maryland state courts dismissed Ms. Murray's case. However, the U.S. Supreme Court reversed the dismissal and also found for *Schempp* and *Murray* stating that the requirements of prayer and Bible reading were in violation of the Establishment Clause of the First Amendment. This decision made unconstitutional all state laws that required public schools to hold prayers or devotional Bible reading.[42] In the majority opinion in *Schempp*, the Court made clear that they supported the study of religion, but not the practice of religion in public schools.

Although Bible reading and prayer in public school classrooms had been ruled unacceptable, prayer still continued in many public schools, both unofficially in class rooms and officially in other school-related activities. Certain ceremonies and events such as graduation ceremonies and athletic competitions were begun with prayer.[43] In 1992, the U.S. Supreme Court heard *Lee v. Weisman*, a case challenging a policy that allowed for opening and closing prayers during public high school graduation ceremonies in Providence, Rhode Island. The prayers were led by clergy, but written such that they were nondenominational. Students who chose not to participate in the graduation ceremony because of an objection to the prayers were given their diplomas; there was no requirement for students to attend the ceremony. The U.S. Supreme Court ruled that because the individuals who led the prayers and the content of the prayers were chosen by the state through the school officials, such activities were unconstitutional.[44]

However, less than a year later, the U.S. Supreme Court remanded back to the Fifth Circuit Court a similar case in which students from a high school senior class chose individuals to lead prayers during graduation ceremonies. The Fifth Circuit Court allowed the practice to continue.[45] The issue of prayer at graduation ceremonies is still controversial and challenges continue with some state courts finding that student-led prayer is not in violation of the Establishment Clause and others ruling that any prayer during such ceremonies is unconstitutional.[46]

In a similar case, parents and students from a Santa Fe, Texas public high school challenged a school policy that allowed prayer by student volunteers at both graduation ceremonies and football games (*Santa Fe Independent School District v. Doe*, 1995). State courts ruled that student-led prayer at graduations was not in violation of the Establishment Clause, but ruled that prayer at football games was. In appeal to the U.S. Supreme Court, the Court chose to hear only the challenge to prayer at football games. The Supreme Court upheld the ruling of the lower court, stating that student-led prayer during football games was in violation of the Establishment Clause.[47]

The controversy continues even after *Lee* and *Santa Fe*. In Alabama, lower courts ruled that genuinely student-initiated religious speech, including at school assemblies, athletic competitions, and graduation ceremonies did not violate the Establishment Clause and was permitted under the student's rights to free speech.[48] Similarly, California and Florida Courts ruled that student-led religious speech during school events was not in violation of the Establishment Clause, but rather was an expression of the students' right under freedom of expression.[49] The U.S. Supreme Court chose not to hear appeals in any of the above cases.

Student-led Prayer Meetings

The next round of challenges came from individuals who felt that student-led voluntary prayer meetings should be allowed on school property. The first such case came from Massachusetts. Students from Leyden, Massachusetts petitioned the school district to allow them to hold prayer meetings in the school building before school began (*Commissioner of Education v. Leyden*, 1971). The Supreme Judicial Court of Massachusetts found the proposal unconstitutional. They stated that because the U.S. Supreme Court had ruled prayer in public schools violative of the Establishment Clause, it was too fine a distinction to allow students and teachers to participate in such a practice on school grounds. The Supreme Court declined to hear the case.

In 1980, a similar case was brought by a group of students who stated that they wanted the right to meet in school classrooms immediately before the start of the school day. Faculty and staff from the school would not be involved in the meetings, the students stated that they simply wanted classroom time for a few minutes in the morning to gather and pray. The Board of Education refused to let the students meet, and the students brought suit (*Brandon v. Board of Education of the Guilderland Central School District*, 1980). The District Court for the Northern District of the State of New York found for the Board of Education and stated that the First Amendment rights of the students had not been violated. The ruling was upheld on appeal. The Supreme Court chose not to hear the case.

Although the Supreme Court chose not to hear the student-led prayer cases that involved public high schools, they did hear a similar case that involved a public university. In 1981, a group of students from the University of Missouri at Kansas City brought suit against the University for refusing to allow them to meet in University facilities. The students were part of a religious organisation and wished to use a room in a University building for meetings. The University allowed other student groups to meet in University facilities, but stated that because the group in question was religious in nature, they could not allow the use of public facilities for meetings (*Widmar et al. v. Vincent et al.*, 1981).

The Federal District Court for the Western District of Missouri found for the University stating that the state could not provide facilities for religious use. The Court of Appeals reversed and stated that by not allowing students to meet in University facilities, the University was discriminating against the students. They further stated that the Establishment Clause does not restrict equal access to facilities when those facilities are open to groups and speakers of all kinds. The Supreme Court affirmed this finding, stating that because over 100 student-led groups were allowed to use University facilities for meetings, it was a violation of the students' freedom of speech to disallow use of facilities based on the content of the speech.[50]

The U.S. Supreme Court stated that religious meetings in universities and the teaching of religion in universities or colleges are more permissible because the students are assumed to be more mature and not as susceptible to influences of religious teachings or peers. 'Religion explored as an academic subject before mature students in a public university was different from prayers in the local public elementary schools'.[51]

17

Following *Widmar*, the Equal Access Act was enacted by Congress in 1984. The Act states that any public secondary education institution that receives federal money and allows groups to use their facilities for non-curriculum related activities could not refuse to allow access to the facilities based on a group's content of speech during the meeting.[52] This opened the door for challenges regarding student-led religious groups being barred from holding meetings in public secondary schools.[53]

Under the Equal Access Act, any public secondary school that allowed the use of its property after school hours to clubs or groups for meetings was classified as a 'limited public forum'. The status of limited public forum made it possible for religious groups to hold meetings in the schools as long as the groups were led by and attended by students.[54] Denial of access could be challenged as a denial of the right to free speech.

A 1990 case involved just such a situation. A group of students wished to organise a Christian club and meet in a school classroom after school hours for Bible study and prayer (*Board of Education of the Westside Community Schools v. Mergens*, 1990). School policy dictated that all clubs have a faculty sponsor, and based on the need of faculty sponsorship, refused to allow the club to meet on school property. The U.S. Supreme Court ruled that because the school met the criteria of a limited public forum the religious student group had the right to meet at the school. The Court stated that although school policy required a faculty member to sponsor the club, the purpose of the faculty sponsor was to 'ensure order and good behaviour' not to lead the religious meetings.[55] The Court ruled similarly in *Good News Club v. Milford Central School* (2001) in which they stated that to deny the club access to school facilities after school hours was in direct violation of the club members' right to free speech and that 'no Establishment Clause concern justified that violation'.[56]

Moment of Silence

A case out of Alabama saw a challenge to three statutes that called for one-minute period of silence to be observed in all public schools.[57] One statute, enacted in 1978, called for the period of silence for personal meditation. A second statute, enacted in 1981 stated that the moment of silence was to be used for meditation or voluntary prayer. The third statute, enacted in 1982 gave authority to teachers to lead prayer for willing students. The prayer was recommended to include reference to 'Almighty God...the Creator and Supreme Judge of the world'.[58]

Lower courts ruled that the statutes were not in violation of the Establishment Clause; thus states were not barred from allowing such activities. The Court of Appeals overturned the lower court decisions stating that the 1981 and 1982 statutes were of the same type that the U.S. Supreme Court ruled on in *Engel v. Vitale*. In Wallace v. Jaffree (1985), the U.S. Supreme Court affirmed the ruling of the Court of Appeals stating that when examined under the *Lemon* test, the Alabama statutes did not even pass the first prong, making it unnecessary to address the issue of advancement of religion. The most persuasive evidence against the secular nature of the statutes came from Alabama State Senator Holmes who stated that he was a sponsor of the 1981 statute because he viewed the statute as an 'effort to return prayer to our public schools' and that he had 'no other purpose in mind' when offering his support for the statute.[59]

After *Wallace*, a number of states attempted to draft legislation that would allow for moments of silence in the public schools.[60] The state of Virginia required public schools to allow for a minute of silence in all classrooms for a daily observance.[61] The Virginia statute was differentiated from *Wallace* because there was no language specific to a religious purpose for the minute of silence. Rather, the statute was deemed to allow for a moment of reflection given recent incidents of school violence. The Fourth Circuit Court applied the *Lemon* test and ruled that the statute passed all three prongs. An existing statute in the State of Louisiana that called for a brief time in silent meditation was amended in 1999 to read: 'allow for a brief time in prayer or meditation'.[62] The Supreme Court ruled that the Louisiana statute was identical to that addressed in *Wallace* and stated that the purpose of the statute was in direct violation of the Establishment Clause.[63]

FREE EXERCISE

The Free Exercise Clause of the First Amendment states that 'Congress shall make no law…prohibiting the free exercise (of religion)'.[64] Challenges relating to the Free Exercise Clause have focused on the rights of parents and students to refuse to participate in school activities that are contrary to their religious beliefs. A number of significant cases attempting to use free exercise as a basis have been heard by the U.S. Supreme Court over the years.

One of the first such cases was that of *Minersville (Pennsylvania) School District v. Gobitis* (1940) which dealt with the nearly ubiquitous requirements that public school students recite the Pledge of Allegiance and salute the flag at the beginning of each school day. A group of parents of the Jehovah's Witness faith objected to saluting the flag and reciting the Pledge, claiming that to do so was directly contrary to their religious belief which calls for individuals to worship only God. The salute of the flag and pledge to America is interpreted by the Jehovah's Witness faith as an act of idolatry, and is therefore in direct contradiction to the second of the Ten Commandments from the Bible as they perceive it.

The superintendent of the Minersville school district felt that allowing one child to refrain from saluting the flag would open the door to others who might object for religious reasons or because they were foreign. The Minersville superintendent's view was the predominant view of educators across the country. Public schools were perceived as a means through which individuals, especially immigrants, would be 'Americanised' into Protestant America.[65]

The District Court for the Eastern District of Pennsylvania found for the plaintiffs and stated that the children would be allowed to attend school without having to salute the flag or recite the Pledge of Allegiance (*Minersville School District v. Gobits*, 1940). The Court of Appeals agreed. However, the U.S. Supreme Court reversed this decision stating that there was no reason why all Americans could not be required to show their loyalty to America through a salute or the recitation of the Pledge.[66]

19

Following this decision, there was much reported violence against Jehovah's Witnesses, including mob violence, and even some attempts to remove Witness children from their parents.[67] Additionally, many school districts adopted rules expelling children who refused to salute the American flag or recite the Pledge.[68] Because of the violence and expulsion of children, public opinion began to change and the *Gobitis* ruling was questioned.

A second case regarding flag salute was accepted by the Supreme Court just three years later. In *West Virginia State Board of Education v. Barnette et al.* (1943), parents of the Jehovah's Witness faith again brought suit to end the requirement of the flag salute and the recitation of the Pledge of Allegiance in public schools. The same argument was made, that the salute and pledge were both directly contrary to the religious beliefs of the Jehovah's Witness faith. Additionally, it was argued that because of the children's refusal to participate and their subsequent forced removal from school, great financial burdens and hardships were faced by the families to find private education facilities. This time, the Court found for the Jehovah's Witnesses, stating that such requirements were beyond the constitutional limitations on governmental power.[69] The State of New Jersey heard a similar case in 1966. In *Holden et al. v. Board of Education* (1966), parents of Black Muslim children in the Elizabeth, New Jersey schools sought to have their children reinstated in school after they had been excluded from school because they refused to salute the American flag. The students had refused to salute the flag, but stood at attention during the flag salute and recitation of the Pledge of Allegiance. The students and their parents stated that to salute the flag and recite the Pledge were in direct conflict with their religious beliefs.[70] The school stated that the children's refusal to salute the flag and recite the Pledge was political, not religious. The New Jersey courts ruled for the reinstatement of the children and recognised the right of the students not to participate in the flag salute or Pledge. The Court further stated that the Supreme Court ruling on flag salute did not pertain only to refusal on religious grounds, but was broader in nature and applied to this situation regardless of the motives of the children's refusal.[71]

The early 1970s saw a number of cases related to flag salutes. Courts in Maryland and Florida have subsequently ruled that children cannot be forced to stand or leave a classroom during the pledge of allegiance. In 1970, the State of Maryland passed a law that required all teachers and students to participate in the flag salute unless there was a religious objection to the activity.[72] The law held that if any individual chose not to participate in the flag salute for reasons other than religious objection, he or she could face disciplinary action, although no specific action was suggested. The Court of Appeals of Maryland ruled that the law was in violation of the First Amendment. Similarly, the U.S. District Court for the State of Florida found that a school policy that called for the suspension of students for refusing to stand during the Pledge of Allegiance was unconstitutional, stating that if a child remained seated and was not disruptive the child could not be punished by being forced to stand or leave the room.[73]

More recently, a father from California challenged the state because he, an atheist, felt that the inclusion of the words 'Under God' in the Pledge of Allegiance made the recitation of that pledge a violation of his daughter's First Amendment rights (*Elk Grove Unified School District v. Newdow*, 2004). The case was dismissed by the District Court. However, the U.S. Court of Appeals for the Ninth Circuit reversed the dismissal and found that the school district's policy of requiring students to recite the Pledge with 'Under God' was in violation of the First Amendment.[74] The United States Supreme Court reversed the decision of the Court of Appeals stating that because the father was not the custodial parent, he had no legal right to challenge on behalf of his daughter.[75]

STATE SUPPORT FOR PRIVATE SCHOOLS

This is an area that has seen profound change over the course of American history. The strong animus exhibited against parochial schools that was present as Catholic immigrants started coming in large numbers in the early and mid-1800s has been nearly totally overcome, as shown by a long series of U.S. Supreme Court opinions, starting with the *Pierce v. Society of Sisters* case in 1925, which made it clear that Catholic schools could exist. After that significant decision, however, the Supreme Court developed a convoluted and meandering course concerning the ability of states to support, in various ways, the system of mainly Catholic schools that has been developed in America. There were also occasional efforts to funnel federal support to these schools, but that too became a battleground in the society.

The end of World War II found President Harry S. Truman proposing federal aid to 'assist the States in assuring more nearly equal opportunities for a good education'.[76] Although some supported the idea because of the potential benefit to children, others were opposed. The National Catholic Association was, of course, supportive of federal aid to parochial schools. Northern politicians from larger areas with many parochial schools would not support a bill that did not offer support to such schools as well as public schools.[77] Meanwhile, politicians from Protestant-majority areas would not support any bill that offered support to parochial schools.[78]

Many states with large Catholic populations experimented with ways to support the parochial schools such as the 'loan' of text books and transportation to and from parochial schools, in an effort to find some methods acceptable to the U.S. Supreme Court.[79] Challenges to such policies were brought to the Court, and these cases became a testing ground for the separation of church and state. Fine and sometimes convoluted lines were drawn between what types of support were acceptable, and at what point such support became an excessive entanglement of church and state.

In *Cochran et al. v. Louisiana State Board of Education* (1930), citizens of the State of Louisiana sued to stop the State's School Districts from purchasing school books that were to be provided to parochial schools free of charge. The U.S. Supreme Court affirmed the ruling of lower courts, which ruled for the School Districts. The Court stated that providing school books to the children of the state was 'aid to the children, not to the schools', which represents the first clear statement of a new 'child benefit' theory that would be used to justify support for parochial schools. Under the 'child benefit' theory, the issue was one of whether children would benefit from the supply of books, not whether the aid was supporting the parochial schools.[80]

Decades later, a second challenge to providing books to all school children in a state was accepted by the U.S. Supreme Court. In *Board of Education v. Allen*

(1968), the Supreme Court heard the case of a School Board of a city in New York State seeking an injunction against a law that required them to purchase books to 'loan' to private and parochial schools. The Supreme Court, apparently wanting to clarify even more this type of support, ruled against the injunction, stating that providing school books to children was for the benefit of the child, not for the aid of the school. This decision led to the consideration of hundreds of legislative proposals to furnish other kinds of aid to parochial schools in states around the nation.

In an earlier major case, transportation to and from school was deemed to fall into the category of 'child benefit'.[81] In *Everson v. Board of Education of the Township of Ewington* (1947), a suit was brought to end the reimbursement of transportation costs by the State of New Jersey to the parents of children who attended private parochial schools. Although the opinion of Justice Black seemed to indicate that a strict separation of church and state was warranted, the Supreme Court found that the reimbursement of transportation costs was not in violation of the First Amendment. As noted earlier, this was the first case in which the U.S. Supreme Court made it clear that the Fourteenth Amendment made First Amendment Establishment Clause protection in the area of religion applicable to local and state law.[82]

Further testing the First Amendment, a Pennsylvania program made it possible for reimbursement of private parochial schools for the salaries of teachers who taught secular subjects.[83] The U.S. Supreme Court ruled that the program led to excessive entanglement of church and state. This is the famous case that resulted in the 'Lemon test' that has been the law of the land since that time, even if most decisions seem to ignore the test.[84] The test involved a requirement that: (1) the law have a clear secular purpose; (2) the law must neither advance nor impede religion; and (3) the law must not foster excessive entanglement of the government with religion. Although there seems to be little difference between the purchase or loan of books, reimbursement of transportation costs for children, and paying salaries in parochial schools, the U.S. Supreme Court ruled that reimbursing parochial schools for salary costs violated the Establishment Clause.

Other programs and statutes developed by states to partially support parochial schools had yet to be tested with the Supreme Court. The Court heard *Levitt et al. v. Committee for Public Education and Religious Liberty et al.* (1973) to further elucidate its position on such support. This case stemmed from a New York State law that provided reimbursement to non-public schools, including parochial schools, for costs incurred because of state mandated testing. New York State Courts found that the reimbursement was too general and that, because testing and record keeping were an integrative part of schools, there was no way to delineate between costs incurred specifically because of the state mandated testing and those costs incurred because of necessary school business.[85] The Supreme Court affirmed this decision, arguing that the law constituted excessive entanglement.[86]

The situation clearly began to shift in a complicated case out of Ohio. In *Wolman et al. v. Walter et al.* (1977), a number of citizens of Ohio State brought suit to challenge an Ohio State statute that provided for specific support to private and sectarian schools. There were six specific actions proposed in the statute: (1) the purchase of textbooks for loan to non-public schools; (2) purchase and supply to non-public schools testing materials; (3) providing speech, hearing, and psychological counselling to non-public school children; (4) therapeutic, guidance, and remedial counselling provided for special needs children; (5) the purchase and loan of secular instructional equipment such as maps and globes; (6) and provision for field trip transportation and services. The Court ruled that the first four sections of the statute were clearly for the benefit of all children, and thus did not violate the First Amendment. However, sections five and six were found to be unconstitutional. The Court stated that the secular instructional equipment and field trips could be used for non-secular learning.

In a later decision, the Court relaxed the limitations of *Wolman* considerably, ruling that, as long as the government was not involved in religious indoctrination, public school districts could loan educational materials such as library books and computer hardware and software to private schools, including parochial schools (*Mitchell v. Helms,* 2000). This very significant decision overruled *Wolman* and in the opinion of some, settled a long standing almost inexplicable contradiction wherein only certain educational materials were deemed acceptable to furnish private schools.[87]

Following the Supreme Court decision in *Wolman,* New York passed a law in answer to the *Levitt* decision of 1973. This time the state provided for cash reimbursement to non-public schools of costs incurred for state mandated testing and required reporting and record keeping as it pertains to the mandated testing. An accounting system was put in place to ensure that only those costs related to testing were reimbursed. State courts found that, because of the new accounting system and the ruling of the Supreme Court on *Wolman,* the New York State law did not violate the constitution. The Supreme Court affirmed this ruling (*Committee for Public Education and Religious Liberty et al. v. Regan et al.,* 1980).

Earlier, in 1973, New York State established a voucher system in which the vouchers could be used by children for attendance at the school of their choice, including private parochial schools. The statute also included the reimbursement of funds to parochial schools for minimum sanitation and lighting requirements that had been set by the state (*Committee for Public Education and Religious Liberty et al. v. Nyquist,* 1973). The U.S. Supreme Court ruled that both the voucher system and the maintenance funds 'aided religion too much and ensured excessive entanglement of church and state'.[88] However, in *Zelman v. Simmons-Harris* (2002) the Court reversed its decision regarding vouchers ruling that, because the challenged statute provided funds to individuals and not directly to private or religious educational institutions, the statute was neutral and did not violate the Establishment Clause.

A similar situation has occurred in the area of tax rebates to parents of children in parochial schools.[89] After initially refusing all such methods of support in a series of cases in the early 1970s (see for instance, *Committee for Public Education and Religious Liberty v. Nyquist,* 1973, a New York case), the Court reversed itself in *Mueller v. Allen* (1983) by a bare five to four majority and ruled that a tax credit program developed in Minnesota was constitutional. As Alexander and Alexander state: 'The repeated attempts to override or change precedents, making them more favourable to parochial schools have apparently now been successful'.[90]

CONCLUSION

Public education in the U.S. began as a means through which to teach Protestant values and ensure that everyone could read and write in order to further their salvation. It then evolved into a way to integrate various ethnic groups into American society. With the increase in the Catholic population, a battle of sorts was undertaken to ensure that children were not indoctrinated into the Protestant faith with no representation from other religious groups. In the end, it seems that the Catholics, with the help of the Supreme Court, won the battle with the removal of religion, especially Protestant teachings and symbols, from public schools.

It is ironic that these two factions, Protestants and Catholics, now work together, again with the help of the Supreme Court, in an attempt to reintroduce some aspects of religion to the public schools and garner financial support for parochial schools, a growing number of which are fundamentalist Protestant in orientation, even though most are Catholic. Rulings regarding state support of private schools have reflected a huge change in public support with early rulings all but eliminating such support and more recent rulings opening the door for state funds and materials purchased with those funds to be used in private schools. The use of the child benefit theory and the coercion test (in lieu of the *Lemon* test) by the U.S. Supreme Court has furthered this trend.

In a similar vein, after elimination from public schools, prayer has recently been reintroduced in a limited fashion to some public school events. Rather than considering religious freedom rights regarding prayer at graduations and sporting events, courts have ruled that such activity is protected under individual freedom of speech. One of the most ingrained 'prayers' offered in public schools, the Pledge of Allegiance, has also been challenged as in violation of the First Amendment, but this challenge has failed.

Although religion is allowed to be taught in public schools as a subject matter, but without indoctrination, in some cases religious prayer and religious meetings are now allowed. Thus it seems that the U.S. Supreme Court has over time turned almost 180 degrees from initial positions on prayer in public schools and public support for parochial schools, and now is sanctioning student-led prayer during some school events and nearly any aid to parochial schools. The controversy continues and will continue to do so. The original supposition of separation of church and state seems to be more an ideal than a reality when it comes to the inclusion of religion in education in the Untied States at this time.

NOTES

[1] J.C. Carper (1998), 'History, religion, and schooling: A context for conversation', in J.T. Sears and J.C. Carper (eds), *Curriculum, religion, and public education: Conversations for an enlarging public square.* New York: Teachers College Press, pp. 11–24.

[2] R.C. McMillan (1984), *Religion in the Public Schools: An Introduction.* Macon, GA: Mercer University Press.

[3] R.A. Baer (1998), 'Why a functional definition of religion is necessary if justice is to be achieved in public education' in J.T. Sears and J.C. Carper (eds), *Curriculum, Religion, and Public Education: Conversations for an Enlarging Public Square.* New York: Teachers College Press, pp. 105–15.

[4]   McMillan, *Religion in the Public Schools: An Introduction*.

[5]   Ibid.

[6]   J.W. Fraser (1999), *Between Church and State: Religion and Public Education in a Multicultural America*. New York: St. Martins Press.

[7]   Ibid.

[8]   Carper, 'History, religion, and schooling: A context for conversation'.

[9]   W.O. Bourne (1870), *History of the Public School Society of New York with Portraits of the Presidents of the Society*. New York: WM Wood & Company.

[10]   Fraser, *Between Church and State: Religion and Public Education in a Multicultural America*.

[11]   Ibid.

[12]   Fraser, ibid.; Bourne, *History of the Public School Society of New York with Portraits of the Presidents of the Society*.

[13]   Fraser, *Between Church and State: Religion and Public Education in a Multicultural America*.

[14]   Ibid., p. 13.

[15]   Ibid.

[16]   Baer, 'Why a functional definition of religion is necessary if justice is to be achieved in public education'.

[17]   C.J. Russo (2006), 'Prayer and religious activities in American public schools', in J.L. Martinez Lopez-Muniz, J. De Groff, & G. Lauwers (eds), *Religious Education in Public Schools: Study of Comparative Law*. Dordrecht, The Netherlands: Springer, pp. 213–234.

[18]   Fraser, *Between Church and State: Religion and Public Education in a Multicultural America*; Russo, ibid.

[19]   K. Alexander & M.D. Alexander (2005), *American Public School Law* (6th edn). Belmont, CA: Thomson West, pp. 195–7.

[20]   Ibid.

[21]   McMillan, *Religion in the Public Schools: An Introduction*.

[22]   Russo, 'Prayer and religious activities in American public schools'.

[23]   Ibid.

[24]   Fraser, *Between Church and State: Religion and Public Education in a Multicultural America*.

[25]   Ibid.

[26]   R.B. Fowler (1985), *Religion and politics in America*. Metuchen, NJ: Scarecrow Press.

[27]   Fraser, *Between Church and State: Religion and Public Education in a Multicultural America*.

[28]   Ibid.

[29]   Ibid.

[30]   Alexander and Alexander, *American Public School Law*.

[31]   *Illinois ex Rel. McCollum v. Board of Education*, 1948; Russo, 'Prayer and religious activities in American public schools'.

[32]   Fraser, *Between Church and State: Religion and Public Education in a Multicultural America*.

[33]   Russo, 'Prayer and religious activities in American public schools'.

[34]   Fraser, *Between Church and State: Religion and Public Education in a Multicultural America*, p. 145.

[35]   Ibid.

[36]   Ibid.

[37]   Ibid., p. 146.

[38]   Ibid.

[39]   *Engle v. Vitale*, 1962, at 4.

[40]   Fraser, *Between Church and State: Religion and Public Education in a Multicultural America*.

[41]   Ibid.

[42]   Ibid.

[43]   Russo, 'Prayer and religious activities in American public schools'.

[44]   Ibid.

[45]   Ibid.

[46]   Ibid.

[47]   Ibid.

[48]   Ibid.

[49]   Ibid.

[50] Ibid.
[51] Fowler, *Religion and Politics in America*, p. 280.
[52] Russo, 'Prayer and religious activities in American public schools'.
[53] Alexander and Alexander, *American Public School Law*.
[54] Ibid.
[55] Ibid., p. 235.
[56] *Good News Club v. Milford*: 1.
[57] Alexander & Alexander, *American Public School Law*.
[58] Ibid., p. 271.
[59] Ibid.
[60] Ibid.
[61] *Brown v. Gilmore*, 2001.
[62] Alexander & Alexander, *American Public School Law*, p. 219.
[63] *Doe v. School Board of Ouachita Parish*, 2001.
[64] Fraser, *Between Church and State: Religion and Public Education in a Multicultural America*, p. 13.
[65] Ibid.
[66] Fowler, *Religion and Politics in America*.
[67] Ibid.
[68] Russo, 'Prayer and religious activities in American public schools'.
[69] Ibid.
[70] Ibid.
[71] Ibid.
[72] *State v. Lundquist*, 1971.
[73] 'Russo, 'Prayer and religious activities in American public schools'.
[74] *Elk Grove Unified School District v. Newdow*, 2004.
[75] *Elk Grove Unified School District v. Newdow*, 2004.
[76] Fraser, *Between Church and State: Religion and Public Education in a Multicultural America*, p. 141.
[77] Ibid.
[78] Ibid.
[79] Ibid.
[80] Fowler, *Religion and Politics in America*.
[81] Ibid.
[82] Fraser, *Between Church and State: Religion and Public Education in a Multicultural America*.
[83] *Lemon v. Kurtzman*, 1971.
[84] Alexander & Alexander, *American Public School Law*.
[85] Fowler, *Religion and Politics in America*.
[86] *Levitt et al.*, 1973.
[87] L.C. Griffin (2007), *Law and Religion: Cases and Materials*. Foundation Press: New York.
[88] Fowler, *Religion and Politics in America*, p. 288.
[89] Alexander & Alexander, *American Public School Law*, pp. 173–4.
[90] Ibid., p. 174.

Janice R. Russell
Interdisciplinary Social Psychology Doctoral Program
University of Nevada, Reno

James T. Richardson
Judicial Studies Program
Sociology
University of Nevada, Reno

PAULINE RIDGE

3. LAW, TOLERANCE AND RELIGIOUS SCHOOLS IN AUSTRALIA

Religious schools in Australia are operated by religious groups to provide a primary or secondary education that satisfies the state's compulsory education requirements within the framework of these groups' religious beliefs and practices. From time to time, public interest in religious schools is sparked by media reports concerning their operation. Often, the public debate concerns the science curriculum: whether creationism or 'Intelligent Design' theories should be taught, for example; however, other aspects of religious schools' operation also receive attention. In August 2004, for example, two media stories concerning religious schools were current. The first concerned an Adelaide secondary school operated by the Church of the Brethren.[1] The school received adverse media attention because it did not allow computers or other information technology within the school.[2] The second story concerned a sect known as the Order of St Charbel.[3] A school operated by the sect came under scrutiny because of the doomsday teachings of the sect's leader whose headquarters were located within the school's grounds.[4] Both schools received substantial federal government funding (a fact that featured prominently in the media discussion).

From a legal perspective, the question that these stories raise is this: To what extent does the law, directly or indirectly, facilitate and regulate the education offered by religious schools in Australia? The question is an important one because public funding of the non-government, predominantly religious, school sector has increased substantially in Australia since the mid-twentieth century.[5] Consequently, while some religious schools, such as those operated by the Roman Catholic and Anglican churches, are established features of Australia's education system and existed before any provision of public, secular education,[6] religious schools in Australia are increasing in number and include a significant, and growing, proportion of schools established by non-mainstream religious groups.[7] It is an understatement to say that this topic has not generated as much attention in Australia as it has in the United States where the First Amendment to the Constitution of the United States has had a very significant impact upon the relationship of the state with religious schools.[8] Notwithstanding this, the law's treatment of religious schools in Australia raises interesting issues in its own right and offers a thought-provoking contrast with the American situation.

In this chapter, I will consider three ways in which the law interacts with the operation of religious schools in Australia; namely, through the conferral of charitable status, the authorisation of Commonwealth funding, and the state and territory statutory requirements for school registration. What will become apparent is that, historically, the law has taken a tolerant attitude towards religious schools, although

E.B. Coleman and K. White (eds.), Religious Tolerance, Education and the Curriculum, 27–39.

regulatory oversight now exists through state and territory registration and reporting requirements.

THE CHARITABLE STATUS OF RELIGIOUS SCHOOLS[9]

The first way in which the law favours religious schools is through a benevolent application of charity law. Religious schools that operate on a not-for-profit basis are able to access extremely favourable fiscal benefits through claiming charitable status.[10] Enforcement and duration privileges also attach to trusts for charitable purposes associated with religious schools.

Australian tax legislation, in common with most Australian legislation, adopts the common law meaning of 'charitable', which can be traced back to the Preamble to the *Statute of Charitable Uses 1601* (the '*Statute of Elizabeth*').[11] Generally speaking, a religious school's purposes will be charitable at common law if they are for the 'advancement of education'[12] and confer a public benefit.[13]

(a) Advancement of Education

The courts have taken a generous approach to what constitutes the advancement of education; notably, the fact that the education relates to a particular religious faith, or is provided within the framework of a particular religious faith, is no barrier to charitable status. Thus, bequests to provide clothing for poor children receiving Roman Catholic education,[14] to provide an education in the Jewish faith,[15] and to continue a school 'for religious teaching, Bible reading, and elementary education'[16] have all been upheld as charitable. The Privy Council decision of *Dilworth v Commissioner of Stamps* is a good illustration of the law's attitude to the type of religious schools now operating in Australia.[17] It concerned a testamentary gift for the purpose of establishing a school in New Zealand for orphan and destitute boys where they would be educated according to the tenets of the Church of England; in other words, an elementary education would be provided within the framework of the beliefs and practices of the Church of England. Lord Watson, on behalf of the Privy Council, held:

> [I]t does not, in their Lordships' opinion, derogate from the charitable nature of the gift that the institution is to be managed by persons of a particular religious persuasion, or that its inmates are to be instructed in the tenets of the same sect.[18]

Advancement of education also extends to the provision of educational facilities such as buildings or scholarships.

(b) Public Benefit

The requirement that charitable purposes confer a public benefit is more problematic. 'Public benefit' has been taken to mean not only that society in general benefit from the charitable purposes, but also that the benefit of the charitable purposes cannot be limited to a section of the public characterised by its relationship to a particular individual or individuals. Thus, the test is whether the purposes are for:

> the benefit of the community or of an appreciably important class of the community. The inhabitants of a parish or town, or any particular class of such inhabitants, may, for instance, be the objects of such a gift, but private individuals, or a fluctuating body of private individuals, cannot.[19]

The leading case on the public benefit element of charity is *Oppenheim v Tobacco Securities Trust Co Ltd.*[20] A trust for the education of children of employees and former employees of a company was held not to be for charitable purposes because the benefit was limited to those who had 'a relationship to a particular individual' (namely, the employer). Similarly, a trust for the education of family members is not charitable.[21] On the other hand, the courts have accepted the charitable status of trusts for the education of 'the daughters of missionaries [or], the children of those professing a particular faith or accepted as ministers of a particular denomination…'[22]

An Australian case on public benefit that raises some interesting questions in the context of the charitable status of religious schools, although, strictly speaking, it concerned neither, is *Thompson v Federal Commissioner of Taxation.*[23] The case turned upon the interpretation of a statutory exemption from estate duty; however, the majority of the High Court considered the question as though the law of charity applied. A testamentary gift was made to the William Thompson Masonic Schools in Baulkham Hills, New South Wales. The schools were only open to the children of Freemasons. The majority of the High Court held that there was no public benefit in such a gift for it was limited by both blood relationship and membership of a private association; namely, Freemasonry.

In determining whether there was a public benefit, Justice Dixon quoted with approval from the judgment of Justice Lowe in a Victorian Supreme Court decision on similar facts:

> Having regard to the composition of the public, certain large groups may readily be recognized, the members of which have a common calling or adhere to a particular faith or reside in a particular geographical area. There is no bar which admits some members of the public to those groups and rejects others. Any member of the public may, if he will, follow a particular calling, adhere to a particular faith, or reside within a particular area.[24]

The assumption being made by the judges here, however, is that membership of a religious faith group is always open to the public at large; hence, the purposes of a religious school that is only open to adherents of the religious group would be charitable. A reasonable question to ask is whether, in fact, all religious groups *are* open to the public in the sense that converts are welcome and encouraged; the judicial assumption appears to reflect a Christian worldview, whereas not all religions take this approach.

The requirement of public benefit is rarely used to deny charitable status to educational purposes;[25] however, it is possible in principle for a court to decide that particular educational purposes have no merit at all and therefore confer no public benefit. A controversial case in this respect is *Re Hummeltenberg*, decided in 1923, where a testamentary gift for 'the purpose of establishing a college for the training and developing of suitable persons male and female as mediums…' was held not to be charitable as the evidence did not establish that it was for the public benefit.[26] It may be that the case would be decided differently today;[27] however, in any event, it is unlikely that a religious school, which was fulfilling the compulsory education requirements of the state, that is, providing a general education albeit within the framework of particular beliefs, would fall foul of the public benefit requirement.

Fiscal Benefits

Religious schools operating on a not-for-profit basis and whose purposes are charitable are eligible for exemption from income tax; in addition, and depending upon the jurisdiction, exemptions may apply in relation to a range of other taxes and charges including fringe benefit tax, payroll tax, land tax, and rates.[28] Tax deductibility may also be claimed in relation to some gifts to schools; this option has been extensively utilised by both government and non-government schools alike in relation to 'library funds' and 'building funds'.[29]

The fact that charitable status is generally accorded to the activities of private schools who thereby receive substantial fiscal benefits is controversial. Some commentators have argued strongly that the charitable status accorded to non-government schools claims a disproportionate share of the government funding available for education, and disproportionately benefits schools that are already wealthy.[30] This is not a criticism that can be levelled at all religious schools, however, and it is undeniable that many schools associated with non-mainstream religious groups would founder if the fiscal benefits associated with charitable status were removed. The Commonwealth Government commissioned a report on charity in 2001 which, among other things, considered this question. The *Report of the Inquiry into the Definition of Charities and Related Organisations* (the '*Sheppard Report*') endorsed the charitable status of schools:

> [T]he Committee does not accept the proposition put in some submissions that education should no longer be recognised as a charitable purpose. In our view, the fact that school education is now compulsory and that it is largely accepted as a responsibility of the state does not detract from it being a charitable purpose. Indeed, the insistence by the state that all children participate in formal education confirms the public benefit that it bestows. The fact that governments also provide education does not deny the charitable status of entities that provide education for altruistic purposes.[31]

COMMONWEALTH GOVERNMENT FUNDING OF NON-GOVERNMENT SCHOOLS

The second way in which the law has facilitated the operation of religious schools in Australia is in allowing the federal government to become involved in the funding of such schools. As a matter of Australian constitutional law, the provision of education comes within the legal powers of the state and territory governments; however, it is now the case that the Commonwealth is the main provider of government funding to non-government schools. This has been a hugely significant factor in the substantial growth of these schools during the late twentieth century.[32]

In the early years of the Australian colonies, primary education was provided, if at all, by Christian denominational groups with colonial government financial assistance (so-called 'state aid').[33] This state aid was provided without regard to sectarian differences and extended to the churches themselves. A public system of schools operated by the colonial authorities also developed during the mid-1800s. During the course of the 1870s and 1880s, and amid some controversy, state aid to church schools ceased in all colonies.[34]

By the middle of the twentieth century, the need for government funding of non-government schools was pressing. The states were struggling to fund government schools and Catholic schools (the largest alternative provider of education) were overcrowded and financially insecure.[35] Furthermore, there was growing political pressure for the Commonwealth Government to take a more active role in education and research.[36] During the 1960s, all states responded to political pressure and re-introduced state aid for religious (primarily Catholic) schools.[37] In 1964, the Commonwealth Government began to make grants for primary and secondary education, including to non-government schools.

Because legislative power with respect to education resides with the states, the federal funding of education relied upon section 96 of the Constitution which allows the Commonwealth to 'grant financial assistance to any State on such terms and conditions as the parliament shall think fit'. The legislative power of the Commonwealth Government to provide such funding was challenged in the High Court case of *Attorney-General (Vic); ex rel Black v Commonwealth*.[38] The case is known as 'the DOGS case' after the lobby group, 'Defence of Government Schools', who initiated the legal proceedings.[39]

One of the grounds upon which the DOGS group challenged the Commonwealth legislation was that federal funding of non-government schools infringed section 116 of the Constitution because it amounted to the 'establishment of a religion' and that therefore the funding legislation under challenge was invalid as being beyond the Parliament's legislative power. The argument relied upon the fact that the overwhelming majority of non-government schools are religious schools. Section 116 provides:

> The Commonwealth shall not make any law for establishing any religion, or for imposing any religious observance, or for prohibiting the free exercise of any religion, and no religious test shall be required as a qualification for any office or public trust under the Commonwealth.[40]

It was argued that section 116 prevented the Commonwealth Parliament from 'making any law which provides any recognition or aid or support to one or more religions or to religion generally'.[41] An analogy was sought to be drawn with the First Amendment to the United States Constitution which provides that: 'Congress shall make no law respecting an establishment of religion...' and with Supreme Court decisions that interpreted that provision to preclude any state financial assistance to religious schools, even for the teaching of a secular curriculum.[42]

A majority of the High Court rejected these arguments and found that the relevant clause of section 116 ('The Commonwealth shall not make any law for establishing any religion...') only prohibited the Parliament from making a law that endorsed a particular religion as a 'national institution'.[43] A distinction also was drawn between the wording of the First Amendment ('Congress shall make no law *respecting* an establishment of religion...') and the wording of section 116 ('The Commonwealth shall not make any law *for* establishing any religion...'). A law providing for funding of religious schools was not a law *for* establishing any religion pursuant to section 116. Although, as Joshua Puls has pointed out, the differences in wording of the two constitutional provisions may have assisted the majority of the High Court to avoid the difficulties that have plagued the American division of church and state:

> [t]he effect of any constitutional provision as loaded with value judgments as one involving religion will inevitably be dependent not so much on the fine wording of that section but on the desired outcome sought by the judges applying it.[44]

That is, as Puls argues, the largely amicable nature of relations between the state and religious groups in Australia before, and at the time of the DOGS litigation, is reflected in the outcome of the case.

I would add to this that the influence of charity law's tolerant attitude towards religious and educational purposes can clearly be discerned in the High Court's judgments in the DOGS case. The majority viewed with equanimity the fact that religious schools have a dual purpose of both education and religion. For example, Justice Gibbs noted that:

> Of course, most church schools give religious as well as secular instruction and, at least in the case of schools conducted by some religious denominations, are intended to serve the purpose of inculcating in their pupils the religious beliefs and values of the church concerned. It may be accepted that in some cases, if not in most, church schools are seen by the church as fulfilling a religious as well as a purely educational purpose: their functioning is regarded as an integral part of the religion which supports the schools.[45]

This passage resonates with the Privy Council's decision in *Dilworth v Commissioner of Stamps*, discussed above, that an education provided according to the tenets of a particular religious faith is still the advancement of education and thus charitable.[46] The passage from Justice Gibbs's judgment also reinforces the impression gained so far that the law in Australia generally takes a tolerant attitude towards religious schools.

The arguments of the DOGS organisation did find favour with Justice Murphy in dissent. In his view, the United States case law concerning the establishment of religion was relevant and should apply by analogy. He went on to emphasise that the funding of religious schools significantly increased the wealth of the religious groups involved:

> The effect of the Grants Acts is that the wealth of the churches is increased annually by many millions of dollars of taxpayers' moneys.[47]

Notwithstanding these views, in the DOGS case, the majority of the High Court endorsed the federal funding of religious schools and thereby avoided the controversies that have beset the relationship of religion and state in the United States.[48]

STATE AND TERRITORY REGULATION OF RELIGIOUS SCHOOLS

The most direct legal regulation of the operation of religious schools in Australia is through the registration requirements that apply in all states and territories to non-government schools; although, again, there appears to be little regulatory intervention in the content of the curricula provided by such schools.[49]

State oversight of non-government schools originated in Victoria in 1905 as a response to public concern regarding the poor quality of education offered by private girls' schools.[50] Nowadays, registration of non-government schools, including religious schools, generally depends upon the provision of adequate health and safety standards and a curriculum that meets prescribed standards. For example, under the *Education Act 2004* (ACT), the criteria for a school to obtain registration are as follows:

(a) the proprietor of the school is a corporation; and

(b) the school has appropriate policies, facilities and equipment for—

    (i) the curriculum offered by the school; and

    (ii) the safety and welfare of its students; and

(c) the curriculum (including the framework of the curriculum and the principles on which the curriculum is based) meets the curriculum requirements for students attending government schools; and

(d) the nature and content of the education offered at the school are appropriate for the educational levels for which the school is provisionally registered; and

(e) the teaching staff are qualified to teach at the educational levels at which they are employed to teach; and

(f) the school has satisfactory processes to monitor quality educational outcomes; and

(g) the school is financially viable.[51]

Although there is little case law concerning the enforcement of these registration requirements, it is clear that they are a valid exercise of legislative power and must be complied with by religious schools. In *Grace Bible Church Inc v Reedman*, the plaintiff,

Grace Bible Church, the governing body of a small Christian school in South Australia, challenged the right of the South Australian Government to impose registration requirements upon its school.[52] The church argued that the compulsory registration requirements infringed its inalienable right to religious freedom. The pastor of the church gave evidence that 'his church was totally controlled by God and registration would mean that the church was controlled by another authority'.[53]

The South Australian Supreme Court, in its appellate jurisdiction, acknowledged that the legislation gave the registration authority 'a very wide discretion as to religious instruction as well as any other kind of instruction',[54] however, it decided that there was no inalienable right to religious freedom in Australia, either under statute or at common law. The *Education Act 1972* (SA) was a valid exercise of the Parliament of South Australia's legislative powers. Justice Zelling spent some time considering what he considered to be the strongest of the Church's arguments: namely, that such a common law right had arisen from South Australia's religious history. He accepted that religious freedom was regarded as important in the state's colonial history, however, he held that there was no such inalienable right established. The state government's regulatory oversight of religious schools, which began in 1915 with the requirement that private schools provide 'returns' and also prevented Lutheran schools 'teaching in the German language', was a valid exercise of legislative power.[55]

It may be that the 2004 amendments to the *Education Act 1990* (NSW) were designed to counter the concerns of religious groups such as the plaintiff in *Grace Bible Church Inc v Reedman*. The NSW Act allows a non-government school to seek exemption from registration because of a conscientious objection to registration on religious grounds.[56] The Minister for Education and Training is authorised to accept an objection to registration if satisfied that the school satisfies the requirements for registration and that 'the objection to registration is conscientiously held on religious grounds'.[57] If a school receives such exemption, then it is regarded as registered.[58] In other words, a religious school may seek an exemption from registration, but only if the school in fact meets the requirements for registration.

A search of the Australian case law reveals only two other authorities dealing with the registration of religious schools.[59] Both are South Australian and both concern whether the registration authority complied with the legislative requirements for de-registration. In one of those cases, *Fountain Centre Christian School Incorporated v Harrington*, which concerned the cancellation of registration of a small Christian school, the Supreme Court of South Australia again stressed the theme of non-interference, so far as possible, in parents' choice of education:

> The primary role of parents in choosing the education which their children are to receive is a feature of free societies which distinguishes them from those which are founded upon totalitarian notions of the role of the State. The State, of course, in all contemporary societies, claims the right to insist upon its future citizens receiving an adequate education and that claim finds expression in Pt VI of the Act. I would not be at all surprised, however, to find that the legislation has exercised great restraint in limiting the right of parents to have their children educated in the school of their choice'.[60]

Such legislative restraint is well illustrated in the *Education Act 1990* (NSW) which shows a tolerance for religious schools in regard to the curricula requirements. While requiring both government and non-government schools to comply with syllabuses of the NSW Board of Studies, there is provision for religious schools to modify such material on application.[61] The then Minister for Education and Training, in his second reading speech on the Bill, stated:

> The Government acknowledges that there will always be a small number of schools that for philosophical or religious reasons will find it difficult to use board syllabuses in their entirety. To allow these schools to continue to offer the choice sought by their communities, items [5] and [7] of the bill provide for parts of the syllabus to be modified on application to the Board of Studies.[62]

The legislation was enacted in response to the recommendations of the *Grimshaw Report 1*, which stated in this regard that:

> In these instances, the Board would need to be satisfied that the school's alternatives have the support of its community and that its proposals address the developmental needs of students and assist them to achieve educational outcomes consistent with the stated aims and purpose of the school'.[63]

In other words, the main concern appears to be that the parents are adequately *informed* as to the content of the curriculum offered by the school.

One area in which there is the potential for the clash of state and religious values in relation to the operation of religious schools is in the practice of corporal punishment. The *Education Act 1990* (NSW), for example, prohibits the use of corporal punishment in both government and non-government schools.[64] The question whether such a provision legally infringes the religious freedom of parents of children at religious schools has been litigated upon in the United Kingdom. In *R v Secretary of State for Education and Employment*, persons associated with four independent Christian schools challenged a provision of the *Education Act 1996* (UK) banning the use of corporate punishment in schools on the basis that this infringed parents' rights under the European Convention for the Protection of Human Rights and Fundamental Freedoms (incorporated into English law by the *Human Rights Act 1998*).[65] Article 9 of the Convention provides that:

1. Everyone has the right to freedom of thought, conscience and religion; this right includes...freedom, either alone or in community with others and in public or private, to manifest his religion or belief, in worship, teaching, practice and observance.

2. Freedom to manifest one's religion or beliefs shall be subject only to such limitations as are prescribed by law and are necessary in a democratic society in the interests of public safety, for the protection of public order, health or morals, or for the protection of the rights and freedoms of others.

The House of Lords upheld the legislative ban on corporal punishment while acknowledging that the practice of corporal punishment by some Christian schools was a manifestation of the parents' religious beliefs. The legislation was justified according to Article 9(2) as well as upholding the rights of children pursuant to the United Nations Convention on the Rights of the Child. The House of Lords' position is summed up by Baroness Hale:

> If a child has a right to be brought up without institutional violence, as he does, that right should be respected whether or not his parents and teachers believe otherwise.[66]

While the European Convention on Human Rights has no force in Australia, an Australian court is also likely to uphold legislation banning corporal punishment for the reasons given by Baroness Hale. Thus, while the statutory registration requirements in relation to religious schools reflect the same tolerance for religious difference as does the case law concerning charity, and the DOGS case discussed earlier, it is clear that this tolerance will not extend to a situation where the rights of a child are infringed.

CONCLUSION

It seems reasonable to suggest that the laws of a society will reflect the mores of that society; and that this is particularly so where the relevant law is contained within case law decided by judges in an incremental fashion over a long period of time. If this is correct, then it suggests that Australian society has taken a tolerant and non-interventionist view of religious schools. Certainly, the law of charity and the High Court decision in the DOGS case show that religious schools have received positive support from the state. Even the state and territory legislative regulation of religious schools shows a clear preference for non-intervention in the educational programs offered by these schools. The one clear exception is the prohibition on corporal punishment. Thus, a review of the law concerning religious schools in Australia bears out the assertion of the *Grimshaw Report 1* that:

> The right of parents to choose the kind of education that their children receive... has not been questioned by any Australian government, State or Commonwealth.[67]

Whether the law's tolerant and supportive relationship with religious schools will continue depends, of course, upon the political climate. If fear of religious difference continues to be heightened due to a perceived or actual terrorism threat to Australia, then it is not inconceivable that a future government at either state or federal level would not be so tolerant. If so, this is likely to provoke consideration of human rights issues in a way that has not happened in Australia to date and will present more starkly, the question of whether religious schools may operate free of state interference.

NOTES

[1] S. Maiden (2004), 'Education grants keep the faith', *The Australian*, 7 August. 'You won't find a computer in the classrooms at the Church of the Brethren's private school because they are feared and believed to "damage children's minds".'

[2] According to the press reports, the school had received exemption from national curriculum guidelines in relation to the use of information technology.

[3] S. Maiden (2004), 'Doomsday cult wins federal cash', *The Australian*, 3 August; 'Cult's school investigated', *The Australian*, 4 August. See also, in relation to government schools and the Steiner education system, M. Rout (2007), 'Questions about Steiner's classroom', *Sydney Morning Herald*, 28 July.

[4] The school's registration was subsequently reviewed by the NSW Board of Studies and the school closed in 2006.

[5] For an overview of the relevant Commonwealth Government policies and their impact upon the numerical growth of non-government schools, see Warren Grimshaw (2002), *Review of Non-Government Schools in NSW: Report 1* (the '*Grimshaw Report 1*'), New South Wales Government, pp. 79–80.

[6] Alan Barcan (1980), *A History of Australian Education*, Oxford University Press, Melbourne.

[7] As at August 2006, 28.2 per cent of all schools in Australia were non-government schools, Australian Bureau of Statistics, *Schools, Australia*, 4221.0, 2006. Between 1993 and 2002, the number of school members of the Christian Schools of Australia (CSA) association grew from 52 to 130. In the same period Muslim schools grew in number from 6 to 24. See Australia Institute (2004), *The Accountability of Private Schools to Public Values*, Discussion Paper Number 71, p. 7.

[8] Joshua Puls (1998), 'The Wall of Separation: Section 116, The First Amendment and Constitutional Religious Guarantees', *Federal Law Review*, 26, p. 139.

[9] See generally, Gino Dal Pont (2000), *Charity Law in Australia and New Zealand*. Melbourne: Oxford University Press; Debra Morris (1996), *Schools: An Education in Charity Law*, Aldershot: Dartmouth Publishing Company.

[10] Michael Chesterman (1979), *Charities, Trusts and Social Welfare*, London: Weidenfeld and Nicolson, p. 333. Strictly speaking, the designation of 'charitable' attaches to the purposes and activities of the governing authority of the school or to the purposes of gifts to the school or trusts for the purposes of the school.

[11] *Ashfield Municipal Council v Joyce* [1978] AC 122; *Central Bayside General Practice Association Ltd v Commissioner of State Revenue* (2006) 228 CLR 168.

[12] *Commissioners for Special Purposes of the Income Tax v Pemsel* [1891] AC 531, 583 (Lord Macnaghten).

[13] *Oppenheim v Tobacco Securities Trust Co Ltd* [1951] AC 297.

[14] *Carbery v Cox* (1852) 3 Ir Ch R 231.

[15] *Re Michel's Trusts* (1860) 28 Beav 39; 54 ER 280.

[16] *Re Hawkins* (1906) 22 TLR 521.

[17] [1899] AC 99.

[18] Ibid., 105.

[19] *Verge v Somerville* [1924] AC 496, 499 (Lord Wenbury).

[20] [1951] AC 297.

[21] *Re Compton* [1945] Ch 123.

[22] *Oppenheim v Tobacco Securities Trust Co Ltd* [1951] AC 297, 318 (Lord MacDermott in dissent but not on this point). See generally, Dal Pont, *Charity Law in Australia and New Zealand*. p. 141.

[23] (1959) 102 CLR 315.

[24] (1959) 102 CLR 315, 323 quoting from *In re Income Tax Acts (No 1)* (1930) VLR 211, 222–223.

[25] Some commentators suggest that there is a rebuttable presumption of public benefit in the case of purposes for the advancement of education. See, e.g., Lawbook Company, *Principles of the Law of Trusts*, [19070] (online service).

[26] [1923] 1 Ch 237.

[27] See e.g., *Funnell v Stewart* [1996] 1 All ER 715 where Hazel Williamson QC held that 'faith healing has by the present time... become a recognized activity of public benefit...'. In that case the testamentary gift was held valid on the basis that it was for the advancement of religion (another recognised head of charitable purpose).

28 *Income Tax Assessment Act 1997* (Cth) Division 50. In relation to fringe benefits tax, see Australian Taxation Office Tax Ruling, 'Income Tax and Fringe Benefits Tax: Charities', TR 2005/21. See generally, Dal Pont, *Charity Law in Australia and New Zealand*, pp. 92–105.

29 See, Australia Institute (2004), *The Accountability of Private Schools to Public Values*, Discussion Paper No. 71, Part 6. *Income Tax Assessment Act 1997* (Cth) Division 30.

30 See, e.g., Chesterman, *Charities, Trusts and Social Welfare*; Australia Institute, *The Accountability of Private Schools to Public Values*. For a detailed discussion in the context of the English education system, see Morris, *Schools, An Education in Charity Law*, chapter 2.

31 I. Sheppard, R. Fitzgerald, D. Gonski, (2001), *Report of the Inquiry into the Definition of Charities and Related Organisations*. Australian Commonwealth Government, p. 169.

32 Ian M. Ramsay and Ann R. Shorten (1996), *Education and the Law*. Sydney: Butterworths, p. 148; Australia Institute, *The Accountability of Private Schools to Public Values*.

33 For a discussion of state aid to religious schools in Australia generally, see *Attorney-General (Vic); ex rel Black v Commonwealth* (1981) 146 CLR 559, pp. 607–608 (Stephen J). Unlike the other states, state aid for religious schools in South Australia was provided for a very short period (five years) and was abolished altogether by the middle of the nineteenth century. Barcan, *A History of Australian Education*, pp. 71–73; *Grace Bible Church Inc v Reedman* (1984) 54 ALR 571, pp. 576–577 (Zelling J).

34 Barcan, *A History of Australian Education*, chapter 9.

35 Australia Institute, *The Accountability of Private Schools to Public Values*.

36 Jane Edwards, Andrew Knott, and Dan Riley (1979), *Australian Schools and the Law*. Sydney: LBC Information Services, pp. 282–3. Barcan, *A History of Australian Education*.

37 Barcan, *A History of Australian Education*, pp. 317–20.

38 (1981) 146 CLR 559.

39 The proceedings were commenced at their request through a relator action by the Victorian Attorney-General.

40 For a discussion of the historical background to section 116 see, Stephen McLeish (1992), 'Making Sense of Religion and the Constitution: A Fresh Start for Section 116', *Monash University Law Review*, 18, p. 207.

41 (1981) 146 CLR 559, 636 (Wilson J).

42 See, eg, *Lemon v Kurtzmann* 403 US 602 (1971).

43 (1981) 146 CLR 559, 653 (Wilson J).

44 Puls, 'The Wall of Separation: Section 116, The First Amendment and Constitutional Religious Guarantees', pp. 139, 164.

45 (1981) 146 CLR 559, 586–7.

46 [1899] AC 99. For other examples of the terminology of charity law in the DOGS case see (1981) 146 CLR 559, 604 (Gibbs J), 656 (Wilson J).

47 (1981) 146 CLR 559, 633.

48 Puls, 'The Wall of Separation: Section 116, The First Amendment and Constitutional Religious Guarantees', p. 139.

49 For an overview of these requirements, see Ramsay and Shorten, *Education and the Law*. Sydney: Butterworths, [2.50]-[2.53]. For recent versions of such legislation, see *Education (Accreditation of Non-State Schools) Act 2001* (Qld); *Education and Training Reform Act 2006* (Vic).

50 *Teachers and Schools Registration Act 1905* (Vic). Ramsay and Shorten, *Education and the Law*, p. 51.

51 Sections 88(6).

52 (1984) 54 ALR 571.

53 Ibid., 572.

54 Ibid., 579 (Zelling J).

55 Ibid., 578; *Education Act 1915* (SA).

56 Division 7.

57 Section 77.

58 Section 78.

[59] *The Queen v Ligertwood* (1982) 30 SASR 328; *Fountain Centre Christian School Incorporated v Harrington* (1990) 53 SASR 361.
[60] (1990) 53 SASR 361, 365 (King CJ).
[61] Sections 8(3) (primary education) and 10(3) (secondary education).
[62] The Hon Dr Andrew Refshauge MP (2004), Minister for Education and Training, NSW Parliamentary Papers (Hansard), Legislative Assembly, 18 February. *Education Amendment (Non-Government Schools Registration)* Bill Second Reading, *Hansard*, p. 6232.
[63] Grimshaw, *Review of Non-Government Schools in NSW: Report 1*, p. 45.
[64] Section 47(h). See also, *Education and Training Reform Act 2006* (Vic) part 4.3.1.6(a).
[65] [2005] 2 AC 246.
[66] Ibid 277.
[67] Grimshaw, *Review of Non-Government Schools in NSW: Report 1*, p. 81.

Pauline Ridge
ANU College of Law
Australian National University

PETER BALINT

4. EDUCATION FOR TOLERANCE

Respecting Sameness, Not Difference

For those who are interested in the successful accommodation of the ethnic, cultural and other diversity that exists in contemporary liberal democracies, the teaching of specific civic virtues to children, and perhaps even to adults as well, will seem a sensible idea.[1] For while the state can do much directly to help with the accommodation of diversity—for example, by reforming laws and practices that may directly or indirectly discriminate against certain groups—much of the successful accommodation of difference will rely on the attitudes of the citizenry. Recent public policy in several multicultural jurisdictions has emphasised the importance of the attitudes and practices of citizens themselves. This has been particularly evident in the language of social cohesion, which is prominent in policy discourse in Canada, Australia and Europe. Yet, this does not settle precisely what type of attitude and approach should be promoted among the citizenry. One approach that has been suggested is the encouraging of respect of difference, and with it an approach of embracing diversity. Another approach would be to promote the importance of respecting sameness, that is, common citizenship, or if one wishes to cast the net wider, common humanity. While both types of approach will have their benefits, in this chapter, I will argue that the respect of difference approach is less likely than respect of sameness to accommodate diversity in liberal societies. While respecting the sameness of another individual will entail several duties (e.g. non-harm), of particular importance here is the duty to respect another individual's right to live/act/be in a way that may or may not be at odds with one's own life and views.

This raises the question of how respect of sameness relates to tolerance. To put it simply, approaches that attempt to encourage a respect of difference try to transcend tolerance (understood as forbearance). If we all respect each other's differences, then the practice of forbearance tolerance will no longer be necessary. On the other hand, respect of sameness neither tries to transcend forbearance tolerance, nor valorises it. It simply acknowledges that, because of the fact of diversity—we live different lives and have different values from each other—forbearance tolerance is a necessary minimum to enable liberal accommodation of difference. The structure of the chapter is as follows. In the first part of the chapter, I turn to the meaning of tolerance, and argue against defining away its unpleasant parts and trying to turn it into something much more positive. In the second part of the chapter, I turn more directly to respect of difference and argue that, perhaps surprisingly, this approach may not turn out to be as accommodating of diversity as it first appears. In the third and final part of the chapter, I turn to the issue of education, both for adults and

E.B. Coleman and K. White (eds.), Religious Tolerance, Education and the Curriculum, 41–51.

children, and defend respect of sameness as the most liberal and most accommodating approach to diversity.

TOLERANCE

A state that practices liberal toleration will be very accommodating of the diversity of its citizens. Such a state will, at minimum, not interfere in the (non-harming) practices of its citizens, and in some cases may even change its own policies and practices to enable particular citizens, or groups of citizens, a greater possibility to follow their own practices and beliefs.[2] Yet, this is only one dimension of liberal toleration, that of the relationship between the state and the citizen. The other dimension that must be examined, particularly in relation to education, is that relationship between citizens.[3] If we care about the freedom of citizens to practice their (non-harming) lives, then it will matter that individual citizens, at least in the public realm, do not unjustly interfere with each other's freedom. A society where both dimensions of liberal toleration are practised will be one where individuals are highly free to follow their own life plans, and it will rightly be described as a tolerant society. Yet the meaning of 'tolerance' here is not settled. At one end of a spectrum[4], we have tolerance involving a very positive set of attitudes and practices. This approach is expressed, for example, in UNESCO's (1995) *Declaration of Principles on Tolerance*, which reads:

> Tolerance is respect, acceptance and appreciation of the rich diversity of our world's cultures, our forms of expression and ways of being human. It is fostered by knowledge, openness, communication, and freedom of thought, conscience and belief. Tolerance is harmony in difference. It is not only a moral duty, it is also a political and legal requirement. Tolerance, the virtue that makes peace possible, contributes to the replacement of the culture of war by a culture of peace.[5]

At the other end of the spectrum, we have a much narrower and more negative view. Here,

> x can be said to be tolerating y's performance of z when x disapproves of y doing z, and when x has the capacity to hinder y in their performing z, and yet chooses not to.[6]

These two views are very different. One view sees tolerance as a type of forbearance, of putting up with things you disapprove of despite having the power to negatively interfere, and the other sees tolerance as something much more than simply not interfering with things you believe to be repugnant or problematic, but much more positively, embracing and appreciating these very things.

Yet when it comes to the question of how we, as citizens, should relate to our fellow citizens within a tolerant society, both of these meanings of tolerance have limited application. If we take the second view that a tolerant society means forbearance towards difference, then this can only capture some instances, and probably very few, of how we both *will* and *should* relate to each other. Many differences between citizens will be quite unremarkable, and will simply be objects of indifference—things such as hobbies, whether you like playing football, cooking, chess or sitting in coffee shops. And there is no good reason to think that these sorts of things should be anything other than objects of indifference. Other sorts of differences may well be objects of respect and appreciation—one thinks here of the way food is treated by many people in multicultural societies. And finally, there will be differences that will need to be the objects of the forbearance type of tolerance—things like ideologies, religious beliefs, customs, and clothing often fall into this category. These examples are meant to be merely suggestive. Many individuals are indifferent to many religious beliefs, respect the followers of certain hobbies, and barely tolerate certain foods.

The main point I am trying to make here is that a well-functioning, generally harmonious society will have instances of all three types of attitude (indifference, appreciation respect, and forbearance-type tolerance) displayed by its citizens towards their fellow citizens, and instances of forbearance tolerance might even be quite rare. A tolerant society as one in which forbearance *always* takes place does not make much sense from a descriptive point of view, and is even more bizarre from a normative point of view.

But this does not mean that the 'respect, acceptance and appreciation' of difference view espoused by UNESCO makes sense either. In this approach, we have the opposite problem: there are only positive attitudes towards difference (or as UNESCO puts it, to 'our world's cultures, our forms of expression and ways of being human'). There is no mention here of the forbearance understanding of tolerance at all, or of the attitude of indifference. Indeed, there appears to be no space for either of these attitudes in this view of a tolerant society.

While it may be nice to have a tolerant society with no negative attitudes towards differences, it is far from feasible. The fact that we do not all want or believe the same thing—the fact of diversity—necessarily precludes it. And as I will argue in the next section, it is not clear that aiming for this type of society is desirable, or at least without significant and important costs. There are two other problems with this positive-type description of tolerance that need to be addressed before moving on. The first is that the more precise meanings of tolerance are lost. This is much more that simply a semantic issue; when it comes to the crunch in issues of difference between citizens, the forbearance meaning of tolerance is a crucially important moral minimum. If by 'striving for a tolerant society' we mean at minimum that such a society should be free from acts of intolerance (hate crimes, serious public discrimination, etc), then we need to hold on to the forbearance notion of tolerance very tightly. We may not like someone because of their background or beliefs, and this might even be quite irrational, but ultimately it must be required that such a citizen practices tolerance and avoids committing a violent or discriminatory act. To lose this notion—which did so much to stop the horrendous bloodshed of the European Wars of Religion—or even to seriously diminish it, seems both dangerous and foolish, and this is the case even if we wish to strive for something more than 'mere tolerance'.

The second problem with the positive-type approach to tolerance is that it conflates a method of achieving a tolerant society with tolerance itself. If we take a

43

tolerant society as one that is as free as possible from acts of intolerance, then it is still a separate question as to how we should achieve that society. While encouraging 'respect, acceptance and appreciation' might be one way of achieving such a society, it is certainly not the only possible candidate. Viable alternatives include encouraging the moral virtue of tolerance (forbearance), or encouraging respect of the basic rights of your fellow citizens (what I have called 'respect of sameness'). Moreover, it needs to be remembered that any (non-radically assimilating) society will still require the forbearance notion of tolerance, and this is true even if it wishes to encourage 'respect, acceptance and appreciation' of difference. What a tolerant society entails and the methods best used to achieve it *are* different things. To conflate these two things means both the serious loss of the traditional notion of tolerance, and the closing down of the question of whether there are any other ways of achieving a tolerant society.

For those concerned about acts of intolerance, it might seem that this view of tolerance is unnecessarily narrow. The opposite of intolerance of difference is 'respect, acceptance and appreciation' of difference, and this is what a tolerant society must look like. But aiming for a society free from intolerance, or at least with much less intolerance, does not mean we need to have the opposite type of society, just that it must not be an intolerant society. We need a separate argument for the 'respect, acceptance and appreciation' of difference type of society than simply that it is *not* an intolerant society.

Finally, there is one further potential misconception that requires addressing. This is the common slippage between 'respect the right' to hold a particular difference and 'respecting the difference' itself, or to put is another way, between respect of sameness and respect of difference.[7] These are very different things, despite respect often being used in both senses simultaneously.[8] A society in which citizens respect the right of each other to hold cultural or other differences is wholly consistent with the forbearance type of tolerance—that is, because you respect the right of citizen X to do action Y, you have a strong reason to then tolerate this action. But the obligation to not negatively interfere in the lives or differences of your fellow citizens does not automatically imply directly respecting their differences.

In sum: a tolerant society is one in which here is a minimal degree of acts of intolerance, such as hate crimes, serious public discrimination etc—this is something that all will agree on. Yet for this to occur, the attitude towards a fellow citizen's differences can be indifference, respect and appreciation, or tolerance. Although all three attitudes are possible, tolerance remains the minimum attitude required by citizens. Finally, the *right* of fellow citizens to follow their own beliefs and practices must be respected for a society to be described as tolerant.

As such, this view of a tolerant society is one of toleration as a political practice, and it encompasses both of the views of tolerance discussed previously, but crucially is wedded to neither. A tolerant society is a free society where people can (within liberal limits) live their lives freely without undue discrimination and harassment from their fellow citizens in the public sphere. So while the 'respect, acceptance and appreciation' of difference may not be required to achieve tolerance, is encouraging is the best way to achieve such a society? This is the question to which I now turn.

RESPECT OF DIFFERENCE *how?*

AH

It is ultimately an empirical question as to which method will best achieve a tolerant society. Yet two preliminary points need to be made. First, there *are* methods other than the 'respect, acceptance and appreciation' of difference available. Legitimate alternatives could involve the stressing and learning of the importance of respecting other citizen's rights, and/or having strong (and enforced) disincentives for acts of intolerance, such as heavy fines or incarceration. Second, we need to stipulate some standard for deciding on what 'best' would mean. We can reject straight away 'most efficient' and 'most efficacious' as the main criteria for 'best'. If it was simply about effectiveness in achieving the goal of a tolerant society, then all sorts of illiberal things would be ideal candidates. If we are taking a liberal approach to accommodating diversity, then we need to understand 'best' in more negative terms, as in 'has the least costs' compared to other methods, where 'costs' are impingements on individual freedom. While a very expensive program would impinge on freedom in one way—by requiring a lot of tax dollars—of more relevance is the impinging on people's freedom to live their lives as they see fit without undue (state-sanctioned) coercion. In a liberal society, this is a crucially important cost.

As such, my aim in this section will not be to propose the precise method to achieve and maintain a tolerant society, nor will it involve a total rejection of the 'respect, acceptance and appreciation' of difference approach. Instead, I will warn against thinking the effects of the respect of difference approach are only good, and thereby question the extent that this approach to achieving a tolerant society is encouraged both in education and in wider community programs.

The 'respect, acceptance and appreciation' of difference approach to building and maintaining a tolerant society can be thought of as either one-sided, or as two-sided (or mutual). In the one-sided approach, people are simply encouraged to respect, appreciate, and value the differences of the people they interact with. In the two-sided approach, the idea of mutuality is stressed—respect and appreciation of difference is to be a mutual affair between citizens. In the one-sided approach, it is easy to see that if a sufficient number of people respect each others' differences, then there is a good chance that these people, at least, will not be involved in acts of intolerance towards the holders of differences they respect. If enough people are involved, intolerance should dissipate. If we add a two-sided or mutual approach to respect of difference, then this possible effect should only be strengthened.

Are there possible limitations on freedom with the one-sided approach? When respect of difference is encouraged in a society, the differences that are mostly likely to be respected are the ones that were previously associated with the attitude of indifference rather than intolerance. Sally might not have thought much (negative or positive) about her local Sudanese community, but after being encouraged to learn about them and most likely sample their food, her attitude towards, at least their food, may well turn to appreciation. 'That's great', you may say. But Sally never had any problem with them in the first place. It may seem like a trivial point, but she could have done other things with her time and energy. Perhaps in some views, her life is now richer for understanding the local Sudanese culture. But this will not limit her intolerance of Sudanese people: she did not have *any* to begin with.

As to making her life go better, surely learning about other cultures and trying their cuisines is simply a hobby, and hobbies in a liberal society should be entirely freely chosen and not state subsidised, or at least not differentially subsidised or encouraged.

Nevertheless, this is not the main problem with respect of difference. The main issue is that it does not, nor can it, engage properly with 'difficult' or challenging differences. While many differences in a society are entirely respectable—cuisine being the obvious category here—there will always be those that are not easily respectable despite being within the bounds of what *should* be tolerable. These differences are often, though not always, ideological or religious. Because these sorts of differences are not easily, and sometimes not at all seen as respectable by many citizens, these differences are left out of, or are minimised in this type of respecting game. And on the other side, because of some citizen's differences, for example their religious beliefs, it is not a game they can easily play: they may not find many common differences respectable at all (issues of modesty and sexuality provide good examples here). It is not equally easy for all citizens to respect the differences of their fellow citizens. Of course, some readers may be thinking, this is the very idea: this approach forces these types of citizens to engage fully with their fellow citizens. But this is its very problem. Why should those who have beliefs that make it hard for them to respect other's differences be strongly encouraged to do so? If there was a necessary connection between the lack of respect of a particular difference and acts of intolerance towards its holder, then a strong case could be made. But this is certainly not the case. It is clearly possible to not respect a difference, and not act intolerantly towards its holder. Most religious people do this everyday towards those with alternative beliefs and practices. Indeed, the man who is commonly viewed as one of the world's most tolerant people, the Dalai Lama, does not respect homosexuality, among other 'deviant' practices.[9]

The problem here is that people's differences are not taken seriously, despite any rhetoric to the contrary. This is a point not lost on those with important ideological differences. Felix Cheung, to provide one such example, argues that multicultural attempts to view Christianity as simply a different, but equal way of seeing God, fundamentally misunderstand what many Christians hold to be a crucial distinction between special and general revelation, and as such fail to take Christianity seriously.[10]

If we take a liberal notion of freedom seriously, then people should be free to live their lives as they please as long as it causes no harm. Acts of intolerance *can* be classified as harm, yet lack of appreciation and respect on its own cannot be. To insist on the importance of respecting difference is simply imposing one view of the good on people who are not necessarily going to be intolerant anyway—either because they never really cared, or because they cared deeply but were still able to practice tolerance where required.

Far from being a better solution, the two-sided or mutual approach to respect of difference is doubly problematic. Here, being a good citizen involves being both respecting *and* respectable. Of course, this is not too challenging for those with 'normal-ish' differences, and, among themselves, these people can quickly become highly virtuous citizens. But if we are going to take people's differences seriously, in the sense that the differences are theirs, and if they harm no-one should be left alone, then there is a problem for those whose differences do not make it easy for them to respect others or easily respectable. The full realisation of mutual respect of difference will clearly never happen; many cultures have values that are directly in conflict with each other. Asking citizens to respect each other's cultures is not a possibility without extreme coercion. It is difficult to imagine a traditional Catholic, for example, and a politically active pro-choice abortion campaigner actually respecting each others differences.[11] But what are the ramifications of at least trying to strongly encourage citizens to mutually respect each other's differences?

If good citizenship, and thus the acceptance of cultural difference, is primarily achieved by a person's beliefs and behaviour being acceptable to their fellow citizens, as opposed to being tolerated by the state, then this can have ramifications not only for what is respected, but for what is tolerated as well. An approach to cultural and religious diversity that places the possibility for difference on both the success of being respectable in the eyes of your fellow citizens and your ability to be respecting in return appears likely to severely limit the freedom for diversity. To be involved in the process of mutual respect, you have to be able to be both respecting and respectable. This will necessarily involve the holders of differences accentuating their most desirable and (quite literally) digestible characteristics, while downplaying their values—things that are much more difficult to make as broadly respectable. This political interference is likely to then narrow the difference range towards the mutually respectable and, worse, quite likely skew the range further towards the majority and their preferences (those who can more easily play the respecting game). What we have, then, seems to be an assimilation of difference under the guise of respect of difference. The boundaries of the tolerable within a society are always going to be significantly broader than the boundaries of the respectable, and there is a real danger to individual freedom of either completely collapsing this distinction or creating strong inducements to become more respecting and respectable.

Returning to the UNESCO approach to tolerance for a moment, we can see that if we remove or drastically reduce the notion of forbearance tolerance, the important question of what should be tolerated in a society can be affected by this type of mutual respect. Instead of discussing the question of whether the intolerant should be tolerated, the question can quickly become whether the disrespecting and disrespectable should be tolerated—especially if people with these traits come to be seen as bad citizens.

An obvious retort at this stage might be: 'but people's lives go better this way!' Indeed, they might. But this is an issue of what the liberal state should do, and the respecting and respectable way of being is clearly a conception of the good. A liberal society is one of free association and belief, and it is a fundamental mistake to believe that all associations and beliefs within such a society must be made liberal. Indeed, attempts to do this with state power and resources are themselves illiberal. A thorough-going comprehensive liberalism is just another view of the good, and as such is an intolerant state act itself.

There are alternative ways to achieving and maintaining a tolerant society, and these alternatives would involve fewer costs to individual freedom and be more accommodating of difference. The simplest alternative is to encourage a respect of sameness (whether citizenship status or common humanity). This is much more of a 'regardless of what you think or feel, all citizens must have their rights respected' approach. Perhaps this could be supplemented by encouraging the virtue of tolerance, but even this would need careful thought. While the virtue of tolerance will be required to underpin a tolerant society, it too must not be thought of as a good in itself and thus maximised. Even if it is found empirically that learning about and respecting each others' differences *is* useful for achieving and maintaining a tolerant society, crucially this does not mean that this approach to difference should be maximised. It must be used in the minimal possible way to achieve its ends.

EDUCATION FOR TOLERANCE

My argument against appreciation or respect of difference has its strongest implication for the various policy programs aimed at adult citizens. But this argument still has consequences for the education of children, particularly for the ways that the issues of diversity are experienced and taught in schools.

Despite the temptation to over-insure, thought needs to be given as to whether respect and appreciation of difference really is necessary *at all* for the maintenance of a tolerant society, as its costs and dangers are high. For the respect of difference approach to be implemented in education to any degree, it would need to be shown that not only does it sustain a tolerant society, but that it does so substantially better than the significantly less-costly methods available. Its limitations on individual freedom are too high to be ignored, as is the fact that it is not necessarily a good servant for those who are commonly the victims of acts of intolerance.

There are least two alternative positions those that who wish to encourage respect difference might try and apply here. The first alternative sees better knowledge and understanding, but not necessarily appreciation, of the differences that exist in our society as the key to greater tolerance. This is a view that holds that if only there is wider knowledge about the details of particular cultures and their practices, then instances of intolerance will be reduced (see Joel Windle's chapter in this volume). To use Islamophobia as an example, the argument would be that misinformation about Islam is causally connected to instances of discrimination against Muslims, and that better knowledge about Islam would redress this problem. While I have no doubt that misinformation about Islam does contribute to Islamophobia, it is not clear that it is an easy situation to rectify. If schools are intended to be the providers of such knowledge, then besides the oft-cited problem of an overcrowded curriculum, what differences should be focussed on? People are ignorant or misinformed about most of the differences that exist within a society. There are two main problems with the focus on knowledge. First, there is the practical problem of there simply being too much information to learn, not only about the variety of differences across a society, but even about the intricacies within particular differences—Islam, for example, is far from one monolithic thing. Each difference itself has important differences within. Second, and much more seriously, there is a danger of making acceptance and respect of rights contingent on education. Even if the first problem

48

is somehow solved, as anyone who has done any teaching will attest, school children (and university students) do not retain lots of things they are taught. It is too dangerous to base the respect of a citizen's rights by another citizen on the hope that they listened in school the day they were taught about a particular difference.

The second alternative position involves training and transforming the emotions of individuals when they meet those who hold differences (see Padmasiri de Silva's chapter in this volume). This has been expressed in empathy-based approaches to education for tolerance.[12] While empathy may have an important instrumental role in achieving tolerant action, it does not seem particularly stable or powerful on its own. The emotion of empathy is quickly manipulated, and it is easy to be more empathic with those we already have little trouble with. How many people can really be empathic with those they find ugly, distasteful, or totally morally wrong? How many liberal-minded people could, for example, engage empathically with a middle-aged man who proudly announced 'I wish it was legal to have sex with children? Tolerance, and its achievement, ultimately require putting up with things we do not like, and as such we need to find methods that deal best with the most difficult and unpleasant cases.

The best method of achieving a tolerant society will be capable of both dealing with all sorts of difficult and unpleasant cases, as well as not targeting all citizens for the sake of the few—and this is particularly problematic if a method is unlikely to even affect those few. I want to suggest that that the best alternative is to focus on the fundamental non-negotiability of respecting other citizen's rights in the public sphere (backed up with appropriate legislative force). This respect of sameness, in which the message can be 'regardless of what you think or feel, all citizens must have their rights respected', provides significant advantages over other alternatives. First, unlike knowledge-based approaches, it is simple; it can be regularly repeated and thus should be easy to impart. Second, it is not contingent on appreciation of difference, empathy to its holder, or knowledge of a difference. Third, it treats all citizens equally in both a moral sense, and by requiring no more from one than any other. And fourth, it is not unreasonably demanding on the citizen, and allows the greatest possible range of freedom for individuals to live their lives as they see fit.

There are two critiques that may be levelled at this position. The first is that children are not capable of separating the personal from the impersonal. As David Heyd writes; 'children tend to view individual persons as constituted by their particular actions and beliefs…[and] they judge the validity of beliefs and actions in terms of their attitude towards the individual holding them'.[13] In order to be able engage in the type of respect of basic rights I am suggesting, the individual must be able to say 'I don't like an action/belief, but, because its holder has the right to express it, I must not negatively interfere'. In other words, they must be capable of seeing the individual as not solely constituted by their actions and beliefs; something that children do not naturally do. However, it is clear that adults *are* capable of such a separation. Education for citizenship in a tolerant society must concern the skills necessary for adult life. There is no reason to think that these skills cannot be fostered in schools, even if they only become fully realised later on (this is hardly an unusual trait for many skills taught in schools). While this may prove difficult for very young children where there are immediate issues like anti-bullying and anti-racism to deal with, we need to be careful of taking what can be a convenient short-term solution and extending it into the longer-term goal of education for tolerance.

The other critique that could be offered is that this type of approach may not be sufficient to actually achieve tolerant behaviour, and that some stronger disposition or attitude will be required. Yet, it is not clear that this type of approach, especially if educated early, could not become a reasonably strong attitude or disposition in itself. I am not arguing that the other types of methods have no role at all, just that they have greater costs and dangers compared to this approach, and must therefore play a secondary role, if any. As such, I am simply arguing that respect of basic rights should be the primary method of teaching for a tolerant society. Moreover, I have no pretensions to solving all the problems of living in a diverse society. There will always be acts of violence and discrimination in a society, and it is worth remembering that our political aim as liberals is to reduce these instances: to stop them altogether is highly utopian. Liberalism is not a cuddly doctrine in which everybody loves and appreciates each other. It is a practical doctrine born out of violent intolerance over difference. It recognises that we will always have different and contradictory views, and the best politics can do is to minimise harm and to help individuals live their lives as freely as possible. Our goal should be to minimise acts of intolerance and to give citizens the maximum freedom possible. If we wish to maintain the important achievements of liberalism, there are some risks we must be willing to accept.

Finally, education for tolerance must be just that—instilling the conditions under which restraint can be practiced in the public sphere. It should not entail trying to avoid the conditions of tolerance altogether. That is, it should not involve trying to 'move beyond' tolerance into a sphere where all citizens' differences are somehow respected by one another (either in practice, or by changing the definition of the term). To do so is both empirically nonsensical, and normatively undesirable.

NOTES

[1] This paper was first presented at the conference Negotiating the Sacred IV: Tolerance Education and the Curriculum. I thank the participants and the conference organisers for their useful comments and suggestions. A version of the paper was published as Peter Balint (2010), 'Avoiding an Intolerant Society: Why respect of difference may not be the best approach', *Educational Philosophy and Theory*, 42(1), pp. 129–41.

[2] For major works dealing with this issue see, for example: Charles Taylor (1994), 'The Politics of Recognition', in Amy Gutman (ed.) *Multiculturalism*. Princeton: Princeton University Press; Will Kymlicka (1996), *Multicultural Citizenship: A Liberal Theory of Minority Rights*. Oxford: Oxford University Press; Susan Moller Okin (1999), 'Is Multiculturalism Bad for Women?' in Joshua Cohen, Matthew Howard, and Martha C. Nussbaum (eds.), *Is Multiculturalism Bad for Women?* Princeton: Princeton University Press; Brian Barry (2001), *Culture and Equality: An Egalitarian Critique of Multiculturalism*. Cambridge: Polity Press; Chandran Kukathas (2003), *The Liberal Archipelago: A Theory of Diversity and Freedom*. Oxford: Oxford University Press; Anne Phillips (2007), *Multiculturalism without Culture*. Princeton: Princeton University Press.

[3] For a discussion of both of these dimensions in relation to the issue of respect, see Peter Balint (2006), 'Respect Relationships in Diverse Societies', *Res Publica* 12(1), pp. 35–7.

[4] Michael Walzer describes five possibilities on the spectrum of toleration: resigned acceptance; benign indifference; principled recognition of the rights of others; openness and curiosity; and even enthusiastic endorsement. Michael Walzer (1997), *On Toleration.* New Haven and London: Yale University Press, pp. 10–11. In a similar vein, Rainer Forst identifies four conceptions of toleration: permission; co-existence; respect; and esteem. Rainer Forst (2003). 'Toleration, Justice and Reason', in C. McKinnon and D. Castiglione (eds), *The Culture of Toleration in Diverse Societies.* Manchester: Manchester University Press, pp. 73–6.

[5] UNESCO (1995) *Declaration of Principles on Tolerance*, Proclaimed and signed by the Member States of UNESCO on 16 November 1995.

[6] This is a slightly modified version of Andrew Shorten's definition, and is view that is widely accepted in the philosophical literature. Andrew Shorten (2005), 'Toleration and Cultural Controversies', *Res Publica,* 11, pp. 275–99, p. 280.

[7] For further discussion of this distinction see Balint, 'Respect Relationships in Diverse Societies'.

[8] This can even happen in legislation, for example in New South Wales, Principle 2 of the *Community Relations Commission and Principles of Multiculturalism Act 2000*, Part 1, Section 3, reads: 'All individuals and institutions should respect and make provision for the culture, language and religion of others within an Australian legal and institutional framework where English is the common language'. New South Wales Parliament (2000) *Community Relations Commission and Principles of Multiculturalism Act 2000.* Sydney: New South Wales Parliament.

[9] He writes;

> A sexual act is deemed proper when the couples use the organs intended for sexual intercourse [the penis and the vagina] and nothing else [anus, hands or mouth].... homosexuality, whether it is between men or between women, is not improper in itself. What is improper is the use of organs already defined as inappropriate for sexual contact.

Dalai Lama (1996), *Beyond Dogma: Dialogues and Discourses.* Berkeley: North Atlantic Books, pp. 46–7.

[10] Felix Cheung (2006), Multiculturalism & Education: an evangelical Christian reflection on multiculturalism and its implications for intercultural education. Box Hill: PTC Media.

[11] This example comes from Kukathas, *The Liberal Archipelago*, p. 34.

[12] See for example Lisa A Hollingsworth, Mary J. Didelot, and Judith O. Smith (2003), 'REACH Beyond Tolerance: a framework for teaching children empathy and responsibility', *Journal of Humanistic Counseling, Education and Development,* 42(2), pp. 139–51; or Mary Gordon, (2005), *Roots of Empathy: changing the world child by child.* Toronto: Thomas Allen.

[13] David Heyd (2003), 'Education to Toleration: some philosophical obstacles resolved', in C. McKinnon and D. Castiglione (eds.), *The Culture of Toleration in Diverse Societies.* Manchester: Manchester University Press, p. 200.

Peter Balint
School of Humanities and Social Sciences
University of New South Wales
Australian Defence Force Academy, Canberra

PHILIP CAM

5. EDUCATING FOR TOLERANCE

Early modern thought on toleration in Europe dealt with issues of religious freedom that arose out of the Reformation; and to this, the Enlightenment added the struggle for more open social and political dialogue and dissent. These developments mark the growth of attitudes and ways of life associated with tolerance that are in tension with other deep-rooted human proclivities and traditions found throughout 'the crooked timber of humanity'.[1] While societies that were heir to these developments have become more enlightened and tolerant because of them, intolerance occurs in all societies, adopting various guises in response to social and historical conditions. Under some conditions, societies fall prey to sectarian violence, while in other circumstances they may become riddled with racial hatred, or succumb to ethnic cleansing, suffer the persecution of religious minorities, or a multitude of other afflictions that feed on intolerance.

In a world set aflame by the unbearable suffering of displaced populations, sectarian violence, religious fundamentalism, terrorism and the 'war on terror', the problems of intolerance in Australia pale into insignificance. Yet it would be a mistake to think that these things do not have their domestic correlatives or that we remain unaffected by events taking place elsewhere in the world. Widespread attitudes towards asylum seekers, the lingering shadows of racism, friction between the values of minorities and those of the wider community, violence involving young ethnic groups, tensions within and between minority groups, and the ostracism of religious and ethnic minorities associated in the public mind with the lingering threat of terrorism—these are among the signs and symptoms of intolerance at home that is all the worse for being so commonly denied.

This chapter is concerned with what can be done to build bulwarks of tolerance in Australian society through school education. While our schools can hardly be charged with the responsibility for eradicating intolerance, they do have a formative influence upon each generation and the school can do much to nurture the kinds of attitudes and understandings needed to combat it. Although schools are constantly attempting to deal with this issue, I am going to suggest that common educational practices may well have the unintended consequence of promoting intolerance, and that schools would do well to consider suggestions for turning this around.

I must admit at the outset that what I have to say about these matters depends upon a conception of tolerance that is lexicographically deviant. So I will begin by attempting to draw a distinction between what I take to be the ordinary conception of tolerance and the one upon which I will rely. In a nutshell, the ordinary idea is that to tolerate something is to put up with it, even though one does not agree with it or finds it distasteful. The idea in which I am interested is more properly a

E.B. Coleman and K. White (eds.), Religious Tolerance, Education and the Curriculum, 53–65.

feature of systems, and bears an analogy to the concept of tolerance in engineering, which applies to the limits of variation within which a system can function without significantly affecting its performance. From that conception of tolerance, we may take both the idea of limits and the necessity of a certain amount of free play in order for a system to function effectively. While in no way wishing to imply the reduction of the social to the mechanical, to conceive of tolerance as a practical requirement for effective functioning may turn out to be a fruitful way of thinking about tolerance in human affairs.

FORBEARANCE AND FACILITATION

While we are all prepared to live with things we find irritating, and nearly everyone agrees that certain things are beyond the pale, we recognise that such judgments are not always and everywhere the same. Things forborne in ordinary circumstances may not be tolerated when societies come to a tipping point; and the history of sentiment reveals that things at one time accepted as facts of life can be viewed with abhorrence by later generations. Even so, in any society at any time, there are bound to be disagreements about whether certain things should or should not be tolerated. One general criterion for sorting out such disagreements is that we should forbear when doing so is conducive to the overall good, but not tolerate that which significantly adds to the burden of harm.[2] Things that turn out to be more or less neutral in this respect, such as matters of taste or personal preference, are not proper candidates for discussion, however irritating or distasteful some may find them to be.[3]

While this criterion may not be of much immediate practical help in resolving conflicts, where people are likely to disagree about what is harmful or good, it points us in the right direction. Political, legal, social, educational and other arrangements that aim to provide the groundwork for tolerance should help to establish rights and restrictions or freedoms and responsibilities that promote welfare and minimise harm.

We can see this principle in operation historically by considering a work such as John Locke's *Epistola de Tolerantia* (*A Letter on Toleration*).[4] Locke wrote the *Epistola* in the 1680s while in exile in Holland, where the problem of toleration was a burning issue not only in Dutch intellectual circles but within the sizeable refugee community that had taken shelter there. Locke's answer to the then widespread persecution and civil commotion over matters of religion was to articulate the now classical basis for the separation of church and state. According to Locke, the state has the function of promoting civil goods—the preservation of life, liberty, property and other earthly goods—and it is the duty of the civil magistrate to protect those goods through the administration of laws established for the purpose. The power of the magistrate is to be strictly limited to this realm. Magistrates and the civil law must deal only with matters that are indifferent to religion and must not impose any form of worship, or forbid people to worship as they please. By contrast, it is the church and not the magistrate that has care of the soul; and any church may enact its own internal laws for such purposes, so long as it does not encroach upon the civil domain. Thus, while a church is not required to tolerate members who break its laws, and may punish them by means of excommunication, it has no right to deprive them of their civil goods; and nor has it the right to punish those of other faiths who are not subject to its laws or sanctions.

Locke provides a set of limitations that separate the powers of church and state, assigning associated rights and obligations, which would establish individual liberty in matters of religion and bring an end to religious persecution. When reflected in the civil and religious domains, these arrangements provide a measure of toleration that is facilitation and not merely forbearance. They enable people to enjoy freedom of worship and protect them from persecution, thus promoting liberty and minimising harm.

All measures of toleration are naturally meant to have their limits. Locke never intended his proposals to extend to atheists, for example, and in his view, they were 'not to be tolerated at all'.[5] In addition, of course, the implementation of such measures may be expected to be subject to further limitations, so that political, legal and social restrictions remain. To that extent, we may speak of *degrees of toleration* of formerly persecuted groups, rather than the kind of facilitation that aims at complete social equity while honouring difference. In the case in question, we may note that in the century following Locke's *Epistola*, British Catholics still suffered from 'limitations of the system of toleration' under the system of penal laws. So that 'even if conscience itself was respected, and freedom in actual belief permitted, there remained further incapacities for non-conformists in respect of education, the holding of public office, the holding of land and even the right to sit in Parliament'.[6]

So much for the idea of tolerance as a political, legal or social arrangement in regard to diversity which provides the free play that is necessary for the furtherance of the general welfare. As such, tolerance may be embodied in the overall order of society, as in Locke's separation of the powers of church and state, or it may be enshrined within particular institutions or codes of practice. In such manifestations, far from being an individual attitude of forbearance, tolerance is a perfectly objective feature of political or social systems that helps to maintain healthy good order.

TOLERATION AND EDUCATION

Having presented a social systems view of tolerance, it can hardly escape notice that the historical struggle with intolerance is not just one of reforming political, legal and social institutions. It also has to do with the attitudes of individuals. While it may be argued that the attitudes of individuals are a result of their socialisation, and hence that the problem of toleration is fundamentally institutional, it can also be said that society is the aggregate construction of countless individuals, and therefore embodies the attitudes of those who have contributed to it. Therefore, we must look at the problem of toleration from an individual as well as a societal standpoint. This does not mean that we should deal with tolerance in individuals as if they existed apart from society. We need to look at the individual in society, and in the particular contexts in which mental outlooks are formed, in order to see how the societal constitution of tolerance can find its analogue in the minds of individuals and relations between them.

Education

The formation of the individual is the business of education and, so far as formal education is concerned, the relevant institution is obviously the school. When children pass through our school education systems, we need to do what we can to teach them to maximise welfare and minimise harm in the ways that they respond to difference in the various social contexts that impinge upon them. That is to say, we need to teach them to work productively with difference within the limits imposed by these criteria. On the present view, that is what educating for tolerance means.

Before discussing the current scene, I want to begin once again with Locke and trace a line of thought that will help to make sense of what I have to say. Locke has much to tell us about the sources of human understanding and the obstacles standing in its way, as well as giving us practical advice about how to surmount them. It is of note that when he turns to the topic of toleration in his *Essay Concerning Human Understanding*, he offers the following advice:

Opinions

> Since therefore it is unavoidable to the greatest part of men, if not all, to have several *opinions*, without certain and indubitable proofs of their truths; it would, methinks, become all men to maintain peace and the common offices of humanity and friendship in the diversity of opinions. We should do well to commiserate our mutual ignorance, and endeavour to remove it in all the gentle and fair ways of information; and not instantly treat others ill, as obstinate and perverse, because they will not renounce their own and receive our opinions.[7]

This passage hits the nail on its head. When we have diversity of opinion, and do not know things for certain, controversy is unavoidable. In the face of this, we would do better to admit our collective ignorance and be decent to each other rather than regard those who differ from us as either pigheaded or vicious. Instead of thus abusing each other, we should attempt to dispel our ignorance, insofar as we can, by inquiring into the matter. Sage advice! Notice that Locke's counsel has two components. One has to do with forms of regard and the other with intellectual operations. On the one hand, we need 'to maintain peace and the common offices of humanity and friendship' and, on the other, we should attempt to overcome our ignorance by engaging 'in all the gentle and fair ways of information'. Attention to this combination of interpersonal attitude and intellectual endeavour forms the basis of sound policy in educating for tolerance.

Locke wrote at length on education, but since a detailed discussion of his educational thought is not to my purpose, I will develop the above remarks by turning to James Mill's pithy reworking of Locke's theme in *The Principles of Toleration*.[8] Mill's central concern is with the manner in which people deal with the evidence for what they believe. Where there are divergent opinions in cases of moment, he argues, proper dealing consists in not only being in the habit of seeking all the relevant evidence but also of looking at this evidence impartially. People are seldom impartial in disputes that affect them, and opinions tend to be shaped by such things as social class, racial attitudes, an overblown sense of self-importance, and familial or other affections. Such factors can present themselves in snobbish, racist, self-serving and

Evidence

56

preferential attitudes that are all too familiar. They tend to bias our judgment and lead us to downplay or elevate the significance of evidence. To the extent that we are governed by such motivating factors, we must make allowance for them, says Mill, by giving greater weight to countervailing evidence than would otherwise seem warranted. Fair dealing also demands that we give due consideration to all the evidence, and not pay greater attention to the evidence that favours some belief or proposition that has otherwise gained our favour. The extent to which less attention is paid to evidence that is not to our liking is the extent to which it is downplayed. Beyond that, we should cultivate the attitude that Locke calls 'indifferency', by which he means not wishing or willing that some opinion is true, but having regard for any opinion only in so far as it is supported by evidence. In order to bolster this attitude, we need to create an interest in truth and fairness that is sufficient to counteract our other interests.

Mill goes on to argue that disregard for evidence in the formation of opinions is not distinct from showing disregard for our fellows, thus drawing attention to the connection between intellectual habits and forms of regard. His argument is worth repeating:

> This habit of forming opinions, and acting upon them without evidence, is one of the most immoral habits of the mind. Only observe what it imports. As our opinions are the fathers of our actions, to be indifferent about the evidence of our opinions is to be indifferent about the consequences of our actions. But the consequences of our actions are the good and evil of our fellow-creatures. The habit of neglect of evidence, therefore, is the habit of disregarding the good and evil of our fellow-creatures…By the habit of believing whatever a man wishes to believe, he becomes, in proportion to the strength of the habit, a bad neighbour, a bad trustee, a bad politician, a bad judge, a shameless advocate.[9]

As Mill's argument makes clear, Locke's concerns with intellectual process and regard for others are joined at the hip. If toleration in matters of opinion can be characterised in terms of a response to difference that, while acknowledging fallibility, attempts to maximise welfare and minimise harm, then the habit of properly adjudicating evidence is as inseparable from tolerance as the habitual neglect of it is inseparable from an unwarranted neglect of the welfare of others.

Mill regards the habit of neglecting evidence as 'a dreadful vice of education', which encourages that habit in later life. And he goes on to say:

> One of the grand objects of education should be, to generate a constant and anxious concern about evidence; to accustom the mind to run immediately from the idea of the opinion to the idea of its evidence, and to feel dissatisfaction until it is known that all the evidence has been before the mind, and fairly weighed…The regard of evidence, as we said before, implies regard to the good and evil of mankind. Regard to evidence, and the strength of mind, of which it is the foundation, necessarily lead to the discovery of error, and the discredit of institutions not useful but hurtful to mankind. What a debt

of gratitude should we therefore owe to an education which would implant this habit; what detestation do we owe to an education which implants the opposite![10]

So Mill's plea on behalf of tolerance is for an education that would have concern for human welfare by instilling a desire and regard for evidence in the minds of students, thereby keeping in check those vices of prejudice, bias and bigotry that an education based on an unquestioning adherence to the authority of the teacher and the textbook would otherwise encourage.

In a discussion in danger of being overburdened with quotations, I hesitate to add yet one more passage to make my point. Yet, I could do no better to enlarge upon Mill's observations than by returning to the following remarks from Locke:

> The business [of education] in respect of knowledge is not, as I think, to perfect a learner in all or any one of the sciences, but to give his mind that freedom, that disposition and those habits that may enable him to attain any part of knowledge he shall apply himself to or stand in need of in the future course of his life. This and this only is well principling, and not the instilling a reverence and veneration for certain dogmas under the specious title of principles, which are often so remote from that truth and evidence which belongs to principles, that they ought to be rejected as false and erroneous.[11]

The respect for truth and evidence in Mill's counter to dogmatism and intolerance is here portrayed as the mark of a well-educated and principled person who has attained that freedom of thought which should be the central concern of education. Educators should not conceive of knowledge as so much material that the student is to learn by heart and repeat without adequate warrant, but as the attainment of an inquirer, who is disposed to seek evidence and weigh it dispassionately, and to keep an open mind when the case is not conclusive. The development of the capacity and disposition to inquire, rather than the unquestioning acceptance of so much subject matter that passes for knowledge, should be the principal business of education.

Let me approach my conclusion by way of one more stepping-stone. In the philosophy of education, it may safely be said that no one since Socrates has done more to forward the cause of inquiry-based learning than John Dewey. Dewey equated inquiry with reflective thinking of the kind that is most closely associated with scientific investigation. While this suggests that science education ought to lie at the core of inquiry-based learning, Dewey's inquiry method is so general that it may be applied across the disciplines and can therefore provide an armature for thinking across the curriculum.[12] Thinking was central to Dewey's aims in education and he went so far as to say that 'all which the school can or need do for pupils, so far as their *minds* are concerned...is to develop their ability to think'.[13] This is Locke's claim in its most unremitting form. It charges the school with responsibility for the cultivation of inquiring minds, thus emphasising the development of intellectual skills, habits and dispositions, and treating the supply of factual knowledge, that

goals *skills*

tends to overburden the curriculum, as so much fodder for thought. These skills, habits and other dispositions include but are not restricted to the following: schools should encourage a questioning outlook and develop the ability to probe problems and issues through the art of questioning. They should make abundant provision for the exploration of students' thoughts and ideas—their questions, conceptions, opinions, suggestions, suppositions, tentative explanations, inferences, and the like. They should encourage the habit of exploring alternative suggestions and different points of view, rather than the habit of following a single line of thought no matter what the problem domain. They should teach students to reason carefully and avoid fallacious and sloppy inferences. They should engage them in the exploration of ideas, through which they can gain a deeper understanding of significant concepts that are embedded in the curriculum. And, as both Locke and Mill emphasised, they should train students to reach reasonable conclusions through an impartial survey of the evidence. In short, school education should immerse students in inquiry in one and another domain and develop the intellectual skills and habits of mind that will enable them to think for themselves about all kinds of subject-matter and gradually take charge of their own learning.

Dewey also placed great emphasis upon the importance of community in his *community* conception of education in a democratic society. For Dewey, democracy is first and foremost a way of life rather than rule by elected representative government; and a democratic way of life is the life of community that is characterised by free-flowing communication and open decision-making that takes account of everyone's interests. It is inclusive rather than exclusionary and treats differences of belief and opinion as occasions for inquiry rather than as grounds for enmity and division. So, an education that befits democracy must not only empower the individual to make considered judgments and choices, it must also engage students with each other in dialogue and discussion, so that they learn to see things from other people's points of view and to take each other's interests into account in making decisions and arriving at judgments. That is to say, it should not treat students simply as individuals, but regard them as members of a cooperative community and seek to strengthen those social dispositions through which they can learn to discuss their differences and be reasonable with one another.

Dewey's blending of community and inquiry continues to offer an educational remedy for the intolerance that so easily takes root in young people's lives. Yet, even though Dewey has had a considerable influence on educational theory and practice, our educational institutions are home to an incongruent mixture of approaches to education, including widespread ways of engaging in teaching and learning that are likely to contribute to intolerance rather than counter it. Having laid the groundwork, it is time to confront some of these practices by unveiling the intellectual and social outlooks that they perpetuate.

REFORMING EDUCATIONAL PRACTICE

If we are going to educate for tolerance, then students will need to acquire the modes of thought and social dispositions that John Locke and James Mill began to articulate and which find their more contemporary expression in the writings of John Dewey. Only then will they learn to maximise welfare and minimise harm in dealing with their differences. As we have seen all along, however, we cannot make provision for greater tolerance without attending to our institutions. This means that, in order to educate effectively for tolerance, we need educational reform.

I am going to address four elements of normal educational practice that are bound to be internalised by students and which will inevitably affect the ways that they deal with differences of belief and value. In each case, these elements coincide with an aspect of intolerance and are likely to promote it. The pity is that these aspects of practice are so deeply engrained in our educational institutions that their ill effects go unrecognised. And so we unwittingly persist in reproducing intolerant attitudes and conduct, even while we introduce special programs and other measures to combat them.

1. The Lack of Open Intellectual Questions

One of the essential ingredients in educating for tolerance is the development of an inquiring outlook. We need to guard against the unquestionable presumption that we are in possession of the truth when we find ourselves in disagreement as to beliefs and opinions, or that we are automatically in the right when it comes to controversy about conduct. When faced with such difficulties and disagreements, we need to inquire of each other and look into the situation. Let us focus on one aspect of this in order to get some idea of what is involved, practically speaking. Since to inquire is to question, we cannot hope that students will become proficient at resolving problematic situations unless they are taught to be questioning. This is not just a matter of encouraging general curiosity, but of teaching students how to use questions in order to probe a problem domain. And yet school education pays little or no attention to the art of questioning.

how to ask questions

While students are certainly taught how to answer questions, they are seldom taught how to ask them. Teachers' uses of questioning do not even present a good model to their students on the whole. The questions that teachers ask about their subject matter are mostly closed questions dealing with comprehension or background knowledge; and most teachers are not even familiar with the distinction between a question that admits of different possible answers that do not call for further investigation and an open intellectual question that calls for inquiry. This is connected with the general approach to subject matter, which is so often presented as if it were unproblematic. Students are fed the desiccated results of the inquiries of others—of scientists, historians, geographers, and so on—instead of being taught to think scientifically, historically, and geographically. Given the manner in which such subject matter is presented, there is nothing for them to inquire into and little or no place for students to so much as raise genuine inquiry questions in the classroom.

Nothing could be more important in regard to educating for tolerance than to have students learn the art of questioning in connection with inquiries into their own understandings and differences of opinion, particularly in regard to social problems and ethical issues. This is not just a matter of allowing for a certain amount of class discussion, which is a fairly common practice, but of using that forum in order to teach students how to question and inquire. At present, of course, very few teachers are sufficiently trained in that art, and this is a major hurdle. It is not the fault of the teachers, of course, but one that lies within the institution. However we look at this issue, it is clear that systematic attention to the development of a questioning outlook would require widespread changes in the approach to subject matter and teaching methods.

2. The Prevailing Concern with Unique Right Answers

Most of the questions and problems that school students are asked to address have unique right answers, which depend upon factual recall, look-up tasks, or being able to correctly follow mathematical or other procedures. Success in school largely depends upon learning the set facts and getting the right answer. It should hardly need to be pointed out that very few problems in life are like that. Practical problems normally present us with alternative possibilities and no such thing as the unique right response. Instead, there are likely to be more and less sensible ways of going about things and better and worse decisions. Similarly, in social life we are constantly faced with different points of view, each of which has something to be said in its favour, rather than being simply right or wrong.

This is particularly relevant to educating for tolerance. If we feed students on a steady diet of right answers, we develop a cast of mind that is unused to deliberation and lacking in skill and sophistication when it comes to dealing with difference. We can also develop an undue reliance upon authority and a 'we're right' and 'they're wrong' attitude to the troubles that divide our world. I do not claim that our education systems are to blame for the prevalence of such an attitude, but it is sad to say that they inadvertently replicate habits of mind that so readily comport with intolerance.

To criticise a heavy reliance on 'right answers' is not, of course, to imply that we should be educating students to think that any opinion or practice is as good as any other, or that there are no limits to the attitudes and conduct we should tolerate. In expressing disapproval of an education wedded to right answers, I am not endorsing one in which 'anything goes'. On the contrary, I am suggesting that students need to learn to respond critically to the different values that are constantly being thrust upon them and to deal intelligently with conflicting points of view.

3. The Emphasis upon Individual Rather than Collaborative Learning

If we are serious about educating for tolerance, we should make discussion among students an integral part of classroom activity. While classrooms are no longer places where it is generally forbidden for students to talk to one another, the basic educational relationship is still between the teacher who knows the subject matter that is to be taught and the students who don't know it, so that teaching and learning involves the transfer of that material from the teacher to the student. Therefore, it is the teacher who communicates with the student, and if the student is going to communicate with anyone it should be with the teacher.[14] When we move away from the closed questions and settled knowledge of the traditional classroom to the open questions and search for knowledge in the inquiring one, we move from a classroom that stresses basic comprehension and memorisation to one in which the thoughtful exploration of alternative possibilities and different points of view come into play. And then it becomes educationally desirable for students to engage with one another.

Let us see why this is so by considering a basic feature of inquiry. In an inquiry that tries to explain what we have observed—to explain the evidence before us or the facts of the case—there must be alternative possible explanations. If there is only one live possibility, then that is the answer, and inquiry comes to an end. When human conduct stimulates moral inquiry it is usually because that conduct is controversial, which is to say that there are different points of view as to how it should be judged. When we inquire in order to develop some significant idea or proposal, we need a source of alternative conceptions, suggestions or strategies. In all these cases we need each other. I may suggest one explanation while you offer another that had not occurred to me. That gives both of us something to think about. If you and I have different opinions, then we are both in need of justification and our views are subject to each other's objections. When I make a proposal, I rely upon others who are reasonably well-placed for constructive criticism in order that my suggestion may be bettered or improved.

This reliance upon others applies equally to classroom inquiry. If we want students to avoid the habit of responding without thinking or dogmatically insisting that they are in the right, then we could not do better than to have them become used to considering alternative possibilities by learning to explore issues, problems and ideas with their peers. In that way they become used to giving reasons for what they say and to expect the same of others. They become used to the give-and-take of reasons and to seeing that there can be reasonable alternative judgments and ways of doing things. This is particularly important if we want them to grow up to consider other people's points of view, and not to be so closed-minded as to think that those who disagree with them must be either ignorant or vicious. Since this is precisely what we do want when we are attempting to educate for tolerance, we need the combination of intellectual and social engagement to be found in collaborative inquiry. And, once again, this means that we would do well to seriously consider making educational provision for it.

4. Mistaken Approaches to Values Education

Finally, I would like to say something about values education. Values education cannot be simply a matter of instructing students as to what they should value—just so much 'teaching that'—as if students didn't need to learn to think about values or exercise their judgment. In any case, it is an intellectual mistake to think that values constitute a subject matter to be learnt by heart. They are not that kind of thing. Values are embodied in our commitments and actions and not merely in propositions to which we may, when prodded, give verbal assent. Of course, students need to learn about the values of their society—and about the values that are expressions of its cultural diversity, as well as about the values of people in other times and places. Historical and social knowledge can help to open students' minds to difference and diversity. But we cannot teach students to be tolerant just by imparting content.

Nor can values education be reduced to an effort to directly mould the character of students so that they will make the right moral choices—as if in all the contingencies of life there was never really any doubt about what one ought to do, and having the right kind of character would ensure that one did it. Being what is conventionally called 'of good character' will not prevent you from acting out of ignorance, from being blind to the limitations of your own perspective, from being overly sure that you have right on your side, or even from committing atrocities with a good conscience in the name of such things as nation or faith. The parties to a conflict all too often take themselves to be upright in character and the obvious champions of good, while their antagonists are the personification of depravity and evil. History is littered with barbarities committed by men reputedly of good character who acted out of self-righteous and bigoted certainty. Far from being on solid moral ground, the ancient tradition that places emphasis upon being made of the right stuff has encouraged moral blindness toward those of different ethnicity, religion, politics, or the like—a blindness that has been responsible for a large portion of the preventable ills in human history.

Whatever else we do by way of values education, we must make strenuous efforts to cultivate good judgment. In situations where there are conflicts over values, good judgment involves distinguishing more- from less-acceptable decisions and conduct. Such discernment needs to be made by comparing our options in the circumstances in which they occur. Any such comparison requires us to ensure that, insofar as possible, we have all the relevant facts. It involves us doing our best to make sure that we have not overlooked any reasonable course of action. It requires us to think about the consequences of making one decision, or taking one course of action, by comparison with another, and to be mindful of the criteria against which we evaluate them. It requires us to monitor the consequences of our actions in order to adjust our subsequent thinking to actuality. In short, good judgment requires us to follow the ways of inquiry.

This approach to values education fits with the emphasis to be placed upon collaborative inquiry. The idea that values are to be cultivated by student reflection rather than impressed upon the student from without does not imply that the pursuit of values is a purely personal affair and that everything must be tolerated. Collaborative inquiry supplies a middle road—a way forward between an unquestioning attitude toward set values, with nothing else to be tolerated, and the kind of rampant individualism that makes each person their own moral authority. The development of good judgment through inquiry with others is the path toward a truly social intelligence that keeps us within the limits of reasoned toleration. Moreover, collaborative inquiry is itself a kind of moral practice that encourages tolerance. Consider such elementary aspects of the practice as: learning to hear someone out when you disagree with what they are saying; learning to explore the source of your disagreement rather than engaging in personal attacks; being disposed to take other people's interests and concerns into account; and generally becoming more communicative and inclusive. Such dispositions and habits are surely among the outcomes to be attained if we are truly to educate for tolerance.

NOTES

[1] The metaphor is from Kant: 'Aus so krummen Holze, als woraus der Mensch gemacht ist, kann nichts ganz gerades gezimmert werden'. Immanuel Kant (1963), *Idea for a Universal History from a Cosmopolitan Point of View*. Lewis White Beck (trans.), Indianapolis: Bobbs-Merrill.

[2] Other general answers are possible, of course, such as that society should tolerate something or not according to its consistency with the will of God, or with the General Will. The first of these reverts to the answer given in the text, on the traditional ground that God wills something because it is good rather than something being good because God wills it. The second alternative succumbs to the ills of totalitarianism.

[3] We cannot be said to tolerate that which we regard as more or less harmless. 'Why shouldn't we tolerate that? It's not doing any harm'. If there were no dispute about whether the thing is harmless, the question wouldn't even arise.

[4] John Locke (1968), *Epistola de Tolerantia*. J.W. Gough (trans.), Oxford: Oxford University Press.

[5] Locke, *Epistola de Tolerantia*, p. 135. This is because he held that 'promises, covenants, and oaths, which are the bonds of human society, can have no hold or sanctity for an atheist' and that 'a man who by his atheism undermines all religion cannot in the name of religion claim the privilege of toleration for himself'. The first of Locke's reasons for the exclusion of atheists falls under the prevention of harm—'the bonds of human society' having no hold upon an atheist, thereby placing atheism beyond the limits of tolerance. The second of Locke's reasons for placing atheism outside the limits of tolerance can only be justified on the ground that he is dealing solely with the toleration of different religious beliefs and practices and not, more generally, with the toleration of convictions concerning matters of religion. Yet this is to say that atheists lie outside his terms of reference, rather than providing positive grounds for discrimination.

[6] Herbert Butterfield (1977), 'Toleration in early modern times', *Journal of the History of Ideas*, 38, p. 580.

[7] John Locke (1924), *An Essay Concerning Human Understanding*, A.S. Pringle-Pattison (abridged) (ed.), Oxford University Press, pp. 337–8.

[8] James Mill (1971), *The Principles of Toleration*. New York: Burt Franklin. Mill's essay was originally published in the *Westminster Review* of 1826. Locke's principle work on education is *Some Thoughts Concerning Education*, but it is complemented by *Of the Conduct of the Understanding*, from which Mill quotes at length. James Mill was, of course, father to the more famous son, John Stuart Mill.

[9] Mill, *The Principles of Toleration*, p. 18–21.

[10] Ibid., p. 19–21.

[11] John Locke, (1966), *On the Conduct of the Understanding*. Francis W. Garforth (ed.), New York: Teachers College Press, pp. 63–4. This passage is also quoted by Mill in a slightly different version. See *The Principles of Toleration*, p. 25.

[12] Dewey wrote extensively about this method in both accessible and more scholarly terms. *How We Think* (1991, Prometheus Books, New York) provides an introduction to teachers, and *Logic: The Theory of Inquiry* (1938, Henry Holt and Company, New York) gives an extensive formal treatment.

[13] John Dewey (1966) *Democracy and Education*. New York: The Free Press, p. 152.

[14] Not that we should forget the long tradition of group work in schools. Many of us will remember doing group projects in primary school or conducting laboratory experiments in pairs or small groups in secondary school.

Philip Cam
School of History and Philosophy
Faculty of Arts
University of New South Wales

JOEL WINDLE

6. WHAT KNOWLEDGE FOR UNDERSTANDING?

Addressing Ignorance of Islam in Australian Schools

This chapter addresses three central concerns. This first is of an ethical nature:
'Should schools teach about Islam and Muslims to a greater extent than they do
now, and should they do so with the objective of displacing particular harmful
views with other views?' This question must be answered with regard to the roles
of school in society in transmitting social norms and creating citizens, but also
with regard to the growth of anti-Muslim sentiment that has come to be called
'Islamophobia'.[1] The second concern is both theoretical and practical: 'Can the
problem of Islamophobia be addressed by confronting ignorance about Islam, or
rather particular kinds of knowledge about Islam, with other kinds of knowledge
about Islam and Muslims?' While prejudice against Muslims and ignorance of Islam
have been connected in empirical work,[2] the nature of the connection between
attitudes and knowledge is far from clear. This chapter will therefore seek to offer
some clarification on this relationship with reference to the social foundations of
anti-Muslim sentiment. Such clarification is essential for my final concern, which
is to identify what educational strategies schools might best adopt in order to promote
tolerance and understanding. I divide these strategies broadly into universalising
strategies, which emphasise shared experiences across religions and cultures, and
particularising strategies, which emphasise the distinctive characteristics of Islam
and Muslim populations and the distinctive history of their reception in the west.

I will argue that schools already contribute to the production of particular kinds
of knowledge about Islam and Muslims, and that a reconsideration of their treatment
in the curriculum is called for as a consequence of the prejudice currently faced
by Muslims in western societies. I will suggest that attitudes may be changed not
through coercion, but through the production of alternative forms of knowledge and
through exposure to new experiences. For antipathetic attitudes to be re-evaluated,
it is necessary first to interrogate the conditions of their development and transmission. The arguments I make about knowledge, power and attitudes draw on radical
traditions of scholarship, however, the case for greater school intervention into this
field can also be justified from a liberal perspective. If a measure of success is to be
taken from increased attitudes of tolerance (and this is accepted as an acceptable
goal for schools to pursue), then common ground between these perspectives is not
too difficult to find.

From the outset, I wish to make clear that knowledge of Islam and Muslims is not
the only question that schools need to concern themselves with in order to promote
tolerance, or that tolerance flows automatically from knowledge. Instead, my

E.B. Coleman and K. White (eds.), Religious Tolerance, Education and the Curriculum, 67–83.
© *2011 Sense Publishers. All rights reserved.*

more modest claim is that improved knowledge and understanding is a condition which is, as Robert Jackson has observed, 'necessary but not sufficient' for reducing prejudice.[3]

OUGHT SCHOOLS INTERVENE TO 'TEACH TOLERANCE'?

The question of whether schools have a duty or a vocation to influence students' judgments of particular faiths and their followers emerges as a potential dilemma. On the one hand, students may be understood to be entitled to form their own judgements free from interference or coercion by schools. So long as such an entitlement is extended to all students, this position accords with Isaiah Berlin's definition of 'negative liberty'.[4] The question is whether an intervention by schools, particularly secular schools, to determine students' views and actions in relation to a particular faith constitutes a violation of freedom from interference or is simply a continuation of their educational work. On the other hand, the entitlement of Muslims to be free to act and be without the interference which flows from bigoted attitudes, particularly when these are translated into actions, may be understood as justifying a strong and even 'coercive' approach by schools in seeking to change attitudes.

As attitudes have hardened against Muslims in the west in recent times, these attitudes have increasingly led to more concrete actions for, as a religious group whose members are often viewed as irrational, greater restrictions are placed on them as a precaution in western liberal societies. As Susan Mendus has noted, freedom to act as one wants may be restricted in some versions of liberalism to freedom to act as one *would* act if one were fully rational.[5] Restrictions may thus be placed on irrational desires and practices with fewer scruples, following this argument. The banning of the hijab in French schools provides one example of restrictions placed on a negatively viewed population engaged in an 'irrational' practice. It is interesting to note that the banning of the hijab in French schools, discussed by Mendus in this volume, represents not merely an effort to maintain neutrality and freedom at school, but to change the minds of Muslim girls who do not know what is good for them.

The impact of draconian 'anti-terror' legislation and ethnic profiling practices by security agencies in Australia and other western nations provides another example of restrictive practices. These measures affect the agency not just of those ostensibly targeted, but also that of all members of the Muslim community through the generation of fear, anxiety, and increased self-regulation. Further, it might be argued that the generation of fear of, and hostility towards, a particular faith group, dehumanises and reduces the agency of individuals beyond that group, thereby frustrating the goal of self actualisation autonomy which is the primary reason freedom is so important in liberal thought.[6]

From a radical perspective, the intrusion of the state on the agency of individuals is of less concern because agency is understood as already powerfully circumscribed. Individual opinions reflect not merely personal choices or the product of rational consideration, but ideologies serving antagonistic social interests. Within this radical perspective, school has been viewed either as a space of potential liberation of the mind, and hence from oppressive social structures (as in the work of Paulo Freire), or a tool for the reproduction and legitimisation of divisions (as in the work of Pierre Bourdieu).[7] Both viewpoints conceive of schools as having an important political function, and as lacking the neutral or un-imposing quality that (political) liberals seek to protect. The question of whether schools ought to intervene is thus less troublesome from a radical perspective because schools are seen as already intervening to protect an unjust capitalist social order, or as potentially intervening to undermine it.

Both liberal and radical perspectives therefore share a concern to protect a human subject from the oppressive interference of either unspecified others (liberalism) or the dehumanising workings of a system (Marxism). Both perspectives might suggest caution as to the duty or ability of schools to influence students' judgments of particular beliefs or religious populations. In educational policy, however, both traditions may be seen as inspiring action in schools. Policies promoting 'multiculturalism' have generally taken on a liberal guise, while some examples of anti-racism education have taken on a more radical guise.[8] To complicate matters further, a radical tradition of secularism has sought to exclude all religion from schools in order to counter the power of religious institutions and strictures, and objections to devoting school time to teaching about Islam might be raised on these grounds too.

A further perspective on school intervention may be distinguished from the liberal and radical traditions by virtue of its questioning of the stable subject, and its interrogation of processes of 'subjectification'. Writers such as Foucault understand subjects as constituted by 'discourses', and their inability to act outside of them.[9] From this perspective, self-regulation becomes more important as a form of power than does interference from the strong arm of the state or capital. A postmodern understanding of the subject does not admit the liberal concern for protection of individual autonomy or the radical concern for liberation of the oppressed subject. While postmodernism lacks the unity of purpose which characterises the liberal and radical political projects, the decentred location of power and regulation in discourses implies that if an intervention were to occur, particular kinds of attention should be paid to the way religious groups are described and characterised. The postmodern techniques of deconstruction have indeed entered some English classrooms in particular, and are reflected in 'critical literacy' approaches to reading and interpreting texts, which are also influenced by radical modes of critique. Nevertheless, postmodern traditions of interpretation, in identifying knowledge as always imbued with the power to dominate, risk condemning the very possibility of representing other cultures without misrepresenting them.[10] Edward Saïd makes this argument in his work on representations of Islam in the west as an exotic 'Other', which he understands as an extension of colonial and post-colonial projects of domination.[11] While this line of thinking suggests an inevitability of misrepresentation, or the impossibility of a 'true' and faithful representation, others who share the premise of the orientalist thesis see the possibility of undermining the claims of a neo-conservative ruling elite from within the west.[12]

In this section, I have outlined objections to school interventions based on desirability and practicality. I have also suggested that forms of intervention may differ according to which perspective is adopted. My arguments in favour of intervention stem from both the harm resulting from negative attitudes when these are dominant in a society and the weak foundation of negative attitudes in 'interested' forms of knowledge. Indeed, attitudes towards Islam and Muslims, as I will outline in the following section, may be characterised as grounded in prejudice, defined according to the famous formulation of Gordon Allport as 'an antipathy based on faulty and inflexible generalization'.[13] I will then outline how the expression of prejudice towards Muslims in Australia warrants special attention to this topic in schools as a means of promoting tolerance.

WHY FOCUS ON ISLAM AND MUSLIMS?

If we accept that it is desirable for schools to 'teach tolerance', and that they are capable of fulfilling this role, then suitable approaches must be identified. One approach is to promote general tolerance of others as a virtue, and a skill that may be transferred into different contexts as students encounter new kinds of difference in the course of their lives (see de Silva this volume). This approach implies that prejudices are too varied and unpredictable to be addressed one-by-one, or that to do so would be ineffective. Another approach, which I suggest has been too often overlooked, is to focus on those areas of greatest intolerance. Thus, if Buddhists were a group faced with particular intolerance in Australia, then efforts should be made to educate students about this group in order to reverse these prejudices. As a religion that is relatively new to Australia, coming primarily via recent migration, many Australians have little knowledge of Buddhism. If Buddhism came to be seen as threatening, it would be logical in these circumstances to propose improving knowledge as a first step to confronting the fear of Buddhism. However, unlike Muslims, Buddhists are a generally well-regarded group in Australian society.

The contrast between the treatment of Buddhism and Islam in Australia is instructive. The numbers of Buddhists in Australia in 2001 stood at 350,000, or just under two per cent of the population. This figure represents an 80 per cent increase in the number of Buddhists in Australia since the 1996 census. The Muslim population is slightly smaller, at 282,000 (1.5 per cent of the population), and grew at half the rate of the Buddhist population over the same period (40 per cent increase since 1996).[14] It is almost unthinkable to imagine an Australian politician complaining about the influx of Buddhists eroding the 'Australian way of life', yet this is precisely the assertion that Pauline Hanson used in relation to Muslims in attempting to re-launch her political career.[15] Another right-wing politician, Fred Nile, has called for an immediate halt to Muslim immigration with a press-release entitled 'No more Muslims', for similar reasons.[16] Nile's Christian Democratic Party complains that, among Muslims, 'the English language is disregarded and Aussie family values are unknown or despised'.[17]

These statements come in the wake of controversy over sexist comments made by the Mufti of Australia[18] and the highlighting of the Muslim background of young men prosecuted in a high-profile rape case. Janette Albrechtsen, in *The Australian* newspaper, for example, wrote of how '*Muslim* brothers were found guilty of the gang-rape of a young *Australian* girl'[19] [my emphasis]. Albrechtsen finds in these events some insight into the nature of Islam. She identifies Islam (although 'ethnicity' and 'culture' are also used interchangeably by her) as the cause of the rapes, which are understood as a weapon in the 'clash of civilisations':[20]

> Transplanted to countries such as Australia, a culture which places so little value on gender equality was always going to have problems when faced with women who not only read and write but think and assume control of their lives. Each of those barbaric gang-rapists showed utter disdain for their young *Western* victims.[21] [My emphasis]

This thesis would not readily withstand a readership that is able to call into question the brittle and homogonous cultural whole in which Islam is construed in this comment, or one that has knowledge of the diversity of perspectives about literacy, education, independent thought and gender relations among Muslims. Knowledge about different Muslim interpretations of the teachings of Islam on gender relations and existing understandings of gender-relations among the Muslim populations of the world appears to be conspicuously absent from commentaries such as the one above, which quotes a French psychotherapist as its only authority. Albrechtsen's claims, while displaying ignorance, also generate a particular kind of knowledge about Islam. This is a reductionist knowledge of Islam inferred primarily from cases of rape, and is reliant on the absence of alternative forms of knowledge that might contradict the inferences drawn and the intolerance likely to flow from them. Intolerance in this instance flows not from total ignorance, but from folk theories.

The notion that there is a 'problem' with Islam above all other religions in Australia is further evident from the *Daily Telegraph's* 'multiculturalism in Australia' 'in-depth' webpage.[22] The feature summary states that 'cultures are clashing as Muslims, Christians and rank-and-file Aussies struggle to live together. Here we hear from those at the heart of the issues'. Thirty-five of the 52 titles on the webpage are related to conflict and controversy involving Islam or Muslims in Australia, while four are related to Christianity, including a condemnation of Islam by a Catholic Archbishop. No other religion or ethnic group is evoked. The remaining 13 articles focus on the tightening of citizenship requirements and the limits of multiculturalism. With this kind of framing, knowledge about Islam becomes knowledge about social conflict, and intolerant 'outside influences'. This webpage invites readers' comments on the issues so framed, and these further build intolerance through the pooling of outrage and vitriol. One reader blandly asserts that:

> Muslims immigrate to Western nations and practise a regime of virtually absolute intolerance to the peoples of their host nations, while stridently demanding that their barbaric, misogynistic medieval creed that masquerades as a religion is accepted.[23]

Like most comments, this one is vague and reductionist in its claims about Islam, which are linked to ethno-nationalist concerns about the preservation of a similarly reductionist white Christian 'Aussie' culture. The status of many Muslims in Australia as non-white, and first or second-generation migrants, provides the basis for racist and xenophobic prejudices that are not replicated in relation to other religious

Media = violence [handwritten annotation in left margin]

groups which hold similar views on, for example, the prohibition of alcohol. A focus on Islam of the kind represented on the *Daily Telegraph* readers forums and on talk-back radio in Australia reinforces the idea that Islam is a problem. Schools attempting to teach their students about Islam must be careful to avoid falling into this trap; however, the danger of depending on current media discourses as the primary source of information about Islam is far greater.

The power of the media as the primary source of information about Islam and Muslims for most Australians[24] is demonstrated by the increase in assaults on people of 'Middle Eastern appearance' following vilification on talk-back radio after the outbreak of the first Gulf War and September 11.[25] The primacy of religion over other concerns confronting Muslim ethnic minorities is revealed by the fact that the greatest form of disadvantage that Turkish-background women in Sydney report, to take the example of one of the largest Muslim groups, is their religious identity.[26]

The involvement of Australia in foreign military campaigns and of Muslims in terrorism appears to draw on and fuel 'Islamophobia'. Nor is hostility confined to Australia. Polling in over 50 countries shows that westerners view Muslims as fanatical, violent and intolerant, while Muslims perceive westerners to be selfish, immoral and greedy—as well as violent and fanatical. Each group views the other as being disrespectful towards women.[27] Beyond promulgating prejudice, the media shows itself to be a poor source of information about Islam in Australia. According to a survey conducted by Kevin Dunn in the early 2000's, half of Australians report knowing little about Islam, while only one in five claims knowledge that is 'reasonable' or better.[28] Of those who lay claim to knowledge, this often comes in the form of a critique of Muslims (38 per cent) or is erroneous (such as, 'they don't eat cows').[29]

It is possible that intolerance might be maintained, even with more complete knowledge of the complexity and diversity of Islam and Muslims. However, my argument here is that, in the instance of Islam in Australia, there is great scope for improved tolerance on the basis of increased knowledge of a certain kind. Current knowledge of Islam in Australia is often ill-founded, as in the Albrechtsen example, and this is a symptom of its production within certain ideological battle-fields. I now turn to a fuller investigation of the relationship between knowledge and attitudes, before turning to the nature of knowledge that I seek to advocate in relation to Islam and Muslims, and the conditions of its production and sharing.

KNOWLEDGE AND ATTITUDE

The relationship between knowledge, understanding and attitude is a complex one. It becomes most troublesome in matters relating to knowledge of oneself and the social world. Religion is one such area where the nature and foundation of knowledge claims are seen to be so troublesome that religious perspectives are generally excluded from the formal curriculum. A moral education may be proffered outside of the mainstay of academic disciplines, but only in the United States have religious knowledge claims made headway into the academic curriculum, in the guise of creationism or 'intelligent design'. When it comes to claims for religious knowledge, 'claims of fact', which may be demonstrated by evidence, become confused with 'claims of value', which must be demonstrated by other arguments.[30] Claims of value draw us further away from knowledge as it is commonly understood as an objective property of the academic curriculum and towards attitude, as a personal property. A distinction is generally drawn between what must be absorbed from the curriculum, and what views students are free to retain or develop independently of that curriculum. Knowledge does not necessarily support attitude, nor are schools always concerned to encourage students to base their attitudes on the knowledge they encounter at school. There are exceptions to this, when students are asked to draw inferences from certain information or to present an argument supported by certain information. Such tasks are, however, often merely academic games and students are not required to sincerely espouse the arguments they devise for these scholarly purposes.

Bullying

The effort to connect knowledge to attitude through education is more clearly present in efforts to modify attitudes that lead to harmful behaviour. Anti-bullying education is one example of such an attempt, although the kind of knowledge that will change the attitudes of bullies is far from obvious because the motivations of bullies are often difficult to establish.

AIDs

A more clear-cut example of an effort to change attitudes, which has generated a considerable empirical literature, is that of AIDS education. The transmission of AIDS has been connected to particular beliefs and attitudes, particularly relating to sex, and hence education programs have been devised with the explicit aim of changing attitudes through increased knowledge of HIV and AIDS. Some researchers have found that knowledge, and even practices, are more easily changed through education than are attitudes;[31] other research points more clearly to the impact of education on attitudes.[32] A range of pedagogical approaches to AIDS appear to be effective in changing attitudes in secondary school settings,[33] although the presence of an HIV positive speaker as part of an education program appears to have a particularly strong impact on attitudes towards both AIDS and homosexuality.[34] It is interesting to note that, even where harm can be clearly identified from particular attitudes, these attitudes are entangled with questions of sexual morality, pedagogy and the goals of education, and can become sites of religious contestation.

Education directed at changing attitudes towards race, ethnicity and religion involve distinct concepts, that are closely tied together in the case of Islam. Despite the ethnic diversity of Muslims, many Australian school students mistakenly believe that all Muslims are Arabs, and that all Arabs are Muslim. Students use insults such as 'towel head', 'sand nigger' and 'terrorist' that carry a combination of religious, racial and ethnic connotations. The thesis underlying these insults is of religious and cultural inferiority or incompatibility which has been termed 'cultural racism'[35] to distinguish it from racism based on purported biological differences.

cultural racism

Some early experimental research into the effects of specially devised curriculum on high-school student attitudes dealing with religious and ethnic groups suggested only a little support for the effectiveness of increased knowledge in changing attitudes.[36] More recent research has been more confident that attitudes are changed by education,[37] even when educational intervention comes later in life.[38] Outside of education programs, contact with different ethnic groups has been shown to positively affect attitudes towards those groups. Multi-ethnic social networks appear to play a positive role in increasing racial tolerance.[39]

The research literature into attitudinal changes, grounded in psychology, generally relies on pre-test and post-test surveys of participants and does not measure longer-term or more gradual changes. Given the repositioning of oneself in the world that changes in attitude often imply, it is reasonable to consider that attitudinal changes are unlikely to be sudden in many instances, and may only emerge once the social pressures of a given set of circumstances alter. Examples of sudden changes of attitude are perhaps more likely to arise from either a particularly intense experience or from a sudden change in circumstances, and not from the classroom.

Further, the empirical literature tends to take a fairly a-social approach to individual change and draws on a limited repertoire of methodologies. Even though social attributes are sometimes controlled for in statistical models, the psychological approach locates behaviour and changes to attitude primarily within individuals, which are understood to be in a fairly mechanical relationship.[40] J. Brynner and his colleagues, for example, establish a causal linear model of the development of political identity (including level of tolerance). According to this model, political engagement can be explained as follows:

interest > attentiveness > knowledge > opinion formation > ideological identity > political participation.[41]

This is certainly a plausible model, and has been used with some success by the researchers, however, its universality and necessity is doubtful.

The nature of particular objects of interest, attentiveness and knowledge will also influence the formation of attitudes. Attitudes towards Islam and Muslims in Australia are often sparked by interest, not in religion, but in conflicts involving Australia overseas or theories of cultural incompatibility developed in the media or neighbourhood interactions. This kind of interest is likely to result in attentiveness to particular attributes that fit in with this thesis or help to explain international conflict. Where some more disinterested knowledge of religion and the religious precedes the formation of opinions, then these are less likely to be prejudicial.

In the Australian context, Dunn has found a strong positive relationship between contact with Muslims and knowledge of Islam, both of which appear to reduce Islamophobia.[42] However, there are good reasons to consider countervailing forces which may maintain intolerance, even in situations of regular social contact. Conflict arises not just from ignorance or fear of the unknown, but from threats to group positioning and the protection of acquired privilege.[43] Those who see themselves in competition with Muslims (over scarce jobs, education, housing, or other resources) are likely to be threatened by and to feel antipathy towards Muslims. As a largely working-class population, Muslims in Australia are positioned in competition with other low socio-economic status groups, among whom anti-migrant sentiment is greatest.[44] Nevertheless, these countervailing forces only suggest that the task of reducing Islamophobia is a particularly challenging one, not that it is unworthy of being undertaken.

To summarise, the current dominant (though not exclusive) pattern of attitude formation in relation to Islam in Australia may be characterised as ignorance supporting misunderstanding leading to prejudice. Attention to the practices and beliefs of Muslims is sustained by the place of Islam in a theory of global and local cultural conflict. It is further sustained by xenophobic anxieties about the preservation of a mythologised social cohesion and white, Christian national identity in a diverse, migrant society. We can also consider an alternative schema of attitude formation that might particularly apply where there is sustained and direct contact between antagonistic groups (such as in Northern Ireland), where certain kinds of knowledge about the other sustain misunderstanding and prejudice. This may be the case in working-class suburbs of Sydney, for example, where close contact with Muslims is combined with suspicion among some non-Muslims. Finally, knowledge that does provide good understanding may sustain negative attitudes, which are perhaps no longer accurately described as prejudice because this term implies an irrationally held and ill-informed attitude. At this point, we have reached the limits of the educational strategy I am concerned with here, and which I will outline in its pedagogical context below.

WHAT FORMS OF EDUCATION SHOULD EDUCATION ABOUT ISLAM AND MUSLIMS TAKE?

As I have already discussed, liberal, radical and postmodernist perspectives point to somewhat different lines of action in the setting of the school. Nevertheless, some common ground exists between these perspectives, just as serious divides exist within each one. My argument here is for education strategies that are grounded in the current reality of widespread prejudice against Muslims in Australia. I will distinguish between a universalising approach to education for tolerance, which is currently represented to some extent in schools, and a particularising approach which emphasises the specificities of Islam in the contemporary context and which has been overlooked for a number of reasons.

The universalising approach places Islam among other belief systems, whose commonalities of purpose and function may be revealed by comparison. This approach engages empathy by relativising different perspectives and showing how they are part of a broader human experience of religion. It is represented in the models of religious education presented below and in policy statements calling on a general level of awareness and the celebration of difference.[45] However, the universalising approach, in addition to smoothing over differences and assuming a universal level of religiosity, is hampered by an inability to recognise the unequal power relationships that are reflected in attitudes towards religion and groups defined by faith in contemporary Australia.

A particularising approach to the study of Islam would emphasise the specificity of the range of Islamic religious belief and expression in Australia as the product of ethnically diverse migration and the insertion of Muslim migrants into particular historical relations of power that have resulted in the construction of Islam as an object of fear. A particularising approach is partly reflected in the anti-racist model, which aims to clearly identify and target an unequal power relationship between groups in society. However, advocates of anti-racist approaches have generally been sceptical of 'religious education' as a vehicle of anti-racism education and have focused on knowledge of structures rather than on the dynamic and overlapping cultural practices, identities and beliefs which are the 'content' of religion. Jackson observes that anti-racist concerns with eliminating categories mobilised in power relations tends to 'homogenise' different communities.[46]

The distinction between universalising and particularising approaches does not constitute a complete break. The UNESCO *Declaration of Principles on Tolerance*, for example, despite being framed in broad universalist terms, draws attention to particular forms of prejudice against particular groups in society.[47] Anti-Semitism is named as a particular form of prejudice and 'religious and ethnic minorities' are named as groups particularly vulnerable to intolerance, for example. Further, structural concerns are raised in the demand for 'systematic and rational tolerance teaching methods that will address the cultural, social, economic, political and religious sources of intolerance—major roots of violence and exclusion'.[48] Both approaches may be effective to achieve a number of common goals, but part ways on others. Starting with minimalist interventions and moving towards more radical and contested goals, these include:

1. Education for awareness and recognition of difference

2. Education for tolerance (as forbearance) of difference

3. Education for acceptance or 'embrace' of difference

4. Education for understanding of a faith and its place in the lives of its followers

5. Education for understanding of the personal and interpersonal processes involved in the formation of attitudes and beliefs

6. Education for understanding of the political and ideological processes involved in the formation of attitudes and beliefs

7. Change in attitudes to dispel 'harmful' prejudices

8. Change in political and personal actions arising from a critique of prejudice.

The first three of these goals reflect the universalising framing of much multi-cultural policy currently informing schools. They are only likely to present a dilemma to liberal advocates of a weak form of tolerance, which does not interfere with an individual's right to hold objectionable views. According to Peter Balint, for example, forbearance represents a cautious model of liberal toleration to be preferred over 'celebration of difference' because it requires minimal interference from the state through schools, and thus the third goal should be rejected. This argument supposes that intolerant attitudes are rarely translated into actions and have no negative or obstructive impact on their own. This objection presupposes that, without the inter-vention of schools, individuals would be free to rationally inform themselves and determine their own view of Islam. However, the media and political discourses in

Australia, and their connections to violence towards Muslims, suggests that this is not the case. Nevertheless, 'embrace' does not appear to me be a particularly realistic goal, nor one that is necessary for the fulfilment of other goals.

Goals 4 and 5 are more focused on religion as a concept, and while they suggest the in-depth study of a range of religions, they do not provide a strong justification for prioritising or privileging any one. A particularising approach might also be adopted in relation to these goals.

Goals 4 and 5 are vital to the development of empathy, which is also necessary for the 'strong' tolerance goal of acceptance. The final three goals are more ambitious in scope. If they are embarked upon, it is likely that they will have a bearing on how the former goals are met because they entail students having a different under-standing of themselves not just as individuals situated interpersonally in a multi-cultural society, but as structurally located *within* a society charged with relations of power that are reflected in, and constituted by, beliefs and attitudes. It is attention to the final three goals that provides the rationale for addressing the treatment of Islam in Australia as a priority through the generation of knowledge about Islam which is not produced by the current dynamic of the 'clash of civilisations'/lack of civilisation thesis.[49]

CURRICULUM MODELS

I will now outline how current curriculum provision fits into these two broad approaches, and what scope exists for extending them, with particular reference to the potential of the particularising approach.

Citizenship education provides a good example of the universalising approach. Australian education has adopted the goal of citizenship education as a 'public' good benefiting society as a whole, rather than as a 'private' good, merely benefiting individuals. *The Future of Schooling in Australia,* a declaration made by state educa-tion ministers in 2007, proclaims that schooling should 'promote social cohesion through sharing values and aspirations underpinned by knowledge and tolerance' and 'prepare for global citizenship'.[50] The introduction of civics as a learning area in schools provides one clear space for them to fulfil this task. However, schools are also expected to form citizens by modelling and exacting particular behaviours and values in the course of the school day.[51] The current approach to promoting inclusive citizenship among school students places emphasis on sensitive teaching styles rather than on any particular content knowledge. Even in addressing cultural diversity directly, in the Victorian setting, for example, the Department of Education currently provides no information or resources specific to Islam or Muslims, and cultural diversity is taught as linguistic diversity, with no reference to religion.

Religious education, in the sense of education about religions, dwells on particular religions, but often with a universalising focus. Islam is typically presented in religious education, but also geography and history, as a 'world religion' that may be fairly easily compared to the other 'religions of the book: Christianity and Judaism.[52] Writing from within this broad 'world religions' framework, Cohn-Sherbok et al. argue that the introduction to religion through spiritual experience or religious artefacts is

thematic & systematic approach

not an appropriate approach to Islam, and instead favour the phenomenological approach of Ninian Smart.[53] Smart's influential work provides for a thematic or systematic approach to seven dimensions of religion—ritual, mythological, doctrinal, ethical, social, experiential and material.[54] However, these dimensions do not relate to equivalent concepts in all religions, which may tend to be judged against the 'gold standard' of Christianity.[55] Jackson instead proposes that:

> Religions can be represented not as homogeneous systems of belief, but in terms of relationships between individuals, groups and wider contextual traditions. Cultures can be pictured as dynamic, internally contested and fuzzy edged, while individuals can be shown as reshaping culture through creating new syntheses which utilize cultural ideas and expressions from a variety of sources, including their own ancestral traditions.[56]

Jackson's proposal takes us towards a particularising approach, where religions are not considered as abstracted, interchangeable cultural equivalents, and I will return to his work below. First, however, I wish to return to Saïd's insight that the knowledge of Islam developed in western academic thought has been guided by the imperative of justifying colonialism and post-colonial imperialist projects.[57] The presentation of the crusades and the Moorish conquests in Europe are two of the few contexts in which students can learn about Muslims in history, and these typically present a jaundiced and Eurocentric perspective, which appears universalising in its authority. An extract taken from a reference book in a Victorian school library gives a taste of the general flavour of representations:

> The rise of Islam is a history of successful campaigns, in which within a hundred years of the Prophet Mohammed's death (632 AD), his followers had brought a huge tract of territory stretching from the Indian Ocean to the Atlantic under their dominion. This was a remarkable achievement, by any standards, but nothing can disguise the fact that it is an almost unrelieved record of bloodshed, brutality, treachery and assassination.[58]

While this passage comes from an old text, it is still in use, and it is far from an isolated example.[59]

This textbook knowledge is supplemented within schools by the media discourse discussed at length above. Media discourse enters the curriculum in classroom responses to media reports of conflict, or as part of teacher encouragement to foster the expression of diverse classroom perspectives. This is particularly problematic when a diversity of perspectives is not represented in the classroom or where negative stereotypes are merely repeated.

Clearly, then, the universalising approach has some shortcomings. Some of these are addressed in the development of critical skills that are universally applicable and transferable, but these must draw on particular knowledge in their application in order to work as anything other than critiques of style and internal logic.

A clear example of the particularising approach exists in the inclusion of indigenous perspectives in school curricula. State and federal education departments have identified the need for indigenous students as a group to have greater cultural inclusion in schools, although this agenda is driven primarily by a desire to improve retention and academic outcomes rather than as an end in itself. The *National Statement of Principles and Standards for More Culturally Inclusive Schooling in the 21st Century* in 2000 extended government commitment beyond general notions of recognition and tolerance to make specific recommendations for curriculum provision which:

(ii) allows Indigenous students to share in the same educational opportunities experienced by other Australian students and at the same time allows them to be strong in their own culture and language and reposition their cultures, languages, histories, beliefs and lifestyles in a way which affirms identity and the ability to operate in cross-cultural situations,

(iii) supports all students to understand and acknowledge the value of Aboriginal and Torres Strait Islander cultures to Australian society and possess the knowledge, skills and understanding to contribute to, and benefit from, reconciliation between Indigenous and non-Indigenous Australians.

In this initiative, the particular history of indigenous peoples in Australia has been taken as a warrant for special attention.[60] New South Wales has even made it mandatory for indigenous perspectives to be included in the curriculum across all key learning areas. The *Principles*, together with the *Model of Culturally Inclusive and Educationally Effective Schools* has provided the basis not only for curriculum interventions, but also for community partnerships and targeted professional development for teachers.[61]

A particularising approach to Islam would take into account the important place of media discourse. It follows from Saïd's orientalism thesis of the self-interested production of western knowledge about Islam that it is knowledge of the particulars of this process rather than knowledge of cultural practices or beliefs that is most important. Knowledge of the motivations guiding prejudicial accounts of Islam may serve to undermine the authority of this perspective and hence reduce intolerance. The English and Media Studies classroom provide spaces where the mechanisms which produce and sustain stereotypes may be investigated. Queensland and Tasmania have both embraced a critical literacy approach in their curriculum guidelines, and some textbook authors have also adopted this approach.[62] More importantly, from a post-colonial perspective, the western monopoly on the production of authorised knowledge about Islam must be broken and challenged.

There is great scope for increasing the level of community involvement in Australian schools around the themes of religion and tolerance as part of a particularising approach which opens schools to different perspectives and epistemologies. Education departments have shown an increased focus on responsiveness to local communities in a devolved system, with state education ministers noting:

Schools must recognise that families and the community provide the context that underpins learning experiences and shapes values and aspirations. Parents and the broader community have a shared obligation with teachers to be the educators of the next generation.[63]

WINDLE *Representation in Curriculum*

The inclusion of Muslim perspectives can be pursued either through curriculum material generated by Muslims or through dialogue with Muslims in the production of school-based knowledge.[64] In practical terms, a dialogical pedagogy that is based on contact and experience produces knowledge that is weakly controlled by school. School-based projects bringing together students from Islamic, Christian and Jewish schools initiated by the Affinity Intercultural Foundation in Sydney provide an example of such action. At one step removed, the curriculum materials developed through the *Warwick RE Project* in the United Kingdom provide another example of the inclusion of Muslim perspectives.[65] However, this is a nerve-wracking proposition for schools, and for educators who are suspicious about the purposes of religious organisations that participate in such a dialogue—as these organisations are also motivated to present themselves in a particular light that is far from disinterested.

To this dialogical pedagogy may be added an analytical pedagogy that is more strongly framed by schools, and which engages critical faculties rather than empathetical faculties used in a dialogical pedagogy. Both an analytical and dialogical pedagogy can contribute to students' interpretations of Islamic practices and beliefs, to the development of attitudes towards them, and the positioning of self in relation to them. They can also contribute to the interpretation of external or 'public' pedagogies provided by talk-back radio and political discourses relating to Islam in Australia. These public pedagogies may find their current central role in the construction of knowledge about Islam displaced by other pedagogies and forms of knowledge that provide an alternative lens for understanding and attitude formation.

CONCLUSION

In this chapter, I have argued that with increased and improved knowledge of Islam and its followers, attitudes would be considerably less negative than they are now. Schools have an important role to play in this endeavour, and must attend to the kinds of knowledge that are most likely to promote tolerance. As Islamophobia is an important form of cultural racism in Australian society, the causes and effects of this phenomenon are worthy of particular attention.

At a time when western knowledge of Islam is focused on the witnessing of terrorist accounts, current highly-selective accounts of Islam provided by the media must be called into question by providing richer accounts of the diversity of Muslim faith and practice. Schools have a responsibility to redress prejudiced social attitudes through knowledge (not just the social environment provided), to equip students to be engaged in informed political and social discussion, particularly in a global context, and to provide tools for understanding how stereotypes emerge and the conditions and sources of religious/social conflict.

While what constitutes 'improved' knowledge is far from settled, numerous examples exist of successful education campaigns that have been directed at changing attitudes through knowledge. The inclusion of indigenous perspectives in all curriculum areas is one example of this agenda which targets an area of great misunderstanding and intolerance. Education campaigns in fields such as AIDS and sex education, as well as intercultural education programs, have also demonstrated success. Similarly, contact with the populations concerned emerges as a particularly important strategy for incorporating non-institutional perspectives in a powerful way. So limited and gross are understandings of Islam in Australia, that the provision of knowledge to understand the diversity and complexity of this group through education in our schools is urgent.

NOTES

[1] Barry V. Driel (2004), *Confronting Islamophobia in educational practice*. Stoke-on-Trent: Trentham.

[2] Kevin Dunn (2005), 'Australian Public Knowledge of Islam', *Studia Islamika, Indonesian Journal for Islamic Studies*, 12(1), pp. 1–32.

[3] Robert Jackson (2004), *Intercultural education and religious diversity, Interpretive and dialogical approaches from England*, Global Meeting on Teaching for Tolerance, Respect and Recognition in Relation with Religion or Belief, Oslo, 2–5 September.

[4] Isaiah Berlin (1969), 'Two Concepts of Liberty', in Isaiah Berlin (ed.), *Four Essays on Liberty*. London: Oxford University Press, p. 131.

[5] Susan Mendus (1989), *Toleration and the limits of liberalism*, Macmillan, Basingstoke, p. 73.

[6] John Stuart Mill (1956), *On Liberty*, Indianapolis: Bobbs-Merrill.

[7] Paulo Freire (1970), *Pedagogy of the oppressed*. New York: Herder and Herder; Pierre Bourdieu, Pierre and Jean-Claude Passeron (1979), *The inheritor:, French students and their relation to culture*. Chicago: University of Chicago Press.

[8] Barry Troyna, Morewena Griffiths, and British Educational Research Association, Conference, 1995, *Antiracism, culture and social justice in education*. Stoke-on-Trent: Trentham Books; Barry Troyna and Jenny Williams (1986), *Racism, education, and the state*. London: Croom Helm.

[9] See, for example, Michel Foucault (1972), *The archaeology of knowledge*. London: Tavistock Publications; Michel Foucault, (1977), *Discipline and punish, the birth of the prison*. London: Allen Lane.

[10] Hastings Donnan (2002), *Interpreting Islam*. London: Sage, p. 6.

[11] Edward Said (1981), Covering Islam, How the media and the experts determine how we see the rest of the world New York, Pantheon Books; Edward Said (1995), Orientalism. New York: Penguin.

[12] Joe L. Kincheloe and Shirley Steinberg (2004), The miseducation of the West: how schools and the media distort our understanding of the Islamic world. Westport, Conn.Praeger Publishers.

[13] Gordon W. Allport (1954), *The nature of prejudice*, Cambridge, Mass.: Addison-Wesley Pub. Co., p. 13.

[14] Australian Bureau of Statistics, 2006, *1301.0—Year Book Australia, Religious Affiliation*, Canberra: ABS.

[15] AAP, 2007, 'Hanson announces election bid'. *Sydney Morning Herald*, February 26.

[16] Christian Democratic Party (2007), *No More Muslims*, Press Release, retrieved 30 September 2007 from http,//www.cdp.org.au/fed/mr/0703010f.asp.

[17] Ibid.

[18] This position was created by the Australian Federation of Islamic Councils, one of a number of organisations whose representative legitimacy is limited and is rejected by many non-Arab Muslims in Australia, most notably those of Turkish background.

[19] Janet Albrechtsen (2002), 'Blind spot allows barbarism to flourish', *The Australian*, 17 July.

[20] Samual P. Huntington (1996), *The clash of civilizations and the remaking of world order*. New York: Simon and Schuster.

[21] Albrechtson, 'Blind spot allows barbarism to flourish'.

[22] *Daily Telegraph*, 2007, Multiculturalism in Australia, retrieved 30 September, 2007 from http,//www.news.com.au/dailytelegraph/index/0,22045,5009120,00.html.

[23] *Daily Telegraph*, 2006, 'Muslims show no tolerance for the tolerant—Your Comments', retrieved 30 September 2007, from http,//blogs.news.com.au/dailytelegraph/piersakerman/index.php/dailytelegraph/comments/muslims_show_no_tolerance_for_the_tolerant/.

[24] Howard Brasted (2001), 'Contested representations in historical perspective, images of Islam and the Australian press 1950–2000', in Shahram Akbarzadeh and Abdullah Saeed (eds.), *Muslim communities in Australia*. Sydney: UNSW Press.

[25] Scott Poynting (2002), 'Bin Laden in the suburbs, attacks on Arab and Muslim Australians before and after 11 September', *Current Issues in Criminal Justice*, 14,(1), pp. 43–64.

[26] Zuleyha Keskin (2007), The voice of Turkish women in Australia today compared to yesterday, an analysis by a second generation Turkish woma., Presented at Immigrants as Citizens Conference, University of Sydney, 6–7 October.

[27] Pew Research Centre, 2006, *Conflicting views in a divided world*. Washington DC: The Pew Global Attitudes Project, p. viii.

[28] Dunn, 'Australian Public Knowledge of Islam'.

[29] Ibid.

[30] Terminology taken from Chris Hart (2003), *Doing a Literature Review*. London: Sage, p. 60.

[31] Jacquelyn Flaskerud and Adeline Nyamathi (1990), 'Effects of an AIDS education program on the knowledge, attitudes and practices of low income black and Latina women', *Journal of Community Health*, 15(6), pp. 343–55.

[32] Carolyn Thomson, Candace Currie, Joanna Todd, and Rob Elton(1999), 'Changes in HIV/AIDS education, knowledge and attitudes among Scottish 15–16 year olds, 1990–1994: Findings from the WHO, Health Behaviour in School-aged Children Study HBSC', *Health Education Research*, 14(3), pp. 357–70.

[33] R. Zimmerman, L. Langer, R. Starr, R, and N. Enzler (1991), 'Evaluation of theory-based high school AIDS education, Impact of teacher vs. peer-led and active vs. passive education, and an HIV awareness campaign'. Paper presented at the International Conference on AIDS, 16–21 June.

[34] Lorraine, Guth, Cynthia Hewitt-Gervais, Sherri Smith, and Manda Fisher (2000), 'Student attitudes toward AIDS and homosexuality, The effects of a speaker with HIV', *Journal of College Student Development*, 41(5), pp. 1–10.

[35] Martin Barker (1981), The new racism, conservatives and the ideology of the tribe. London: Junction Books.

[36] Milton Kleg (1970), 'Race, caste, and prejudice, the influence of change in knowledge on change in attitude'. Unpublished PhD thesis, University of Georgia, Athens.

[37] Felix Neto (2006), 'Changing intercultural attitudes over time', *Journal of Intercultural Communication*, 12, August; Mirium Hill, and Martha Augoustinos, 2001, 'Stereotype change and prejudice reduction, Short- and long-term evaluation of a cross-cultural awareness programme', *Journal of Community and Applied Social Psychology*, 11(4), pp. 243–62.

[38] Leon Feinstein, Cathie Hammond, Laura Woods, John Preston and John Bynner (2003), *The Contribution of Adult Learning to Health and Social Capital, WBL Research Report No. 8*. London: Centre for Research on the Wider Benefits of Learning.

[39] T. Pettigrew, J. Jackson, J. Ben Brika, G. Lemaine, R. Meertens, U. Wagner, (1997), Outgroup prejudice in Western Europe, *European Review of Social Psychology*, 8, pp. 241–73.

[40] Martin Fishbein and Icek Ajzen, 1975, *Belief, Attitude, Intention and Behaviour*. Reading MA.: Addison-Wesley.

[41] J. Bynner, D. Romney, and N. Emler, (2003), 'Dimensions of political and related facets of identity in late adolescence', *Journal of Youth Studies*, 63, pp. 319–335, p. 330.

[42] Dunn, 'Australian Public Knowledge of Islam'.

[43] Lawrence Bobo and Vincent Hutchings (1996), 'Perceptions of racial group competition, extending Blumer's theory of group position to a multiracial social context', *American Sociological Review*, 61(9), pp. 51–72.

[44] Wafia Omar, Philip J. Hughes, Kirsty Allen, and Australian Bureau of Immigration Multicultural and Population Research, 1996, *The Muslims in Australia*. Canberra: AGPS; R. Davis and R. Stimson

(1998). 'Disillusionment and disenchantment at the fringe, explaining the geography of the One Nation Party vote at the Queensland Election', *People and Place*, 6, pp. 69–82.

[45] Ministerial Council on Education, Employment, Training and Youth Affairs (1999). *The Adelaide Declaration on National Goals for Schooling in the Twenty-first Century*. Adelaide: MCEETYA.

[46] Robert Jackson (1995), Religious education's representation of 'religions' and 'cultures',. *British Journal of Educational Studies*, 433, p. 275.

[47] United Nations Educational Scientific and Cultural Organization. 1995, *Declaration of Principles on Tolerance*. Paris: UNESCO.

[48] Ibid, p. 4.

[49] Huntington, The clash of civilizations and the remaking of world order.

[50] Council for the Australian Federation (2007), *Federalist Paper 2, The future of schooling in Australia*. Melbourne: Council for the Australian Federation.

[51] Department of Education, Science and Training (2007), 'Values education for Australian schools', retrieved 30 September 2007 from http,//www.valueseducation.edu.au/values/values_homepage,8655. html.

[52] Dan Cohn-Sherbok, Lavinia Cohn-Sherbok, and Mark Halstead (1997), 'Teaching about Judaism and Islam', in Lelie J. Francis and Willian. K. Kay (eds), *Religion in education*. pp. 191–214. Leominster, Gracewing; Emma Barnard, Costain Cho Asia Education Foundation, and Deptartment of Education Science and Training (2005), *The really big beliefs project*, Carlton: Curriculum Corporation.

[53] Ibid, p. 207.

[54] N. Smart, (1969), cited in Cohn-Sherbok et al., (1989), 'Teaching about Judaism and Islam', p. 208.

[55] Jackson, 'Religious Education's Representation of 'Religions' and 'Cultures'', p. 278.

[56] Jackson, Intercultural education and religious diversity, Interpretive and dialogical approaches from England.

[57] Said, Covering Islam, how the media and the experts determine how we see the rest of the world; Said, Orientalism.

[58] Alan Bullock (1970), *The Rise of Islam*. London: Marshall Cavendish Books, p. 1.

[59] H. Kharem (2004), 'The great European denial, The misrepresentation of the Moors in Western education', in Kincheloe and Steinberg, *The miseducation of the West, how schools and the media distort our understanding of the Islamic world*.

[60] Ministerial Council on Education, Employment, Training and Youth Affairs, 2000, National statement of principles and standards for more culturally inclusive schooling in the 21st Century. Canberra: MCEETYA.

[61] Ministerial Council on Education, Employment, Training and Youth Affairs, 2000, *Model of culturally inclusive and educationally effective schools*. MCEETYA: Canberra.

[62] See, for example, Roger Dunscombe (2004), *Heinemann media 1. Units 1 and 2*. Port Melbourne: Heinemann.

[63] Council for the Australian Federation (2007), Federalist Paper 2, The Future of Schooling in Australia.

[64] Susan Douglass and Ross Dunn (2002), 'Interpreting Islam in American schools', in Donnan, *Interpreting Islam*, pp. 76–98.

[65] Jackson, Intercultural education and religious diversity: Interpretive and dialogical approaches from England.

Joel Windle
Faculty of Education
Monash University

WINIFRED WING HAN LAMB

7. 'THE TRUTH LOOKS DIFFERENT FROM HERE...'[1]

Faith, Education and Dialogue

TOLERANCE: THE CONTEMPORARY EDUCATIONAL CHALLENGE

Young people today grow up in a world of radical pluralism and consumer omnipotence, for theirs is 'the age of over-exposure to otherness'.[2] Esoteric as postmodern philosophy is, something of its 'incredulity towards metanarratives'[3] has filtered into popular consciousness with the sense of suspicion towards those who profess bold truth claims about their beliefs. Along with a new postcolonial consciousness, we have become more aware of the ethical challenge of 'the other'. However, recent world events have also complicated our consciousness with the spectre of growing terrorism and fundamentalism. Who wields the totalising metanarrative? Who is the other? To whom should we extend tolerance? Is tolerance always a virtue? Should it be nurtured? What are its limits? What part should education play?

These are big questions and hide further ones addressed by contributors to this volume. While the concept of tolerance suggests something of value and has obvious educational appeal, it also raises its own complex questions as we have seen. For this reason, it is more fruitful in the educational context to focus on the notion of 'dialogue' to address the concerns raised by tolerance—in particular, the achievement of mutual understanding and coexistence. Furthermore, it can be argued that 'dialogue' in its various senses is intrinsic to the aims and processes of education, exemplifying relationships that occur within it of an inter-personal and intra-personal kind. The former includes interactions between students, teacher and students and between learners and the content of learning. The latter refers to what the learner experiences in her effort to gain understanding of knowledge, a process which involves rationality (obviously), but less obviously, also emotion, imagination, empathy and will as well as epistemic virtues like courage, humility and concern for truth.

Now it is often supposed that the capacities for dialogue outlined above are significantly reduced if not totally inhibited within those who hold strong conviction, especially of a religious nature. Indeed, the belief that religious faith leads to closed mindedness is a deeply held presupposition in western philosophical thought. The perception may be based on the common sense deduction that those who believe they hold true beliefs are unlikely to seek illumination from the views of those of a different persuasion. Of course, the case of religious fundamentalism looms large in public consciousness today to reinforce that perception. While this presupposition has historically occasioned extensive debate between philosophy and theology, as

E.B. Coleman and K. White (eds.), Religious Tolerance, Education and the Curriculum, 85–98.

Relativism

shown in papers in this volume, we have recently been faced with an analogous presupposition in contemporary thought. Widespread relativism in our societies (paradoxically with growing fundamentalism in others) has weakened traditional notions of truth and conviction, giving rise to the parallel perception that unless one is relativist with respect to truth claims, one cannot be tolerant. The view, in short, is that only relativists can engage in genuine dialogue because only they are able to hold their own opinions lightly and exercise some detachment from them.[4]

Q's

In view of the fact that most adolescents and teenagers in western societies today are relativists in inclination, their teachers (and not only those of religious studies) are faced with a challenge. How do they speak about truth claims, values and personal conviction? Can they defend the idea that non relativism is compatible with open mindedness and dialogue? How should educators conceive of truth in our pluralistic environment?

These are complex questions, but teachers of religious education are attuned to analogous ones within religion and theological debates. Questions such as: *Is religious conviction necessarily fundamentalist? Does conviction produce closed-mindedness? What kind of open-mindedness is consistent with faith? What does it mean to believe in transcendent truth?* have produced a range of interesting responses that are relevant and illuminating to the educational questions.

Main focus Christianity

In this chapter, I will assume this narrower focus within the religious debate to consider whether dialogue is compatible with religious conviction, further confining myself to the example of Christian faith. Theological discussions on these questions within Christianity are illuminating to the broader questions also because they bring an important distinction into focus: *viz.* the distinction between the 'epistemology' and the 'psychology of dialogue'. The first aspect of dialogue refers to the evaluation of truth claims in interpersonal dialogue, that is, when individuals consider arguments for their positions and reasons that count against them. The second refers to the personal capacities of individuals for dialogue, that is, as mentioned earlier, qualities of emotion, imagination, empathy and will, as well as virtues like courage, humility and concern for truth because of the significant part they play in how well dialogue fares between people.

aspects of dialogue

It can be argued that education is concerned with both aspects of dialogue: the first corresponds broadly to its cognitive aims and goals and the second to its affective and attitudinal ones. However, the two senses, while distinguishable, are not distinct. The capacity of individuals to engage in dialogue do, to a greater or lesser extent, also depend on the question of truth, in particular, on how individuals *conceive* of truth. Both senses must be born in mind in the educational task. While the 'epistemology' of dialogue directs attention to the educative role of developing the capacities of individuals to understand the assumptions behind and arguments for various positions that people hold, the 'psychology' of dialogue refers to the part education plays to develop depths of the self sometimes referred to as 'inwardness'.[5]

The discussion that follows proceeds on the assumption that contemporary education faces us with the challenge of promoting well-informed tolerance. Furthermore, it is based on the assumption that the educational challenge can be illuminated by analogous religious questions outlined above. However, the picture for contemporary education is complicated by recent political and international developments in which religion is perceived as part of the problem of tolerance in public consciousness. By giving voice to the theological responses, we are enabling a dialogue with popular perceptions of religion that unhelpfully equate religious belief with fundament-alism. Furthermore, by laying bare the relationship between the epistemological (the conception of truth in religious belief) and psychological aspects (how individuals exercise faith) of belief, we can open up the discussion on the educational questions, in particular, of how individuals' conceptions of truth affect their capacity for dialogue.

We will begin by setting the context for the charge against religious faith, *viz*, that by its nature, faith cannot make room for dialogue. Turning to a range of Christian thinkers, including Søren Kierkegaard, Samuel Taylor Coleridge, Lesslie Newbiggin and Janet Martin Soskice, we will consider ways in which their views of faith can provide arguments against the charge. A picture of inwardness emerges that elucidates the two aspects of dialogue discussed above and which holds lessons for education. Out of this, we will draw some lessons for education.

'THE GOD'S EYE VIEW':[6] RELIGIOUS FAITH AND DIALOGICAL CLOSURE

When individuals seriously discuss their different views, the question of truth is clearly at stake. However, there is more going on than epistemological issues, such as in what is assumed by the views held and the reasons and arguments given to support them. Situations of dialogue involve concrete situations and people, each with complex histories and agendas that may either be conscious or unconscious. Indeed, people who are experienced with dialogue remind us of the obvious fact that the process requires an attitude of openness in the exchange. They also note the equally obvious fact that dialogue partners need to be attentive listeners to the other, in such a way that they should even expect to be changed in the encounter. Indeed, genuine dialogue involves risk and requires courage.

If individuals can either facilitate or hinder dialogue, when does dialogue become a fruitful engagement? We could begin by proposing the following four conditions for dialogue:

– First, dialogue is possible and worthwhile only when discussions do justice to the distinctiveness of the positions of the dialogue partners involved. Those experienced with inter-religious dialogue make the point that if one is to take the other seriously one must recognise their distinctiveness and difference.[7]
– Second, those involved in dialogue need to exercise openness. We may contrast this with the closed-mindedness that comes with fundamentalist belief, a mindset that is represented by oppositionalism.[8] As a stance that is governed by the dualistic categories of 'inside' and 'outside,' fundamentalism regards openness to what is 'outside' as both dangerous and unwise.[9] In contrast, in exercising openness, parties to dialogue may have to put their most cherished beliefs at stake and risk the challenge of refutation.[10]
– Third, parties to dialogue need to exercise judgement regarding the truthfulness, plausibility and/or attractiveness of the positions that they encounter. In other words, they need epistemological criteria for the evaluation of claims and positions.

87

Why?

- Fourth, parties to dialogue need to be sustained by the conviction of its worth-
  whileness such as that it could lead to learning, the possibility of a larger understanding and the benefit of shared understanding.[11]

Stephen White puts it well when he describes dialogue as 'a willingness to hold
open an intersubjective space in which difference can unfold in its particularity'.[12]
A convincing account of dialogue must therefore recognise the various dimensions
of intersubjective space. In addition to the importance of 'rhetorical space',[13] that
is, a fair and non-threatening context for discussion as noted above, fruitful dialogue
also depends upon certain interior qualities of the participants, such as trust, care,
resilience, humility and hope.

Now what is being claimed about religious believers is that unless they are
relativists about their beliefs, or take an unqualified position of inclusivism with
regard to other faith claims, they will experience insuperable psychological impediments to genuine dialogue. Given their conviction that they hold true beliefs,
they would be incapable of taking an opposing position seriously. At best, they will
be closed to them, at worst, hostile. This is well exemplified by J.J. Rousseau's
assertion in the *Social Contract* that 'theological intolerance' must lead inevitably
to 'civil intolerance' since '[one] cannot live in peace with people one regards as
damned'.[14]

Contemporary philosophers express a similar assumption about the nature of
metaphysical beliefs of all kinds. Jacques Derrida describes metaphysical thinking
as that 'which receives only what it gives itself' and which merely 'neutralises' the
other rather than genuinely engages with it.[15] The feminist philosopher, Donna
Haraway, connects the notion of transcendence to domination because of its claims
to a 'disembodied infinitude' and to 'the god's eye view'. Reference to transcendent
truth is a 'god trick' because it is based on the illusion that we are in charge of a world
of which we have an unmediated grasp. It cannot take in the 'surprises and ironies
at the heart of all knowledge production...' and necessarily leads to irresponsibility,
reductionism and epistemological closure. In contrast, she proposes a 'dialogical
process of making knowledge' which is reverent and attentive to what is there in
the world.[16]

Foucault

Christopher Falzon makes a similar point in his illuminating reading of Michel
Foucault's philosophy as one of 'social dialogue'.[17] He argues that all metaphysical
beliefs, especially religious ones, block dialogue and openness in at least two ways,
first, the all-encompassing nature of these beliefs is such that the other is obliterated
and reduced 'to a mere function of [its own] categories'.[18] Second, in the case of
religious beliefs, those who hold them often adopt a posture of self-negation and
'deferential attentiveness',[19] towards others, or God, and thereby loses his or her
own point of view. This occurs through forms of subjectivity that encourage both
docile subordination to its own beliefs and fundamental resistance to others.[20]
However, as Falzon rightly argues, for dialogue to occur, we must neither deny our
own contribution to the encounter, nor the contribution of the other. He argues that:

> ...[o]penness towards others demands that we reject such absolutisations, that
> without simply abandoning our standpoint we remain open to the possibility
> of learning something about how to live from those we judge.[21]

In the spirit of postmodern critique, Falzon targets not only religion but the whole western philosophical tradition. While Hegelian thought purports to advance a dialectical philosophy and Kantian ethics is founded on respect, Falzon argues that both are in reality framed by a totalising system that has no room for an exterior other, and that is only concerned with showing how 'the Other, the Distant, is also the Near and the Same'.[22] This is not the place to respond to the postmodern critique of western philosophy, but I cite this example to reflect the challenge to education from contemporary philosophical relativism, which presents the contention that metaphysical and non relativist notions of truth disable genuine dialogue.

But is the charge against religious belief a fair one? It could, of course, be based on an empirical observation about religious believers. Rousseau's remark was no doubt inspired by real people and events. But is he right about all believers? Does his observation reflect an epistemological and psychological necessity? Does every metaphysical belief obliterate ones different from itself? What does it mean to believe in transcendent truth? Does faith produce a passive and docile mentality as Falzon claims? Can believers be open to learn from those they judge? We will now consider some Christian responses.

'SUBJECTIVELY LESS CERTAIN TO US...': CHRISTIAN FAITH AND POSSIBILITIES FOR DIALOGUE

In answering the charges against them, Christians will need to show that their faith has been mischaracterised. This is not to deny that, as a matter of fact, believers can and do display the traits described in the critique above. But they need to show that believing in a transcendent truth is not synonymous with claiming that they possess an ultimate unmediated grasp of reality in a 'god's eye view'. They will need to give an account of what it means to exercise religious faith and show how such faith is not a form of static dogmatism. In short, they will have to show that their faith leaves room for dialogue, both in its epistemological and psychological aspects.

It is a well known fact that Kierkegaard's philosophy was in part a reaction against the idea that philosophy or religion can be summed up by a metaphysical system of thought. He attacked Hegelian thought on such grounds, not only because he believed it misrepresented the nature of truth, of faith, and of the human condition, but also because he claimed that it led to the complacency that greatly weakened Christian experience. Referring to the 'make believe in which the system has made itself fancy that it knew what faith is',[23] Kierkegaard particularly criticised that 'system' of 'Christendom' which, by means of Hegelian thought, represented (that is, misrepresented) Christianity as the highest form of religion.[24] He further rejected the attempts to give Christianity 'objective' foundations, either evidentially in historical scholarship or metaphysically in the 'speculative thought' of Hegelian philosophy. Both, Kierkegaard argues, are misconstrued attempts to establish the Christian faith on points of reference outside time, as if such measures are accessible to finite human beings. According to Kierkegaard, the 'holism' of the Hegelian system comes at the cost of denying our humanity, which is the condition of faith.

Far from endorsing the argument (which we have met in Falzon) that Hegelian philosophy articulates Christianity, Kierkegaard emphasises that the two ways of thinking are actually utterly incompatible.[25] While the lure of a metaphysical system tricks individuals 'into becoming objective',[26] Christianity is not a system of coherent thought that elucidates everything, since Christian faith, by its very nature, cannot deliver epistemic certainty. As an existential quest for God, an 'infinite personal interested passion',[27] faith is marked by an irresolvable tension between the spiritual and the temporal. As such, it is at times maintained at the cost of clarity and coherence to the believer.

It is significant that when Kierkegaard warns that faith must not be turned into 'another kind of certainty',[28] he is pointing us away from the traditional philosophical understanding of faith as a form of cognition, a misconception that Augustine centuries earlier had debated with reference to his own account of coming to faith.[29] Augustine traced this erroneous understanding of faith to its early depiction as *pistis* (opinion or belief as distinct from knowledge) which, in Plato's well-known image of the Line in *The Republic*, is located in the lower half of the Divided Line on knowledge. Here, it is presented as an inferior mode of cognition, and one directed toward the wrong objects (that is, the sensible world). In the other well-known allegory, *pistis* belongs to the dark world of the Cave in which it is cut off from the sunlight of reason (*episteme, noesis*).[30]

In Books Seven and Eight of his *Confessions*, Augustine rejected the idea that the question of faith and reason was an issue of opinion and knowledge. Speaking from experience, he showed how the achievement of epistemological certainty about God did not for him ease the burden of guilt.[31] Augustine's breakthrough into faith is, therefore, not described as a transition from *pistis* to *episteme* or *noesis*, but the reverse. The process of coming to faith proceeded:

> from a certainty already achieved to faith as a whole new way of life, indeed,
> a whole new framework for interpreting and evaluating his life…[t]he primary
> issue is not the degree of certainty but the direction of the will.[32]

Accordingly, Kierkegaard draws the distinction between 'approximation' and 'appropriation' to underline the point that faith is not the quest for increasing epistemic certainty, or 'approximation' to objective truth, rather it is a self involving 'appropriation' of truth. In this view of faith, the believer does not claim possession of truth as the 'god's eye view', nor does her appropriation of truth foreclose new learning since she is driven by an existential and passionate need to understand truth.[33] Her decisive commitment, such as it is, does not rest on the grounds of perfect or certain knowledge, for such is the disparity between human beings and the infinite God that faith will always remain a quest that is characterised by non-arrival. By its very nature, therefore, the exercise of faith provides a training ground against complacency and epistemic arrogance.

However, complacency and closed-mindedness can and does arise from a misplaced sense of loyalty to one's particular faith tradition and it is partisan forms of allegiance that Samuel Taylor Coleridge warns against. He does so on theological grounds.[34] Coleridge's point is that narrow loyalty does not reflect the God that

Christians worship since a theologically sound notion of truth for Christians must be faithful to the nature of the Godhead. Accordingly, the exercise of will and reason should reflect the dynamism of pluralism in unity of the Trinitarian God. To be faithful to something less than truth is to fail to participate in the Trinity and to engage in an idolatrous form of knowing. It is to enter 'a downward spiral which produces atrophy and closure and whose end [is] self-love'.[35] He writes:

> He who begins by loving Christianity, better than truth, will proceed by loving his own sect or church better than Christianity, and end in loving himself better than all.[36]

Christians should therefore stake their ultimate loyalty in 'truth' itself, rather than in particular interpretations of it, and allow this practice of nimbleness to train them in courageous forms of openness and learning. The clear distinction that Coleridge drew between faithfulness to institutionalised truth and faithfulness to truth itself was designed to warn believers against the self affirming illusion that '[their] words are God's words'.[37] Coleridge also recognised that the exercise of vigilance has direct social implications. He writes:

> The soul that hath the deepest sense of spiritual things and the truest knowledge of God, is most afraid to miscarry in speaking of Him, most tender and wary how to acquit itself when engaged to speak of and for God.[38]

While Coleridge and Kierkegaard provided both philosophical and theological arguments against a closed minded and complacent faith, it is clear that religious believers do not always exhibit appropriate tolerance. According to Janet Martin Soskice, this can be attributed to the conception of truth that they hold.[39] Citing a negative example of dialogue from the sixteenth century between John Calvin the reformer and Cardinal Sadolet as representative of Rome, Soskice identifies the conception of truth that drove the interlocutors far apart. From their exchange of letters, Soskice notes the profound doctrinal differences that form the background of their antagonistic exchange. However, she argues that the two men are as much divided by the assumptions they share as by their doctrinal differences. Importantly, those assumptions centre on their concept of truth.

Contrary to Coleridge's view, Sadolet presents loyalty to the church as a supreme priority. Accordingly, he is able to argue convincingly that the Reformers have torn the church in pieces and destroyed the one Truth, for 'Truth is always one, while falsehood is varied and multiform' for 'the glory of God', 'both his with us, and ours with him' consists solely in the one true and united church.[40] In reply, Calvin insists that he is not rejecting the one true Church, but *rescuing* it from Rome. Vitriolic as he is about the corrupting work of Rome, Calvin shares with Sadolet the view that there is a clearly identifiable true church that stands in opposition to what is corrupt and of man. Their shared monolithic view of truth, and their clear and certain identification of its source, encouraged and enabled each man to relegate the other to profound error: As Soskice writes, 'Black and white, saved and damned, in no sense are the two men in this exchange agreeing to differ'.[41]

In interesting ways, this early modern exchange prefigures the twentieth century phenomenon of fundamentalism, defined as the attempt to 'freeze' truth in some form.[42] When North American fundamentalism was born at the beginning of the twentieth century, the polemical exchanges between Protestant fundamentalists and those they criticised within the church, reflect the same monolithic view of truth which also enabled clear and confident reference to what is God given and to and what is man made. For example, the theologian, Gresham Machen, insisted that the Christian faith is based on immovable 'facts' that have a fixed significance revealed by God himself. Therefore, the task of historical scholarship is to *discover* the 'true' facts and their significance, rather than interpret them.[43] In fact, so insistent was Machen that the human mind should not impose its categories on reality that he took exception to the modern use of the word 'interpretation', saying that it is a word 'that has been custodian of more nonsense, perhaps, than any other word in the English language today'.[44] Machen's anti-hermeneutical position continues to this day in fundamentalist understandings of truth.[45]

Theological discussions since the development of Protestant fundamentalism have addressed the question of the influence of modern epistemic canons on the development of theology in the modern period. For example, it has been pointed out that modern theology has simply assumed the idea of truth as correspondence to reality and the value of a neutral standpoint in enquiry. According to Lesslie Newbigin,[46] such epistemic ideals and the ensuing false dichotomy between 'objectivism' and 'subjectivism' have not served Christian theology well since both positions miss the place of personal responsibility in coming to know and in making knowledge claims. Indeed, something of that dichotomous thinking may lie behind the charge against religious faith and belief in transcendent truth discussed in the early part of this chapter, for the charge assumes that the only alternative to a fundamentalist conception of truth is a subjectivist and constructivist conception, that is, the idea that all the utterances of the human subject reveal nothing more than the thought world and perspective of the subject itself.

What conceptions of truth will serve the claims of theology? According to Soskice, the idea of one monolithic truth cannot be maintained on either epistemological or theological grounds. On epistemological grounds because we now recognise that our account of the world relies on a system of concepts that is framed by the paradigm that we have chosen. Accordingly, theology seeks to represent a complex reality by means of multiple models and metaphors. In this way, the task of theology reflects a critical realist conception of truth and the recognition that 'the truth looks different from here'.[47] However, Soskice adds that, for Christian theology, critical realism is also underpinned by its view of the human condition, which recognises the 'dark side' of our languages and cultures, and of 'injustices…so built into the fabric of language' that we may not even be aware of them. These theological reasons alone would caution an epistemic modesty. Soskice therefore cites the thirteenth century theologian and philosopher St Thomas Aquinas' articulation of the position as follows: 'There is nothing to stop a thing that is objectively more certain by its nature from being subjectively less certain to us because of the disability of our minds'.[48]

However, critical realism besides, a further conception of truth has emerged in our discussions of faith. Implicit in the views of Coleridge and Kierkegaard that we have considered is the idea of the responsibility of knowledge. Coleridge has urged

Christians to exercise a faithfulness to truth itself, wherever it will lead. Similarly, Kierkegaard has insisted that the question of truth is inseparable from truthfulness in the person one becomes.

According to Richard Campbell, this lived conception of truth has been eclipsed in philosophical discussion by the 'linguistic conception of truth'.[49] However, it is reflected in our common speech acts, such as promises and avowals of true love or true friendship. What is pledged in such instances is not only genuineness and authenticity, but also the assurance of reliability and dependability in the long term. Campbell further observes that this conception of truth as the faithfulness of persons and of their dispositions over time is an insight built into many natural languages. It is particularly striking in Hebrew in which *emeth* means 'the reliability, the un-shakable dependability, of a thing or a word, and accordingly the faithfulness of persons'.[50] *Emeth* is sustained by openness of character, that is, 'a binding directed-ness, to think of, to speak of, and act towards reality—entities and other persons—in a way faithful to their own way of acting'.[51] The meaning of *emeth* exemplifies the views of Coleridge and Kierkegaard on how Christians should live in the light of their faith. When corroborated by the epistemological notion of critical realism, faith can be born with both steadfastness and openness of character and also with appropriate epistemic modesty. It is now time to draw out some broader educational lessons.

'VALUES ARE WHAT WE DO': IMPLICATIONS FOR EDUCATION

In drawing our lessons from the example of Christian faith, we do so fully aware of the fact that religious dogmatism and close-mindedness differ in content from their non-religious counterparts. However, in a formal sense, the issues are analogous. If certain forms of religious faith are dialogically open because of the notions of truth on which they are based, we could raise the following questions with respect to education: first, how can those twin ideas of truth, as critical realism and as faithful-ness and reliability, be promoted through the academic curriculum? Second, what habits of mind can be developed within the curriculum and culture of schools?

These are big questions involving detailed examination of curricula, pedagogy, school and classroom culture that cannot be adequately discussed in this chapter. However, the recent Australian debate on values education provides a focus for how some of these questions may be addressed. The former liberal Howard govern-ment's initiative to address what it saw as a values vacuum in public school education issued in the Schools Values Poster[52] designed to articulate a list of 'Australian values', such as 'Care and compassion', 'Fair Go', 'Freedom', 'Understanding, Tolerance and Inclusion', centring around the historical memory of the ANZAC legend. Even though they have been subject to criticism, these values were also meant to be treated with seriousness and respect rather than critical appraisal.[53] When it comes to values associated with patriotism and loyalty to country, such as celebration of the ANZAC legend, we are faced with matters approached by some with a respect that borders on religious reverence. Education has a clear role to play.

Critical realism enjoins all citizens to examine the nature of truth claims that surround the promotion of patriotism. The history wars[54] in Australia reflect differences in opinion on how national history should be represented. Accordingly, the contested nature of history should feature in the curriculum to underline the complexity of the issues represented by the diversity of perspectives. Where patriotism is concerned, educators should be concerned with such questions as: *When does patriotism become unhealthy and when does it descend into uncritical nationalism? When does patriotism block understanding of those who are different?*

Coleridge's warning against parochial religious loyalty is relevant here. The distinction drawn between loyalty to partisan truth and faithfulness to truth itself is clearly relevant to the question of loyalty to one's nation. The notion of 'critical nationalism'[55] challenges the parochial loyalty that Coleridge identified as a dangerous and anti-social form of faithfulness. It challenges the passionate defence of 'our way of life' or of the defence of 'our' free and democratic society with reference to values higher than those of loyalty to a narrow conception of who 'we' are.[56]

The notion of critical nationalism like Coleridge's notion of Christian faithfulness is clearly important to dialogical openness within a social context. At a time when questions of identity (whether national or religious, or in combination) are rallying cries for political policies (foreign policy or domestic policies on refugees), we must be vigilant that notions of identity are not determined and fixed by the permanent categories of 'them' and 'us', 'inside' or 'outside'.[57] On this subject, the philosopher Jacques Derrida has reminded us that a critical notion of identity is a requirement for justice. [58] He writes:

[I]t is because I am not one with myself that I can speak with the other and address the other...I can address the Other only to the extent that there is a separation, a dissociation, so that I cannot replace the other and vice versa...It is a relation in which the other remains absolutely transcendent...I cannot reach the other. I cannot know the other from the inside and so on. That is not an obstacle but the condition of love ...[59]

How is such vigilance promoted in education and how are such supporting habits of mind cultivated within individuals? What part does the academic curriculum play? It is important to note that, despite their differences, all areas of knowledge within the curriculum have a part to play to promote both aspects of dialogue, first, in developing an awareness of arguments for and against truth claims as well as introducing students appropriately to the complexity of issues which will militate against easy reference to 'the facts' or to simple dichotomies. Second, all areas of knowledge can help to develop attitudes of mind and intellectual virtues which are intrinsic to enquiry within them, such as concern for truthfulness, lucidity and objectivity.[60]

In his discussion of how an appreciation of objectivity is cultivated in education, R.K. Elliott makes an important distinction between 'public' and 'private' objectivity.[61] The former refers to the public standards of enquiry integral to areas of knowledge, and the latter to the enquirer's need to overcome subjective hindrances to truth. The distinction recognises that beyond the observation of public conventions and standards of proper procedure in enquiry, the subject needs to be 'in right relation to the reality to which he transcends'.[62] Here, Elliott echoes the Kierkegaardian idea that the individual enquirer cannot implicitly trust common assumptions and collective subjectivity, but needs to exercise her own sense of accountability in the cause of truth. The practice of 'private objectivity' can be demanding to individuals, at times requiring them to 'an intense and sustained effort of self examination and individual inwardness'.[63]

Pedagogically, the use of community of enquiry[64] as a way of conducting philosophical discussions with school students at all levels reflects the recognition that the two dimensions of 'objectivity' need to be coalesced. It also recognises that values are caught rather than taught, that they are best learnt through practice, through joint respect for important forms of regard, such as attentive listening and waiting for one's turn to speak, as well as the practice of self and group evaluation. But there are broader educational considerations. When it comes to values necessary for dialogical openness, further questions arise for education:

– How can schools create intersubjective spaces in which 'difference can unfold in its particularity'?
– Are there non-threatening rhetorical spaces at all levels of the school?
– How can education nourish 'private objectivity' and the depths of the self so that truthfulness is not overruled by our evasive consciousness?
– Finally, if forms of regard integral to dialogue are caught rather than taught, what does this require of educators at all levels?

These are challenging questions indeed and, if too challenging, only serve to show how the task of values education and educating for dialogue should not be taken lightly. The cultivation and practice of such qualities are demanding to the best of us, not only in our public roles as educators, but also to us in our private lives, whether or not we are people with religious faith. Highlighting this irony, for those who presume to take on the task of 'teaching ethics', Gordon Marino shows that besides confronting first and foremost the challenge of their own 'private objectivity' and evasiveness of consciousness towards the requirement of ethics, teachers also need to help students to develop honesty at this level. Marino writes:

People who presume to teach ethics should help their students to be honest with themselves about their own interests. Such candour is, of course, part of the Socratic curriculum of coming to know yourself. But it is hard psychological work, which we do not value much in these post-Freudian times. Unless our ethics students learn to examine themselves and what they really value, their command of ethical theories and their ability to think about ethics from diverse perspectives are not likely to bring them any closer to being willing and able to do the right things.[65]

Responding to the Values Poster for Australian Schools, a Year 12 student of mine has wisely observed, 'values are not we say, they are what we do'. C.J. Sautelle continues:

[I]f the government wishes to infuse a particular set of values into the youth of Australia, then these values must be manifest in the lives of those in contact with the students themselves, their teachers...However, beyond this, to see values manifest in our education system the government must itself first begin to model the values it wishes to inspire. They must begin to truly show a commitment to equality, tolerance and compassion, both through policy and through their interactions with the community. Only then will these values permeate our society and our schools.[66]

All this points to a dimension in education that is not often acknowledged—the living of values through action and practice. When it comes to the practice of dialogical openness, we must confront the question not only of how we cultivate this capacity in education, but of whether young people see genuine capacities for dialogue embodied in those who lead them in important spheres of their lives.

NOTES

[1] Janet Martin Soskice (1992), 'The truth looks different from here', in Hilary Regan and Alan J. Torrance eds., *Christ and Context*. Edinburgh: T & T Clark, pp. 43–59.

[2] Walter Truett Anderson (1995), *The Truth about the Truth: De-confusing and Re-constructing the Postmodern World*. New York: Tarcher/Putnam, p. 5

[3] Jean François Lyotard (1981), *The Postmodern Condition: A Report on Knowledge*. Translated by Geoff Bennington and Brian Massumi, Minneapolis: University of Minnesota Press, p. xxiv.

[4] Richard Rorty, 'Ironists & metaphysicians', in Walter Truett Anderson, *The Truth about the Truth: De-confusing and Re-constructing the Postmodern World*, pp. 100–4.

[5] See, for example, later discussion of faith as 'appropriation' and 'private objectivity'.

[6] Donna Haraway (1998), 'Situated knowledges: The science question in feminism and the privilege of the partial perspective', *Feminist Studies* 14(3), pp. 575–99.

[7] See, for example, Harvey Cox (1988), *Many Mansions: A Christian's Encounter with Other Faiths*. Boston: Beacon Press,; J. DiNoia (1993), 'Teaching differences', *Journal of Education*, 73(1), pp. 61–8; Thorwald Lorenzen (1999), 'Towards a Christian theology of religions: Christianity in dialogue with other faiths', in 'Postmodernism and Theology', Graeme Garrett and Winifred Wing Han Lamb (eds.), *Interface* II(1) May, pp. 39–55.

[8] Martin E Marty (1992), 'Fundamentalisms compared', *The 1989 Charles Strong Memorial Lectures*. Adelaide: Flinders University Press, p. 1.

[9] Nancy Ammerman (1991), 'North American Protestant fundamentalism', Martin E. Marty and R. Scott Appleby (eds.), *Fundamentalisms Observed*. Chicago: University of Chicago Press, pp. 1–65; vii–viii, also chapter 15; (1999), 'Human like us: Some philosophical implications of naturalising fundamentalism', *Australian Religion Studies Review*, 12(1), pp. 5–17; Niels Nielsen (1993), *Fundamentalism, Mythos and World Religions*. Albany: State University Press.

[10] For a fine discussion on the phenomenology of openness, see RK Elliott (1974), 'Education, love of one's subject and love of truth', *Proceedings of the Philosophy of Education Society of Great Britain*, VII(1), pp. 135–53; see also Shaun Gallagher (1992), *Hermeneutics and Education*. New York: State University of New York Press.

[11] Elliott, ibid.; Winifred Wing Han Lamb (1998), 'The open heaven: Understanding other faiths in God's world', in V Pfizner and H Regan (eds.) *The Task of Theology Today: Doctrines and Dogmas*. Adelaide: ATF (1998); (Edinburgh: T & T Clark, 1999) pp. 163–89.

[12] Stephen White (1991), *Political Theory and Postmodernism*. Cambridge: Cambridge University Press, p. 99.

[13] Lorraine Code (1995), *Rhetorical Spaces. Essays on Gendered Spaces*. New York: Routledge. The notion highlights the effect of inequality in power relations in discussion.

[14] Jean-Jacques Rousseau, *The Social Contract*, cited in Richard J. Mouw and Sander Griffioen, *Pluralisms and Horizons* (Grand Rapids: Eerdmans, 1993), p. 159. I am indebted to ideas and insights in this book.

[15] Derrida (1981), 'Violence and Metaphysics', in *Writing and Difference*. Trans. Alan Bass, Chicago: University of Chicago Press, p. 96.

[16] Cf. Sally McFague's notion of 'the loving eye'. See her *Super, Natural Christians: How We Should Love Nature* (Minneapolis, Minnesota: Fortress Press, 1997), p. 35.

[17] Christopher Falzon (1998), *Foucault and Social Dialogue: Beyond Fragmentation*. London: Routledge.

[18] Ibid, p. 62.

[19] Ibid, p. 37.

[20] Ibid, pp. 64–6.

[21] Ibid, p. 62.

[22] Quoted in ibid, p. 18.

[23] Søren Kierkegaard (1944), *Concluding Unscientific Postscript*. Trans. David F. Swenson, Princeton: Princeton University Press, p. 18.

[24] See G.W.F. Hegel, *Lectures on the Philosophy of Religion*, Peter C. Hodgson (ed.) (Berkeley and Los Angeles: University of California Press, 1984–5). G.W.F. Hegel (1975), *Lectures on the Philosophy of World History: Introduction*. Translated by H.B. Nisbet, Cambridge: Cambridge University Press. The extent to which Kierkegaard was fair in this interpretation of Hegel is discussed in Merold Westphal (1996), *Becoming a Self: A Reading of Kierkegaard's Concluding Unscientific Postscript*. West Lafayette: Purdue University Press, pp. 42–3.

[25] Westphal, ibid, p. 55.

[26] Ibid, p. 34.

[27] Kierkegaard, *Concluding Unscientific Postscript*, p. 30.

[28] Ibid, p. 15.

[29] I am indebted to Westphal for this idea. See his *Becoming a Self*, pp. 40–1.

[30] The 'Simile of the Divided Line' is at the end of Book 6 and its exposition in the Allegory of the Cave in Book 7. Plato, *The Republic* (London: JM Dent, 1992), pp. 509–11 & 515–21.

[31] Augustine writes, 'Now the truth is certain, and you are still weighed down by your burden', *Confessions*, 8.7, quoted in Westphal, *Becoming a Self*, p. 41.

[32] Ibid, p. 41.

[33] The dialectical tension between approximation and appropriation is developed throughout *Concluding Unscientific Postscript* in terms of our relationship to 'objective' and 'subjective' truth. The former is based on the quest for knowledge to be completed and describes a detached relationship, the latter is an existential relationship to truth, also described as 'inwardness' in which the subject does not gain mastery and detachment of what is known. Belief is described as, 'An objective certainty, held fast through appropriation with the most passionate inwardness, is the truth, the highest truth there is for the existing person'. Kierkegaard, *Concluding Unscientific Postscript*, p. 203.

[34] I have based this discussion of Coleridge's position on Dan Hardy's (1989) essay 'Created and redeemed sociality', *Being the Church: Essays on the Christian Community*. C.E. Gunton & Daniel W Hardy (eds), Edinburgh: T & T Clark. See also Coleridge's discussion as the Trinity as the primary Idea out of which all other ideas are evolved in *Notebooks* 4, 5294, discussed in C. E. Gunton (1994), *The One, the Three and the Many: God, Creation and the Culture of Modernity*. Cambridge: Cambridge University Press, pp. 136–54.

[35] Ibid, p. 24.

[36] Samuel Taylor Coleridge (1825), *Aids to the Formation of a Manly Character*. London: Taylor and Hessey, p. 101. Quoted in ibid., p. 22.

[37] Stephen E. Fowl and Gregory L. Jones (1991), *Reading in Communion: Scripture and Ethics in the Christian Life*. Grand Rapids: Eerdmans, p. 110.

[38] Coleridge, *Aids to the Formation of a Manly Character*, Aphorism, XLII, pp. 117–8.

[39] Soskice, 'The truth looks different from here', pp. 43–59.

[40] Ibid, p. 45.

[41] Ibid, pp. 45–7.

[42] Marty and Appleby, *Fundamentalisms Observed*.

[43] Gresham Machen (1925), *What is Faith?* New York: Macmillan, p. 249.

[44] Quoted in George M. Marsden (1991), *Understanding Fundamentalism and Evangelicalism* Grand Rapids: Eerdmans, p. 192.

[45] For example, the Southern Baptist Paige Patterson has charmingly claimed, 'Space scientists tell us that a minute error in mathematical calculations for a moon shot can result in the total failure of the rocket to hit the moon. A slightly altered doctrine of salvation can cause a person to miss Heaven also. Quoted in Marsden, ibid. p. 119.

[46] Lesslie Newbigin (1991), *Truth to Tell: The Gospel as Public Truth*. Grand Rapids: Eerdmans. On the influence of modern philosophy on early Protestant fundamentalism, see Winifred Wing Han Lamb (1998), 'Facts that stay put; Protestant fundamentalism, epistemology and orthodoxy', *Sophia* 37(2), pp. 88–110.

[47] Soskice offers this summary of the position of critical realism: 'The world informs our theories even though our theories never adequately describe the world.' Soskice, 'The truth looks different from here', p. 50.

[48] Ibid.

[49] Richard Campbell (1991), *Truth and Historicity*. Oxford: Clarendon, pp. 395–429.

[50] Ibid, p. 437.

[51] Ibid.

[52] The list of Values can be found at http://www.civicsandcitizenship.edu.au/cce/default.asp?id=9500 Accessed 16 September 2010.

[53] National Framework: Nine Values for Australian Schooling. See http://www.curriculum.edu.au/values/val_nine_values_for_australian_schooling,14515.html from where the Values Poster can be downloaded. Accessed 16 September 2010.

[54] See Stuart MacIntyre and Anna Clark (2004), *The History Wars*. Melbourne: Melbourne University Press.

[55] See Richard J. Neuhaus (1984), *Naked Public Square: Religion and Democracy in America*. Grand Rapids, Eerdmans.

[56] Richard Neuhaus reminds us that neither democracy nor democratic freedom are self sustaining but require a higher order of values to nurture them. He argues that the sense of accountability to something higher to what is 'ours' and what 'we' love provides the critical spirit of self interrogation.

[57] I am interpreting Derrida's discussion of identity in John Caputo (ed.) (1997), *Deconstruction in a Nutshell: A Conversation with Jacques Derrida*. New York: Fordham University Press, pp. 13–5.

[58] Ibid, p. 14.

[59] Ibid.

[60] R.S. Peters called these traits 'rational passions'. See his 'Reason & passion', in R.F. Dearden, P.H. Hirst and R.S. Peters (eds) (1972), *Education and the Development of Reason*. London: Routledge & Kegan Paul.

[61] R.K. Elliott (1982), 'Objectivity and education', *Journal of Philosophy of Education*, 16(1), pp. 49–62.

[62] Ibid, p. 57.

[63] Ibid, p. 59.

[64] see Philip Cam, *Thinking Together: Philosophical Enquiry for the Classroom* (Alexandria, NSW: Hale & Iremonger, 1995), an excellent introductory text for promoting and facilitating community of enquiry.

[65] Gordon Marino (2004), 'Before teaching ethics, stop kidding yourself', *The Chronicle Review*, 50(24), p. B5. http://chronicle.com/article/Before-Teaching-Ethics-Sto/12923/Accessed 16 September 2010.

[66] C.J. Sautelle, 'Theory of Knowledge'. Essay addressing the question: Discuss the idea of values and the challenge of setting forth values for all Australian schools?, August, 2005.

Winifred Wing Han Lamb
Philosophy
Australian National University

PADMASIRI DE SILVA

8. TOLERANCE AND EMPATHY

Exploring Contemplative Methods in the Classroom

The faculty of voluntarily bringing back a wandering attention, over and over again, is the very root of judgment, character, and will. An education which should improve this faculty would be the education par excellence. But it is easier to define this ideal than to give practical instructions for bringing it about. William James, *Principles of Psychology* (1890).[1]

As Jon Kabat-Zinn observes, William James was not aware of the practice of mindfulness when he penned this passage but he would have been delighted to have discovered that, in the practice of mindfulness, there was certainly an education for improving the faculty of voluntarily bringing back a wandering attention over and over again.[2] What this chapter attempts to do is to locate the place of tolerance and empathy in a multi-cultural and multi-faith setting, in society and in the classroom, and to explore the role of contemplative education in fostering this objective. Thus, this chapter attempts to locate the development of empathy and tolerance within the recently expanding domain of contemplative education. As diversity work is basically reflexive, this implies that we must ask ourselves how do we engage constructively with those who are not like ourselves? Institutions like the Naropa University, which have taken a lead in the development of contemplative education, though Buddhist in inspiration, have a broad ecumenical vision, and this practice cuts across all religions, and accommodates a dialogue across religions. Their curriculum has cross-cultural dimensions, and woven into their curriculum are sitting meditation, t'ai-chi ch'uan, aikido, yoga, Chinese brushstroke and ikebana.

Also, the great contemplatives may be located across a wide spectrum, from those who have interiorised their outlook like the Christian desert fathers, the Himalayan yogis, some of the Sufi saints, Thomas Merton and the Buddhist forest monks, and at the other end, we find those who emphasised the interconnectedness with the world, like the present Dalai Lama, Hildegard of Bingen, Thich Naht Hanh, Gandhi and Martin Luther King.

EMPATHY IN THE CLASSROOM

A philosopher discussing issues pertaining to 'Diversity and Relativity', Mike Martin observes: 'Tolerance and respect are virtually important in the increasingly multicultural, global environment in which we live today. They are important not only because our self-interest is promoted by being able to work, trade, and live with diversity within a global economy, but because people deserve respect for their

E.B. Coleman and K. White (eds.), Religious Tolerance, Education and the Curriculum, 99–110.

individuality, which includes their religions, family and cultural traditions'.[3] He says that tolerance and respect are needed to avoid ethno-centricism. In the context of education trends today, 'empathy' is the skill to be cultivated and then tolerance would be a natural ally. Tolerance without empathy would look like a kind of paternalism. Daniel Goleman, discussing the gulf between 'Us' and 'Them', says that 'it is the silencing of empathy' that generates this gulf.[4]

> As a psychiatrist who grew up amid the ethnic turmoil of Cyprus put it, groups that are so much alike move from Us to Them via the 'narcissism of minor differences', seizing on small features that set the group apart while ignoring their vast human similarities. Once the others are stationed at a distance, they can become a target for hostility.[5]

While reason and argument may back the case for tolerance, it is by the development of 'contemplative education' in the schools that we could build up a real base for the cultivation of empathy. First we need to foster the habit of *deep listening*. In our academic culture most listening is critical listening. It has been observed that we pay attention long enough to develop a counter argument; when we critique the student's or the colleague's writings, we mentally grade them. Deep, open ungrudging reception of the other person has a great deal of empathy and what is *present* before the listener is not merely an argument, but a person. Second, we have developed a whole culture of techniques focused on speed, accuracy, rigour and certainty, extending its hegemony not only to education and work, but also to the way we spend our leisure and even how our kids play We also need a less deliberative and a slower, more intuitive approach to deal with situations more intricate, shadowy and, at times, seemingly paradoxical. In this world of speed and certainty, at least in a discipline like counselling, there is a context to slow down, relax, listen and respect the flow of life. 'Flow' is a state in which people are so absorbed that nothing else matters. Developed by Mihaly Csikszentmihalyi, the notion of 'flow' is a new model in education.[6]

The great success of contemplative methods has opened up space for contemplative education in the classroom. Kabat-Zinn, a pioneer in developing contemplative education, observes: 'When you are grounded in calmness and moment-moment awareness, you are most likely to be creative and to see new options, new solutions to problems. It will be easier to maintain your balance and sense of perspective in trying circumstances'.[7] Thus, contemplative education is not merely a training to do a trade; it is a training for life. I see tolerance and empathy as natural allies and a pedagogy and a curriculum that fosters empathy would also foster tolerance.

I will first deal with the epistemological aspects of empathy and contemplative education, second with the psychological aspects, and third with the ethical dimensions. Finally, I will focus attention on how contemplative education may be integrated into different world-view orientations and religious perspectives. It is at this level that empathy and tolerance may work together.

EPISTEMOLOGICAL FRAMEWORK FOR CONTEMPLATIVE EDUCATION

Critical thinking is important as it helps us to delve into the coherence of thinking, the validity of the ideas expressed, and the examination of assumptions made in an argument. It also emphasises the importance of information and data on which we base our theories and the deduction of inferences from them. Clarity of thinking and focus are excellent philosophical virtues for building our learning skills. Also, it helps to integrate information from different sources and disciplines. But, in addition, we need to have education that is also focused on the experiential, the self-reflexive and the contemplative dimensions of learning. An exponent of contemplative education, describing its nature, says that the epistemology of contemplative education includes the natural human capacity for knowing through silence, looking inward, pondering deeply, beholding and witnessing the contents of our consciousness.[8] Entering into the experience of another is empathy. According to Toby Hart, current education trends in the schools emphasise calculation, explanation and analysis. Contemplative education is not a substitute but a supplement to this dominant rational-empirical approach in the schools. Though the contemplative approach has a wide range of ingredients, ranging from poetry to meditation, there is a common thread running through them: these methods are designed to quiet and shift the habitual chatter of the mind, so that the mind develops skills for deepened awareness, concentration and insight.

An important facet of contemplative education is that it does not seek quick answers to questions. The kind of answers we search for are not information seeking, statistical and computerised, but rather a different type of ability to become absorbed and immersed in the questions themselves; as almost living the questions:

> Have patience with everything unresolved in your heart and *try to love the questions themselves* as if they were locked rooms or books written in a foreign language. Don't search for answers now, because you would not be able to live them. And the point is to live everything. Live the questions now. Perhaps then, someday far in the future, you will gradually, even without noticing it, live your answer.[9]

One of the most important facets of contemplative knowledge is its self-reflexive quality: as Krishnamurti observes—listening to the operation of our own minds. He considers self-knowledge as the beginning of freedom. One who listens to one's own mind would open up to others as well. 'When you begin to inquire into the operation of your own mind, when you observe your own thinking, your daily activities and feelings, you cannot be taught because there is no one to teach you'.[10] He also observes that if a person is weighed down by accumulated layers of facts and theories, these may act as impediments to understand his own mind or those of others.

Guy Claxton says that we have been inadvertently trapped into 'a single mode of mind that is characterised by information gathering, intellect and impatience, one that requires you to be explicit, articulate, purposeful and to show your reasoning', a mode which he symbolises as the 'D mode' due to its deliberative nature.[11] Claxton's book, *Hare Brain and Tortoise Mind*, offers a graphic metaphor to distinguish contemplative knowledge from the kind of knowledge people develop to live in the accelerated times, where the mind seeks decisive and business-like ways of thinking—working like the hare brain. He recommends the tortoise mind to balance our patterns of thinking. Claxton picks up a metaphor from Native American medicine cards to give a graphic description of the contemplative process:

> 'Turtle buries its thoughts, like its eggs, in the sand, and allows the sun to hatch the little ones.' Look at the old fable of the tortoise and the hare, and decide for yourself whether or not you would like to align with the turtle.[12]

Like the tortoise laying eggs, we sit on our anger, impatience, anxiety, stress, tension and fear and we do not try to destroy these states—but contain them in their disorganised form, and see them with the gift of listening that calms and energises us.

Without throwing them away, this valuable material may be converted with a bit of magic into forgiveness, patience, confidence and self-assurance. The mind in the D-mode is much different from the way of the contemplative mind. The D-mode:

- is interested in finding answers and solutions rather than examining questions;
- treats perception as unproblematic, and assumes that the way it sees the situation is the way it is;
- sees conscious, articulate understanding as the essential basis for action and thought as a problem-solving tool;
- values explanation over observation;
- likes explanations that are reasonable and justifiable rather than intuitive;
- relies on language that appears to be literal and explicit and is suspicious of language that is evocative and metaphorical;
- operates at a level where language can be received, produced and processed; and
- prefers to break a problem into manageable parts.[13]

The contemplative mind is described differently as it is directed towards paying close and patient attention to even the most insignificant situation or idea. When the mind is still and not everlastingly occupied, it is easy to see one's connections with others and the world—and that how empathy is born.

The point that I wish to emphasise is that this model of contemplative education, which may be constructed across different religious traditions, offers pathways for building bridges across different religious, ethnic and cultural groups. This adds a creative dimension to education and a context to slow down the hectic process of information gathering, by learning to turn inwards. There is a great deal of time spent on religious symbols and dress and rituals across different community groups, but turning inwards provides a point for convergence. A decade ago, Aldous Huxley said that in the field of education, we do everything possible to keep us away from 'exploring inner space' and that 'non-verbal humanities, the art of being directly aware of the given facts of existence is completely ignored'.[14] This paper opens up Huxley's quest to allow us to have a fresh look at the school and university curriculum. In a meditative culture, if one reads a religious text, there is a resonance of their meaning that goes beyond any scholarly exegetical analysis.

CONTEMPLATIVE ETHICS: ETHICS FOR THE ROUGH ROAD

The more narrowly we examine the actual language, the sharper becomes the conflict between it and the other requirement. (For the crystal-line purity of logic was not a requirement was, of course, not *a result of investigation:* it was a requirement). The conflict becomes intolerable; the requirement is now in danger of becoming empty. We have got on to slippery ice where there is no friction and so in a sense the conditions are ideal, but also, just because of that we are unable to walk. We want to walk; so we need *friction.* Back to the rough ground.[15]

The meaning of friction in Wittgenstein's statement above refers to the uncertainties and chaos around our lives. And this feature has today emerged in forms of catastrophe and chaos of a greater magnitude. This is seen not only in the conflicting models of ethical theories and moral dilemmas, but also the claim made by Bernard Williams: 'I shall argue that philosophy should not try to produce ethical theory, though this does not mean that philosophy cannot offer any critique of ethical beliefs and ideas. I shall claim that in ethics the reductive enterprise has no justification and should disappear'.[16] While people need images and conceptions to organise their lives, it would be a very abstract claim to say that people face life armed with theories. Williams feels that there is a great need for moral reflection and perhaps a more contemplative approach to the moral life. Margot Caines, for instance, looking at the scenario of working life observes:

> Reality, it turns out, isn't always the way we would like it to be. Living is full of ups and downs, downs and sideways—bumps, glitches and trials....I have found that is exactly why work is a wonderful learning for emotional and spiritual transformation.[17]

The idea is that we need to work at a radically deeper level and it is the rough road that is the ground for a reflective and contemplative turn in morality.

In keeping with the epistemological framework outlined earlier, it is also necessary to develop a more broad-based ethics, as recent currents of critical reflection on ethics and education have called for ideas to broaden and diversify methods and tools of teaching ethics—ranging from the rigours of logical reasoning and findings of hard data and statistics, to more imaginative encounters through narrative ethics, stories, case studies, fiction, drama and the film. While we do not learn ethics only in times of crisis and uncertainty, as a contemporary medical ethicist says, 'abstractions of ethics' have to be counterposed with 'the chaos of advice', and he observes that this is the ethics we need in the midst of medical emergencies, car accidents and fires. This does not mean that we have to basically feed our moral perspectives with a diet of moral dilemmas and tragic conflicts, but that the hypothetical moral situations examined in the class room need to have some contact with the real world. We need to close the psychological distance between ethics in the classroom and the real world.

The more important type of ethics is not the ethics that emerge when one makes a decision but, as Iris Murdoch observes, they 'emerge continually and not something switched off between choices'.[18] It is here that we can build a tradition of 'contemplative ethics'. We have to confer a sense of majesty and clinical sacredness to our routine lives—the moment-to-moment flow of life, which comes within the range of mindfulness practice. It is because our routine lives get infected with habitual forms of deception, automatic and thoughtless behaviour, that we expect the spark of a crisis or a dramatic choice situation to make us re-think the whole tenor of our routine lives. As I have stated in another article, 'But we must remember that it is in the routine, prosaic, silent, ordinary life, that we like ants build moral dexterity, industriousness and integrity. Thus, ethics can add a sense of enchantment, and beauty to every moment of our lives. The little details, real situations, the particulars are important—reminding us of Iris Murdoch's 'nostalgia for the particular'.[19] She says that the moral life unfolds in the moment-to-moment flow of attention: 'I regard the (daily, hourly, minutely) attempted purification as the central and fundamental 'arena of morality''.[20]

This is not to deny the value of learning ethical theories and principles, which do play a role in moral thinking, but their use and application need to be followed by a deep immersion in the reflective concerns of morality, real challenges, existential encounters, as well as the concerns of routine life. We need to be in touch with the wellsprings of morality that keep us awake and fresh, and then we may not collapse in a moment of crisis.

The final point I wish to make is that ethical issues that concern us as matters of public and social policy need to be discussed in the dialogic spirit of a conversation. However, we often find what Deborah Tanner calls the development of an 'argument culture'.[21] In this culture, we set up debates and develop an adversarial frame of mind and there is a kind of ritualised opposition. Good dialogue fosters close listening and understanding other points of view and is able to see contrasting perspectives so that it can sometimes help us to see that the truth may have many sides to it. Through the study of paradoxes, we get used to the idea that sometimes both sides are correct and we convert apparent contradictions into real moments for reflection. This is *transformative dialogue* and here the spirit of tolerance reigns supreme. To conclude this section, as John Cuttingham observes in his reflections on the good life, we need to replace the excessive manoeuvres of ratiocentric ethics and move towards a more transformational perspective, acknowledging our fallibility and vulnerability, be open and listen.

THE PSYCHOLOGICAL AND THERAPEUTIC FRONTIERS OF EMPATHY

While contemplative education has attracted educationists during very recent times, an important thesis emerged around the mid-nineties with the publication of Howard Gardner's work on multiple intelligence.[22] It was Daniel Goleman's best selling work, *Emotional Intelligence* that built on Gardner's work, bringing the notion of emotional intelligence to the attention of professionals and educationists. He argued that our view of intelligence is too narrow and the concept of EQ (emotional intelligence) needs to supplement our concept of IQ. EQ consists of the ability to monitor one's feelings moment-to-moment and manage one's own emotions, being sensitive to the emotions of others (a dimension of empathy), the ability to use emotions to reach desirable goals, and the art of handling relationships. I have written extensively on this subject and held a number of workshops in Melbourne and Sydney so I do not wish to pursue this subject in this paper, except to note the importance of empathy as a facet of emotional intelligence.[23] In fact, Goleman has more recently located empathy as a facet of social intelligence, which is a central concern when we deal with inter-group tensions and conflicts.[24]

Goleman says that much work has been done about the ways to bridge the gulf between 'Us' and 'Them' and that a social psychologist, Thomas Pettigrew has shed light on the subject of closing the hostile divide: he found, for instance, that having a childhood playmate from another group typically inoculates people against prejudice in later life. This point came out clearly in one study of African-Americans who played with whites as children.[25] Mere casual contact is not sufficient—to overcome prejudice, there has to be a strong emotional connection. Cognitive categories of stereotypes are cool abstractions, but it is the feelings that matter. Holding negative feelings about a group is more prone to conflicts than having an unflattering stereotype of '*Them*'.

What comes out of Goleman's study is the importance of social intelligence, or what Gardner described as 'interpersonal intelligence'. He observes that, 'while cognitive science has served well in linguistic and artificial intelligence, it has limits when applied to human relationships. It neglects non-cognitive capacities like primal empathy and synchrony that connects us to other people'.[26]

In the schools, at a very simple level, cultivation of social skills and, at a more advanced level, the development of social intelligence, would be a very important complement to contemplative education. While empathy is an integral component of good counselling, and while counselling offers us some of the fine-grained metaphors of empathy, the concept of social intelligence takes us to a broader basis for locating empathy.

Darwin's analysis of emotions and the face recently developed by Paul Ekman basically revolved around anger, fear, sadness, happiness, disgust and surprise. But recent work in the Life and Mind Institute by Richard Davidson, with the backing of the Dalai Lama, brings out an interesting link between compassion and meditation. This work also indicates that, in addition to the Darwinian analysis of emotions, compassion may be basic and linked to physiology. Robert Solomon making a very insightful analysis of the relationship between sympathy, compassion and empathy observed that in the eighteenth-century, the natural moral sentiment view of Hume, Rousseau and Smith was that compassion is a basic human emotion.[27]

I take compassion and empathy to be of enormous importance in understanding our emotional lives; they are part of our natural ability to tune into the emotions of others. Without the intermediary of a rich empathetic imagination, we are less able to feel the urge to respond without the need for a great deal of thought. Thought, however, needs to come soon after, so our responses are in fact helpful rather than merely expressive. Thus, sympathy, however 'natural', is a combination of both inherent dispositions and acculturation and education.

If there is such an implicit sense of solidarity in human nature, education and culture may help to bring out these qualities in a more tangible form. Solomon concludes by saying that, against the perennial cynicism that depicts human nature as selfish, we need to recognise the lasting importance of these eighteenth-century theories and similar religious messages in Buddhism, Confucianism and Christianity.

CONTEMPLATIVE PSYCHOTHERAPY

This human being is a guesthouse
Every morning a new arrival

A joy, a depression, a meanness,
Some momentary awareness comes
As an unexpected visitor.
Welcome and entertain them all!
Even if they're a crowd of sorrows,
Who violently sweeps your house
Empty of its furniture'
Still treat each guest honorably.
He may be clearing you out
For some new delight.
The dark thought, the shame, the malice,
Meet them at the door laughing,
And invite them in.
Be grateful whoever comes, because each has been sent
As a guide from beyond.[28]

Contemplative psychotherapy is a discipline that was first developed at the Naropa Institute in Colorado (now Naropa University) where I was fortunate enough to spend a summer vacation with some teaching. Mostly inspired by the Tibetan Buddhist tradition, the basic teachings of contemplative psychotherapy may be considered as one of the richest extensions of contemplative education. It is said that there is a rich centre of sanity within us, but we are not always in touch with this 'brilliant sanity'. However, we experience glimpses of it when we relax. This kind of sanity is characterised by the capacity to be open to all aspects of experience. There is a kind of clarity that is precise and enables the direct experience of every aspect of what comes and goes in our minds, our emotions, our thoughts, our desires, and so on. It is also characterised by compassion and thus, we have an innate compassionate nature. All the problems that emerge obstructing our understanding of our true nature are due to a false centre, that we have been building over years, a solid reference point, which we refer to as the ego. Even if we experience confusion, we could still be sane, if we are open to the experience of this confusion in the moment. We need to be precise and clear with it and have a quality of friendly acceptance and compassion. If we are sane we do not have to get rid of anything or to destroy anything. This is the pathway to uncovering our sanity.[29]

To illustrate this method, let us take the example of working with emotions: a strong sense of anger. One strategy is to push it out of awareness, where we do not want to know we are feeling it. Repressing emotions in this way is not very helpful. The second therapy, unfortunately even used by some therapists, is the acting out, get it out so that you may not be stuck with it. But rather than getting rid of the anger, this approach builds up and feeds on the anger. We are getting more caught up with it due to the strong identification with the ego. In both of these experiences, we do not experience the anger as it is. Anger is a moving emotion and often does not last long if seen in its true nature. First, acknowledge that the experience is yours, then you do not project the anger onto X, saying he was responsible for it; second, you do not get attached to it, but see it as a passing state, and if you are mindful and honest, you may learn from this experience. Repressed anger often gets converted into hatred. But if you look at your anger, and be very transparent and even a bit playful, you may see its roots: frustration, envy, shame, conceit or fierce compassion.

At a deeper level, there is a method known as *choiceless awareness*, a term very much associated with the philosophy of Jiddu Krishnamurti. As described in the poem, 'Guest House', the mind is able to open itself, and instantly know and recognise what is arising, and instantly discern its true nature, non-conceptually by the mind itself. In that moment, the anger, envy and shame are seen as thought bubbles, or as the Tibetans would say, 'touching a soap bubble'.[30] When one sees that they have no essence, they dissolve.

During the last two decades, mindfulness-based therapies have emerged aligned to most of the dominant western traditions.[31] Carl Rogers introduced the notion of empathy into the western traditions: 'an accurate understanding of the (patient's world as seen from the inside. To sense a patient's private world as if it were your own, but without losing the 'as if' quality—this is empathy'.[32] With others, it came to be regarded as an observation tool, a bond, a curative factor, and a necessity for mental health. It is basically a process where the therapist tunes into the patient's world.

THE SHARING OF MULTI-RELIGIOUS DISCOURSE AND WORLD VIEW

If contemplative practice is to be introduced to schools as an extra-curricular program, it is necessary to have a clear idea of how this can be done independent of any religious orientation and how it may be integrated into different religious orientations. As a test situation, I wish to take the predominant concerns today with crisis, uncertainty, and tensions around the unpredictable nature of, natural disasters, like the tsunami experience. The vulnerability to psychological disturbances following the tsunami has been the subject of studies in terms of culture and religion. Janoff-Bulman argues that the individual's shattered assumptions about the universe and self raise fundamental concerns regarding our beliefs that the world is benevolent, the world is meaningful and the self is worthy.[33] A major catastrophe makes one feel that the world is not safe, is not benevolent, and that one is vulnerable. In the healing and rehabilitation of people subject to catastrophic events, religion and culture have played an important role.[34] In the context of this background, Martha Nussbaum, a great advocator of a liberal arts curriculum, says in an article entitled 'compassion and terror', that we need to build on classical and enlightenment thought to develop a critical theory of compassion:

> an education in common human weakness and vulnerability should be a profound part of the education of all children. Children should learn to be tragic spectators and to understand with subtlety and responsiveness the predicaments to which human life is prone. Through stories and dramas, they should learn to decode the suffering of others, and this decoding should deliberately lead them into lives both near and far, including the lives of distant humans and the lives of animals.[35]

She also says that the chances of the success of such an enterprise would be greater if the society in question does not overvalue external goods of the sort that generates envy and competition, and not compassion. Such a scenario of 'restlessness in the midst of plenty' is of course the subject of Alan de Botton's best selling book, *Status Anxiety*: 'the strange melancholy often haunting inhabitants of democracies in the midst of abundance'.[36]

Compare this scenario, cited by de Botton, with the post-tsunami generosity of children in Australia, who graciously donated their savings and pocket money to the tsunami fund. The idea that 'you may gain happiness by giving things away' does not automatically come to a child's mind. When you give, you locate your self in a more lasting world of wealth— 'wealth beyond measure'. This creates a new spaciousness in the mind and values beyond any form of greed and acquisitiveness. Such great values are found in all major religions and traditional cultures. *An education in true values* and the embracing of uncertainty and the tragic would thus form an important ingredient of contemplative education, and learning such values embedded in religions other than one's own religion, as well as the wisdom of the elders in traditional cultures.

CONCLUDING THOUGHTS

I have discussed a range of dimensions of a contemplative education project in the classroom: the epistemological framework of contemplative education, the case for contemplative ethics as a facet of contemplative education, the psychological and therapeutic frontiers of contemplative education with a focus on empathy, and locating contemplative education in the context of multi-religious discourse. The multi-faith context is important, and here we need to explore especially the place of contemplative approaches in Christian mysticism, Sufi Islam, strands of mysticism in Hinduism and Judaism. Such an approach is also being used in more secular contexts as in mindfulness-based cognitive behaviour therapy and action, and commitment therapy. Contemplative approaches in Asian traditions have primarily developed around Buddhism and Hinduism, but the philosophy of Taoism that took root in China and Zen Buddhism in Japan are rich in their contemplative strands. Taoism has rich material on environmentalism, and Zen Buddhism is not only known for its mystical *satori*, but also for the charming Japanese garden and a subtle and deep sense of humour.

I ventured on a pilot project introducing a course in contemplative education at the Dhammasarana Buddhist temple in Keysborough with the assistance of the temple committee and teachers. The course of lectures held during the weekends was given over two months. About forty young students, mostly undergraduates drawn from Monash, Melbourne, La Trobe and Deakin universities, attended and completed the course. Meditation practice and the practical application of mindfulness to stress management, managing grief and anger, along with some basic doctrines, were the key features of the course. It was offered free, and it was certainly a great success. The value of this experience was also greatly appreciated by the Sri Lankan community and specially the parents of the students. The university courses focused on highly specialised academic units do not *always* offer students a context to reflect on their lives, instead they tend to run on speed, demand course work which is accurate and certain, and foster a subliminal competitive instinct to survive in a society with challenges and uncertainty. Perhaps, contemplative education courses during summer could be a promising project to enhance the role of multi-faith work in Australia. Contemplative education is an important kind of education during these challenging times of uncertainty, stress and conflict. Values such as tolerance, empathy and compassion grow well in a contemplative setting.

NOTES

[1] William James (1950), *The Principles of Psychology*, vol. 1. Dover Publications, p. 424.
[2] Jon Kabat-Zinn (2005), *Coming to our Senses*. New York: Piatkus, p. 117.
[3] Mike W. Martin (2007), *Everyday Morality*. Belmont: Thompson/Wadsworth, p. 56.
[4] Daniel Goleman (2006), *Social Intelligence*. London: Hutchinson, p. 299.
[5] Ibid.
[6] Mihaly Csikszentmihalyi (1990), *Flow: The Psychology of Optimal Experience*. New York: Harper-Perennial.
[7] Jon Kabat-Zinn (1990), *Full Catastrophe Living*. New York: Delta, p. 269.
[8] Toby Hart (2004), 'Opening the Contemplative Mind in the Classroom', *Journal of Transformative Education*, 2(1), pp. 28–46.
[9] Rainer Maria Rilke (2001), *Letters to A Young Poet*. Translated by Mitchell Stephen, New York: Modern Library.
[10] Jiddu Krishnamurti (1997), *Krishnamurti: Reflections on the Self*. Raymond Martin (ed.), Chicago: Open Court, p. 7.
[11] Guy Claxton (2000), *Hare Brain and Tortoise Mind*. New York: Harper Collins.
[12] Ibid., p. 1.
[13] Ibid., pp. 7–11.
[14] Aldus Huxley (1998), 'Doors on the Wall', in Helen Palmer (ed.) *Inner Knowing*. New York: Penguin Putnam, p. 6.
[15] Ludwig Wittgenstein (1953), *Philosophical Investigations*. Trans. G.E.M. Anscombe, Oxford: Basil Blackwell, p. 46e.
[16] Bernard Williams (1987), *Ethics and the Limits of Philosophy*. London: Collins, p. 17.
[17] Margot Cains (1998), *Approaching the Corporate Heart*. Sydney: Simon Schuster, pp. 3–4.
[18] Iris Murdoch (1970), *The Sovereignty of Good*. London: Routledge and Kegan Paul, p. 37.
[19] Padmasiri de Silva (2002), *Buddhism, Ethics and Society: The Conflicts and Dilemmas of Our Times*. Clayton: Monash Asia Institute, p. 183.
[20] Ibid., p. 293.
[21] Deborah Tanner (1998), *The Argument Culture*. London: Virago Press.
[22] See Howard Gardner (1993), *Frames of Mind: The Theory of Multiple Intelligences*. 2nd edn., London: Fontana Press.
[23] de Silva, *Buddhism, Ethics and Society*.
[24] Goleman, *Social Intelligence*.
[25] Ibid., p. 303.
[26] Ibid., p. 334.
[27] Robert C. Solomon (2007), *True To Our Feelings*. Oxford: Oxford University Press, pp. 70–1.
[28] Jalal al-Din Rumi (1955), 'The Guest House', in *The Essential Rumi*. Trans. Coleman Barks with John Moyne, Reynold Nicolson Books.
[29] Karen Wegela-Kissel (2003), 'Contemplative psychotherapy', *Ordinary Mind: An Australian Buddhist Review*, 1. http://www.ordinarymind.net/Feature/feature2_jan2003.htm. Accessed 15 September 2010.
[30] Kabat-Zinn, *Coming to our Senses*, pp. 262–3.
[31] Padmasiri de Silva (2008), *An introduction to mindfulness-based counselling*. Sarvodaya-Vishvalekha, p. 165.
[32] C. Rogers (1961), *On Becoming a Person*. New York: Houghton Mifflin, p. 284.
[33] R. Janoff-Bulman (1992), *Shattered Assumptions: Towards a New Psychology of Trauma*. New York: The Free Press.

34 Padmal de Silva (2006), 'The tsunami and its aftermath in Sri Lanka: Explorations of a Buddhist perspective', *International Review of Psychiatry*, 18(3), pp. 281–7.

35 Martha Nussbaum (2003), 'Compassion and Terror', *Daedalus,* Winter, pp. 10–26.

36 Alain de Botton (2004), *Status Anxiety.* London: Hamish Hamilton, Penguin, pp. 52–3.

Padmasiri de Silva
School of Philosophical, Historical and International Studies
Faculty of Arts
Monash University

RONALD S. LAURA AND AMY K. CHAPMAN

9. CAN HOW WE COME TO KNOW THE WORLD DISCONNECT US FROM THE WORLD WE COME TO KNOW?

Within the context of philosophy, a significant literature has accumulated that characterises the ostensible goals of education in socio-political terms. Much of this discussion has certainly centred on the work of political philosophers such as, John Rawls, whose commitment to liberalism has been translated educationally into a rich and varied discourse about the role played by schools in producing 'good citizens'. Given the multicultural societies in which many of us now live, the question naturally arises as to exactly how tolerant a liberal society and the schools that express its values can be, not only in encouraging but in sustaining cultural and religious perspectives that directly or indirectly collide. Our aim in this chapter is to suggest that the debates that have arisen out of this context can be better understood, and made more amenable to resolution, when the covert values that shape and inform the more comprehensive educational epistemology of our schools are made explicit. When such values are made explicit, it will become clearer that the hope of authentic tolerance in a multicultural society cannot be achieved, if the very concept of knowledge that dominates the curriculum of our schools is driven at a deeper level by the preoccupation we have as a putatively 'liberal culture' with power. We shall argue here that power is, in its own right, a defining condition of social identity whose importance has not been sufficiently acknowledged within the current debate on multiculturalism and socio-religious tolerance. We shall now turn directly to the task we have set for ourselves.

However one ultimately defines education, there is no doubt that our present system of education involves at least the transmission of knowledge. While much has been written about the concept of knowledge in the vague hope of ensuring that what is taught in schools corresponds to what is actually known, that is, that what is taught is truth, far too little attention has been paid to the question of whether what we know is really worth knowing, and thus truly worth transmitting. In what follows we shall argue that much of what we know is not worth knowing and, thus, that much of what we teach is not worth teaching. The ideal of authentic tolerance of conflicting religious persuasion will inevitably be subverted because the form of knowledge propagated in our schools encourages a philosophy of power that is fundamentally divisive and inimical to the integrity of our social and personal relations to each other.

UNDERSTANDING THE PROBLEM

According to what might be termed 'the dominant paradigm of educational epistemology', the objectivity of scientific knowledge ensures that what we know is value-free,

E.B. Coleman and K. White (eds.), Religious Tolerance, Education and the Curriculum, 111–120.

as is the technology that derives from it. The idea here is that what we come to know is neither good nor bad, but rather value-neutral.[1,2] It is how people use knowledge and the technological innovations to which it gives rise that determines its moral status. This point is popularly put euphemistically when it is said: 'Guns don't kill people; people kill people with guns'. While we have no wish to deny that there is a truth in this way of looking at the matter, we shall in what follows be concerned to establish that there is a much deeper and more comprehensive truth that it conceals. The implications of this deeper truth have monumental implications for understanding the covert values that are structurally enshrined in our system of education and how they impact on the goals of liberalism.

Part of the problem is that so much of educational research is spent addressing the issues surrounding how teachers can effectively transmit knowledge. Far too little research is undertaken on what knowledge is, and especially on its impact on the subtler aspects of how we relate to the world around us and to each other. On the conventional presumption that knowledge is value-free there is obviously little sense of personal responsibility on the part either of those who 'discover' it, or of those who teach it, to worry about whether what they discover or teach as knowledge is truly worth discovering or teaching at all. Having failed to make these distinctions explicit and then to explore them philosophically, we have, as a society, become woefully ignorant of the foundational values that have covertly come to define the context for teaching and learning.

We shall discuss this issue more determinately when we introduce the concept of 'transformative subjugation', intended in this context as a heuristic, by way of which we hope to bring to bold relief a much neglected dimension of the debate on value-ladenness as it relates to educational epistemology.[3,4,5] Suffice to say here that the debate about whether and how value questions should be integrated into the formal curriculum is largely rhetorical, so long as we remain blinded to the hidden agenda of value we covertly promulgated by the epistemology that continues to underpin it.

It is tempting to think that scientific knowledge is somehow outside the bounds of intellectual history in the sense of having avoided the 'contamination' of such influences as socio-cultural prejudices, religious assumptions, mythology, and political bias, to name only a few. Reflection upon the development of contemporary empiricist science, however, makes palpably clear that all pretence of its virgin birth is misleading and meretricious. Despite its pretensions to methodological purity and the virginal symbolism of the 'white coats' worn by scientists who inadvertently parade it, the ascension of the highly quantified formulation of knowledge proffered in our educational institutions is not without its own historical biography of conceptual dogmatism, religious fanaticism, gender bias, and vested interests. We shall argue that the foundations of educational epistemology have not successfully been sanitised, despite the conventional wisdom that would have us believe otherwise. In the last analysis, the dominant view of knowledge upon which so much of the school curriculum presently rests represents only one form of knowledge from among a wide array of ways in which we can potentially come to know the world.

Similarly, the political history that reflects the attempts of science to discredit and systematically eliminate a number of unorthodox aspirants to the crown of knowledge itself constitutes an important facet of the historical development of the dominant paradigm of science. Despite its privileged position of epistemic priority, the dominant paradigm of knowledge may arguably be more socio-culturally embedded than epistemically entrenched. In the west, scientific knowledge in its empiricist, quantitative and statistical guise has been socially legitimated as the ultimate standard against which other aspirants to the accolade of knowledge are to be measured. When all is said, the dominant paradigm of knowledge is itself as conditioned socio-culturally, as is the socio-cultural phenomenon of religion. In this sense, the logical priority we ascribe to the dominant paradigm of knowledge is at least partly gratuitous and needs to be recognised. Doing so, makes a significant difference not only to how we come to know the world, but also to what it is that we come to know.

THE IDEOLOGICAL PRESUMPTIONS OF EDUCATIONAL KNOWLEDGE

Far from being neutral, every piece of information accepted as knowledge is what we shall here call *structurally encoded* to ensure a covert measure of control over some aspect of our lives. And if the primary form of knowledge we transmit in our schools is conditioned and shaped by our obsession with power, both its form and application will reflect the value we place on power and dominance. If what we claim to know is defined implicitly by the capacity of what is 'known' to provide us with a power advantage over the world in which we live, the orthodox educational view that knowledge is neither good nor bad in itself can be exposed for the illusion that it is. As Chet Bowers states:

> The dominant forms of rationality, which include both discursive and purposive forms of rationality…reinforce a competitive approach to knowledge. As these two approaches to knowledge are also dependent upon the assumptions that ideas and values are individually centred, the individual becomes the ultimate arbiter of what knowledge and values will have authority—before being displaced by the authority of new knowledge that may have equally transient existence. As the source of thoughts and values, individuals thus experience themselves as separate from the world.[6]

In the light of the ideological dimensions of the presumption of knowledge encoded as power, it is easier to appreciate that there exists within the educational curriculum, a conceptually endogenous bias in favour of an epistemology, not only of domination, but of subjugation, and that both domination and subjugation are value terms that have significant ramifications for the way in which education in turn actually informs and shapes the interplay between the attitudes and behaviours that characterise our very capacity for tolerance of any kind.

When knowledge is itself substantively defined by the preoccupation with power, dominance and control, the resultant form of knowledge will enshrine as a fundamental educational value, the propriety of subjugation as the measure of our interaction with the world around us and each other. We thus form our socio-cultural identities by rigidly defining the boundaries of the similarities and differences we share with each other. Jeremy Rifkin describes this process as follows:

> The scientific method...reflects our consuming passion for predictability and order. We have transformed all of physical reality into a giant testing site and then attempted to discover predictable patterns of behaviour that can be exploited over and over in such a way as to advance our control over the forces of nature. The more successful we are at imperializing our environment, the more secure we feel'.[7]

From this it follows that, independently of the good intentions of the persons who use the technologies that derive from a theory of knowledge driven by a lust for power, virtually every application of that form of knowledge will in some covert way serve the aim of knowing, only insofar as it guarantees a measure of dominance, control and subjugation. As noted by Laura and T. Marchant:

> By obliging schoolchildren around the globe to think primarily and increasingly in ways that are circumscribed by the machines we create, we have also covertly encouraged in our schools an invidious conformity of *thinking* about the world in *machine-like* ways. By virtue of the process of reinforcing a progressive movement towards the intellectual conformity which results from seeing the world through the eyes of the computer, education has coincidentally encouraged progressive movement towards the demise of intellectual imagination. If there is a difference between indoctrination and education, it must surely lie in the different things we do either to stimulate and nurture the intellectual imagination or to stifle and diminish it.[8]

As a culture, we have failed to acknowledge that the price we pay for an epistemological posture of dominance and subjugation is not only the desacralisation of nature, but the depersonalisation of our relationships. This, in turn, leads to the dehumanisation of those who are excluded from the circles of power that parade as the dominant icons of socio-cultural identity. This is an enormously complex insight, and we make no pretence that in the space available to us here that we shall be able adequately to develop the many strands of argument that sustain it. It is to be hoped, none the less, that the fragments of insight we are able to weave with tolerable conceptual coherence will serve to prompt constructive discussion, debate and, accordingly, future opportunity for us and others to elucidate more satisfactorily these important issues.

THE THEORY OF TRANSFORMATIVE SUBJUGATION

It is nearly twenty years ago that Ron Laura first sketched his theory of 'transformative subjugation'.[9] According to Laura, the concept of transformative subjugation is

Def

construed as the logical outcome of embracing a form of knowledge motivated by our insatiable appetite for power. In essence, we socially legitimate our craving for power by enshrining it in a way of knowing the world designed to control and dominate it. The more predictable a thing, process or event is, the more control we have over it, and thus the more secure we think we are. What follows from this recognition becomes particularly interesting for those of us concerned to explore the reciprocal nexus between education and the epistemological value presumptions to which it gives rise. While there are many plausible explanations for this pre-occupation with power, one of the most alluring is the idea that the more we can dominate and control the natural, socio-cultural, political and economic environment in which we find ourselves, the more secure we can make ourselves feel, and the easier it is to construct our socio-cultural identity through the boundaries of control that express it.

Because the pragmatic goal of an epistemology of dominance is to make the world as predictable as possible, the pressure will be to strip the world of its qualitative dimensions so that what remains for analysis are the quantitative components amenable to calculable precision or, in some cases, precise probability. The more quantitative a domain, the more readily can its subject matter be subsumed under the laws of science. The more amenable a subject matter is to scientific laws that can ensure predictability, the more 'objective', or so the power-based dominant epistemology would contend, are the empirical investigations undertaken. What is not amenable to quantification is relegated to the subjective domain of metaphysics, however interesting its ratiocinations might be.

To put another gloss on this point, the subject matter of science reduces to a universe of discourse in which every claim to knowledge is entitled by virtue of being quantifiable. What falls outside the aegis of quantifiable science becomes the subjective prerogative of the arts, metaphysics or religion. Given what is now fashionably termed as 'accountability', is it any surprise to be faced increasingly with such conspicuous disparities in the funding available for these respective enterprises, especially within universities? Although this is admittedly an argument for another occasion, it should nevertheless be useful to make explicit the present epistemological considerations that prompt distinctions of logical divergence between the arts and science in the first place.

THE VALUE-LADENNESS OF EDUCATIONAL EPISTEMOLOGY

Let us now revert to our discussion of the other value-considerations associated with the dominant theory of knowledge and the theory of transformative subjugation. Given that the primary form of knowledge that underpins the curriculum is driven by our obsession as a culture with power and dominance, much of the technology that follows from it will be designed and deployed in ways that allow us to restructure the world so that it suits our interests. This being so, our interactions with nature and the cultural determinants of the value we place upon it, are subsumed under our technological attempts to reconstruct the world to make it oblige to our desires and more readily to submit to our will. This process means, so it would seem, that we can spend less of our time having to adapt to the world around us, while spending more of our time enjoying the world we have fabricated to adapt to us. When night falls upon us sooner than we would like, we deploy our technologies of power to turn night into day by artificially lighting our world. If our homes, workplaces or means of transport are hotter or colder than we would like, we create technologies to turn warmth into cold or cold into warmth. When our food crops do not grow fast enough, or as abundantly as we would like, we coax them into obedience by chemically fertilising the soil in which they grow, or by genetically engineering the plants themselves to grow faster, get bigger, and produce more to eat. If the food we harvest does not transport well, we simply engineer it to make it travel better; so the tomatoes thus conformed have skins not unlike durable plastic, are big, red and beautiful, but have lost that delectable tomato flavour and alluring fragrance that make them worth eating in the first place. If our foods do not have a shelf-life long enough to maximise the financial return they are designed to bring, we either irradiate them with nuclear energy, dose them with preservatives to inhibit their rapid demise, wax or otherwise chemically wrap them in ways to maintain the appearance of a freshness that in fact they no longer have. For other foods, such as bread, we technologise them by removing from them the very parts (and nutrient components) that define them as alive. Thus, in the technologisation of bread, the wheat germ or living kernel of wheat is excised to ensure that a once living loaf of bread is converted into a fabricated product so processed and inert that it has become almost invulnerable to decay.

According to the theory of transformative subjugation as we construe it here, the way in which technology achieves this measure of control is not only to transform the living things of nature into things that are synthesised, artificial and inert, but further to take the things we have fabricated and convert them into other things that are ever more processed, chemicalised and inert. Within the context of the epistemology of power, the covert preoccupation with dominance and control—a fundamental value presupposition in itself—is attained by means of technological transformations that reconstruct the living world in such a way that the behaviour of the fabricated things produced can be subsumed under laws of nature. For the more alive and vital a system is, the more difficult it is to predict and control its behaviours. The more inert our technology can make the world and the more synthetic and chemicalised are its components, the easier it is to manipulate these components in ways that make their relationships to each other sufficiently determinate to predict and thus control their behaviours. The paradox or antinomy of the epistemology of power process is that our technologies of power succeed in providing us with a measure of predictable control of the world around us only by transforming the world into a fabricated museum of quantitatively regimented, chemicalised, increasingly inert and, all too often, dead things. The paradox is that the technological kingdom of which we have become rulers is not the living world *per se*, but the fabricated world of chemicalised, inert and lifeless things of our own making. In addition to the many health issues that result from these changes, 'the price of this predictability and control, however, is depressing conformity at the expense of exhilarating creativity'.[10]

alienation

Having welcomingly surrounded ourselves with so many of our lifeless fabrications, is it any wonder that we ourselves and especially the children whose minds are institutionally inculcated with this 'technological bluff' should feel increasingly less healthy, less vital, less connected and less spiritually alive than ever.[11,12,13]

At the group level, the importance of creativity to the growth, health, and well-being of society cannot be understated…The history of creative products and ideas can be thought of as an extension from past to future generations—a cross-generational interconnectedness fostered by the generative possibilities of the human mind.[14]

MIND CONTROL

Sufficient examples have now been provided to demonstrate that western society's insatiable appetite for power leads to the systematic fabrication and reconstruct-tion of the whole of nature. What we have yet to consider is the extent to which the pattern of transformative subjugation extends to the field dimensions of the human mind. Just as we synthesise the world of nature, both surrounding ourselves and literally consuming the lifeless products of our technology, so we synthesise even our experiences of the world and open our minds to the multifarious images of death (violence set in the context of news, murder mysteries, action films, real-life videos of police encounters and even documentaries, to name only a few). In the presence of TV, videos, film and the Internet, we experience much of life vicariously, through the scripts of those who have reconstructed social reality for us.

We willingly receive unto our minds not only synthesised images of people, either dead or dying, but we also open ourselves to the deadened images of people tormented and broken by the misfortunes and adversities of life. What we witness are broken promises, broken relations, broken hearts and broken lives. With what must approximate a religious fervour, we pursue as much information as possible on the vicissitudes of soap-stars, as if their TV lives were real. Not only are we distracted by this medium from experiencing life directly, but much of what we experience vicariously is itself a scripted unreality. Here, we have yet another synthesised environment, but this time it is the environment of mind that has fallen prey to the process of transformative subjugation.

One way in which we convert our experiences, or what may be called our 'endemic experience', of nature is through technologies of visual and experimental media, such as virtual reality 'computechnology', which has the power to present ever more powerful images of synthesised experiences as if they were actual ones. In this sense, the synthesised world of virtual reality is tantamount to a whole new technology ostensibly designed to ensure the control of the mind. Moreover, because so much information can be processed at once, cybertechnology also provides new ways of exploiting and expropriating the precious resources of the earth at phenomenal speeds.

THE HIDDEN AGENDA OF EDUCATION

Our educational institutions have been organised in such a way that the development of power-based technology stands as the ineluctable consequence of our unbridled commitment to an epistemology of power. Western culture has lured generations of school children into the false belief that scientific knowledge, and the technologies deriving from it, are the ultimate tools of social and personal salvation. The more we trust in the advocates of scientific knowledge, the more resources, human and otherwise, we commit to the development of ever more powerful and controlling forms of technology. We have failed to see that our progressive technological intrusions of control over nature serve not only to manipulate and transform the things of nature, but also to disrupt the established harmony of the natural order, including its capacity to reproduce itself and the contexts of social organisation within which we have a genuine chance of living purposefully and well.

THE LOSS OF FACE: THE HUMAN FACE

That computechnology has assisted and expanded the forms of communication now available to us is incontestable. It is salutary to remind ourselves, however, that the more forms of communication we embed to expand the culture of computechnology, the less intimate and depersonalised the face-to-face human interactions become that they were designed to replace. Simply put, the argument advanced here affirms that the depersonalisation of human relationships and the dehumanisation that follows from it are an inevitable consequence of universalising the highly mechanised modes of communication that characterise computechnology. Obsessive infatuation with computechnology, what we call 'compuphilia', thus comes to represent a socially legitimated syndrome that implicitly encourages the love of computers, without adequately understanding the extent to which their universality is, by its very nature, a threat to the love we have for humans. This is why, as a culture, we tend to anthromophormise our machines while dehumanising each other. Consequently, these contrary dispositions give rise to serious moral issues that have been badly neglected. For example, humans are expected by their employers— or we demand it of ourselves—to work at our computers, not only throughout the day, but sometimes tirelessly into the night. One promise of computopia was to give us all, even school children, more leisure time, but the truth is that if we have more leisure time, we all too often spend it working or 'playing' at the computer in virtual isolation. I-Pods are just another symptom of this growing trend towards 'technological isolationism'. It is well worth noting that to date insufficient attention has been paid to the deleterious physical and mental effects of these new forms of social isolation.

Because we spend progressively more time communicating through or working in isolation at our computers, we tend not to notice that we are spending less time, and certainly less quality time, with each other. In particular, within such technologically structured contexts of learning the potential for creating deep and bonding relationships between teachers and students is decidedly diminished. Potentially intimate and vital personal relationships are in essence being channelled without much, if any, notice on society's part, into impersonal one-dimensional, mechanistically mediated ones. We have slipped, that is to say, almost imperceptibly into a new condition or culture of human relationships, which structurally encourages the substitution of face-to-face forms of human interchange with technologically-mediated forms of communication, even when face-to-face communication is available.

CONCLUSION

The problem with our unwitting educational commitment to this epistemology of power and the transformative subjugations of technologies that derive from it is not just the obvious ramifications that relate to our systematic desacralisation of nature. Neither is the problem simply the resultant despoiling of our lakes and rivers, our toxic assault upon our seas, the pollution of the air we breathe and the water we drink, the mindless rape of the earth's forests, land and soil, as horrendous and egregious a wounding of the earth that these violations represent. The ramifications of transformative subjugation are far more pernicious and relate to the philosophy of value that the technology of transformative subjugation presupposes. The particular theory of knowledge we have institutionally entrenched within our educational system is far from an innocent and innocuous way of 'knowing the world'.

The epistemology of power enshrined within it is a fundamental presumption of the value of power and dominance, and the underpinning of an ideological posture that aggrandises gratuitously the freedom those in power have to use other humans and the earth as resources for their own ends. Along with society's commitment to the technologisation of nature is the value system that the process of transformative subjugation entails. The values of power, dominance, expropriation of environmental and human resources, if not the presumed right to play God, are deeply embedded within the curriculum, not necessarily explicitly, but covertly as a feature of the hidden agenda that defines the more general goals of education itself. 'If there is a critical urgency confronting educators, it is to redefine our relationship to nature and to each other by redefining the fundamental concept of educational knowledge in a way that dignifies rather than diminishes our humanity by doing so'.[15]

If our technological interventions are implicitly designed to deconstruct the living world so that its components can be used to fabricate a far more synthesised, chemicalised and inert world of predictable outcomes, then the hidden agenda of education is, on this occasion, in desperate need of critical reflection and assessment. What is needed is not more of the kind of power-based educational epistemologies we already have. What is needed is ultimately a reconceptualisation of the very concept of knowledge which, at the present time, has become so entrenched in our educational institutions that we think it impossible to survive without it.

However, the truth is that we cannot survive with it. The task of critical urgency for educators is to redefine our relationship to nature and to each other by redefining the fundamental concept of educational knowledge in a way that dignifies rather than diminishes our humanity.

NOTES

[1] I. Hacking (1996), 'The disunity of sciences', in P. Gallison, & D. Stump (eds), *The Disunity of Science*. Stanford: Stanford University Press.

[2] M. Jacobs (1988), *The Cultural Meaning of the Scientific Revolution*. New York: Alfred A. Knopf.

[3] W.E. Doll and N. Gough (2002), *Curriculum Visions*. New York: Peter Lang.

[4] C.A. Bowers (2001), *Educating for Eco-Justice and Community*. Athens: University of Georgia Press.

[5] E. Riley-Taylor (2002), *Ecology, Spirituality, and Education: Curriculum for Relational Knowing*. New York: Peter Lang.

[6] C.A. Bowers (1995), *Educating for an Ecologically Sustainable Culture*. Albany: State University of New York Press, p. 27.

[7] J. Rifkin (1985), *Declaration of a Heretic*. New York: Routledge and Kegan Paul, pp.17–8.

[8] R.S. Laura & T. Marchant (2007), *Don't Let Technology Steal Your Soul*. New York: University of America Press.

[9] See, for example, his *Philosophical Foundations of Health Education* with Dr S. Heaney; *Hidden Hazards* with Dr J. Ashton; and more recently, *Empathetic Education* with Dr M. Cotton and *Don't Let Technology Steal Your Soul* with Dr T. Marchant.

[10] R.S. Laura & T. Marchant (2000), *Surviving the High Tech Depersonalisation Crisis*. Wellers Hill: Godbold Publishing, p. 51.

[11] M.E.P. Seligman (1998), 'What is the 'good life'?' President's column. *APA Monitor*, 2.

[12] M.E.O. Seligman and M. Csikszentmihalyi (2000), 'Positive psychology: an introduction', *American Psychologist*, 55, pp. 5–14.

[13] C.R. Snyder & S.J. Lopez (2002), *The Handbook of Positive Psychology*. New York: Oxford University Press.

[14] V.J. Cassandro & D.K. Simonton (2002), 'Creativity and genius' in C.L. Keyes & J. Haidt (eds), *Flourishing: Positive psychology and the life well-lived*. Washington DC: American Psychological Association, pp. 164–5.

[15] R. S. Laura & M. Cotton (1999), *Empathetic Education*. Philadelphia: Falmer Press.

Ronald S. Laura and Amy K. Chapman
School of Education
University of Newcastle

ANTHONY MANSUETO

10. FOR SAPIENTIAL LITERACY

Why (and How) Religion Belongs in the Core

It was...necessary that, besides the philosophical sciences...there should be a sacred science ... Other sciences are called the handmaids of this one...it transcends all others whether speculative or practical... Thomas Aquinas[1]

The criticism of religion is the premise of all criticism...The basis of irreligious criticism is this: man makes religion; religion does not make man. Karl Marx[2]

These two quotations, it would seem, represent two very different approaches to fundamental questions of meaning and value. Thomas not only argues for the necessity of theology, as a sacred science, but also claims that theology is the noblest of the sciences, to which all others are ordered. Marx, on the other hand, treats religion as, without remainder, a human social product. And yet both, I would like to argue, take for granted something which has largely been forgotten by the modern university: that an engagement with religion is central—is the premise even—of any serious intellectual engagement whatsoever.

The debate at Harvard University regarding the place of religion in the liberal arts core curriculum in 2007 served to focus attention on this issue. It has long been taken for granted that courses in *philosophy* ought to be part of the liberal arts core curriculum, though too often even these requirements have eroded as schools have opted for distribution systems which allow students to fulfil a 'humanities' require-ment with courses (or even a single course) in any of a number of disciplines. But it has generally been only at religiously-affiliated colleges that courses in theology or religious studies have had a separate place in the core, and while many such institutions now allow that requirement to be met by courses in comparative religion or some other non-theological discipline, the rationale for including such courses, at least originally, was confessional in character.

Harvard's (now apparently abortive) move to require a course on 'reason and faith', therefore, represented a new departure—a demand that students reflect on religious questions, and on the role of religion in society, not as members of a particular religious community, but rather as members of an ideologically pluralistic body politic in which fundamental questions of meaning and value are *contested*. This proposal was resisted, and eventually defeated, by members of the faculty—led by Steven Pinker among others—who argued that it would give religion more pro-minence than it deserves. Their arguments reflect the agenda of a group, drawn mostly from the physical and biological sciences, and often called the 'Brights', who believe that religion is simply hogwash, and has been shown to be so by modern science, and is thus not a worthy object of scientific or scholarly inquiry.[3]

E.B. Coleman and K. White (eds.), Religious Tolerance, Education and the Curriculum, 121–129.

This chapter will argue that, on the contrary, the study of religion—including especially the study of religion from a non-confessional perspective is it in fact integral to the basic aims of a liberal arts education—and belongs in the core curriculum as a separate field of study, as well as a dimension of courses in history, literature, philosophy, and the social sciences, even at public institutions. I will begin by situating the liberal arts in historical context and show how and why philosophy and theology were both marginalised in the modern academy. I will then go on to show why this is a mistake and why both philosophy and religious studies need to be part of the liberal arts core curriculum. I will specify precisely what needs to be included and explain why this probably entails dedicated course requirements in religious studies. I will conclude by answering the two principal objections to this proposal: Pinker's claim that it gives religion too much importance, and the often associated claim that, in public institutions at least, it represents a violation of the principle of separation between church and state.

WHAT ARE THE LIBERAL ARTS?

Let us begin by defining the liberal arts. The term 'art' translates the Latin *ars*, which in turn translates the Greek *techne*. *Techne* is one of the intellectual virtues, and involves excellence in *making*. There are, generally speaking, three different sorts of art or *techne*. The *instrumental arts* involve excellence in making things which are useful—things which are a means to some other end. This includes all sorts of traditional crafts as well as engineering and other sorts of applied physical science, medicine and other applications of the biological sciences, and business administration and other applications of the social sciences. The *fine arts* involve making things which are ends in themselves—hence 'fine', from the Latin *fine* or end. This includes painting, sculpture, and the other visual arts, music, and literature. The *liberal arts* are those that make a human being free. The question, of course, is just what one can make which, in the course of the making itself, sets one free. The answer is simple: an argument. The liberal arts train us to make arguments, and to evaluate arguments made by others, and thus put us in a position to make decisions for ourselves. This is especially true when the arguments in question concern fundamental questions of meaning and value, questions about what it means to be human, and about how we should live our lives individually and collectively.

This discipline of debating fundamental questions of meaning and value, which we call *dialectics*, and thus the whole enterprise of the liberal arts, came into being during what Karl Jaspers called the 'axial age', the period between 800 and 200 BCE, which was characterised by both religious rationalisation (a shift from mythological to philosophical discourse) and religious democratisation (the opening up of full participation in religious life to those who were not members of hereditary priest-hoods).[4] This was era of the Jewish prophets, of Socrates, Plato, and Aristotle, of the Upanishads, Mohair, and the Buddha, Lao Tzu and Confucius. Interestingly enough, it was also the period during which petty commodity product developed in the principal centres of Afro-Eurasia civilisation. The emergence of market relations at once brought people into contact with other cultures and forced them to ask how their particular myths related to those of other peoples, while the experience of living in a market society created the basis in experience for more abstract thinking. The emergence of markets also created new privileged strata of people, which demanded access to the public arena, and new impoverished strata whose resistance catalysed the emergence of a new discourse about justice.

Throughout the next era of human civilisation during which Africa, Europe, and Asia were bound together by the Silk Road[5] trade networks (roughly 200 BCE–1800 CE), training in the liberal arts and especially in dialectics was fundamental to full participation in the public arena. While the rulers themselves remained, for the post part, warlords who lived by taxing the trade routes they controlled, they were advised and partly hegemonized by advisors drawn from the ranks of clerics and civil servants whose training was based in the traditional liberal arts and dialectics. It was the existence of a common, abstract, philosophical language which, furthermore, made possible, if not a fully global dialogue regarding fundamental questions then, at the very least, an indirect dialogue linking Christendom with *Dar-al-Islam*, *Dar-al-Islam* with India, and India with China.[6]

Each of the great civilisations of the Silk Road had its own specific way of preparing leaders,[7] but all involved training in languages and mathematics and in the physical, biological, social—and sacred—sciences. In medieval Europe, the liberal arts included the *trivium* (whence the term 'trivia') and the *quadrivium*. The *trivium* included grammar, which teaches us to use language correctly, rhetoric, which teaches us to make persuasive arguments, and logic, which teaches us to make arguments which are consistent and complete and in which each term follows necessarily from the others. The *quadrivium* included pure and applied mathematics: arithmetic, geometry, harmonics, and astronomy. These disciplines were regarded as preparatory to the study of physics or natural philosophy (the term was used to describe both the physical and the biological sciences), and of metaphysics, ethics (including politics), medicine, the law, and theology, all of which depended on a finely tuned ability to make and evaluate arguments. But there was an especially close relationship—if also often profound tension—between the faculty of arts and the faculty of theology, for the simple reason that both were concerned with first principles, even if they approached them in different ways. And no one would ever have doubted that those disciplines which deal with first principles are the most important.

The Renaissance, the Reformation, and the scientific revolution changed the way the west, at least, does liberal arts education in three ways. First, a revival of interest in classical and scriptural texts accelerated development of the hermeneutic disciplines and focused attention, in what came to be called the humanities, on the meaning of those texts, as opposed to the fundamental questions of meaning and value which those texts addressed. Over the course of the past 500 years, being a humanistic scholar has ceased to mean leading humanity in reflection on fundamental questions and has come to mean being a master at the use of specialised interpretive techniques. Second, the scientific revolution marked a profound change in the way we do science. Where medieval science sought to explain the physical universe teleologically and thus terminated, quite naturally, in metaphysics, modern science describes the universe using rigorous mathematical models. The result was a rift between the humanities and the sciences, with the social sciences divided by partisans of mathematical formalism and interpretive particularism. Third, philosophy and theology, towards the study of which the liberal arts had historically been ordered, were pushed to the margins of the academy—and radically transformed. Philosophy in the Anglo-American world came to be associated with a sort of linguistic analysis which rejected the fundamental questions which had historically occupied philosophers as, quite literally, meaningless. Elsewhere, what came to known as 'Continental' philosophy persisted a while longer in engaging fundamental questions, but did so in an increasingly indirect way that shaded increasingly into a sort of critical commentary on the larger philosophical tradition. The same is true of theology which—where it has not been reduced entirely to scriptural hermeneutics—has been largely parasitic on developments in Continental philosophy.

SAPIENTIAL LITERACY

The Foundational Role of Philosophy

This marginalisation of philosophy and theology is, I would like to suggest, a serious error, and indeed undermines the fundamental purpose of a liberal arts education.

Let it be said, to begin with, that there *are* other legitimate reasons to study the foundational liberal arts such as grammar, rhetoric, logic, and mathematics, or to explore the sciences or the hermeneutic disciplines, other than the exploration of fundamental questions of meaning and value. These disciplines prepare students for the exercise of professions which require correct, persuasive, logical communication (written and oral), the use of formal, mathematical models, the analysis of cause and effect in physical, biological, and social systems, and the interpretation of such texts as laws and regulations. But if an education stops short at this point, it is not authentically liberal. This is because it falls short of cultivating the virtues necessary to a free human being and citizen. Free human beings must be able to decide *for themselves* not only *how* various systems work or what some positive law or regulation *means*, but *what (if anything) is actually true, good, and beautiful*, and they must be able to do this both in the foundational decisions they make in their own lives, and in their public lives as workers and citizens. This requires a formal study of the traditional disciplines of philosophy:

- epistemology, which asks 'What do we know and how?',
- cosmology, which asks 'Is the universe ultimately meaningful?', metaphysics, which asks 'Is there some first principle in terms of which the universe can be explained and human action ordered? If so, what is it? If not, is there some other basis on which meaning and value can be grounded?', and
- ethics, which asks 'On what basis, if any, can we make moral judgments?' 'What is an excellent human being?' and 'What is just society?'

The importance of these disciplines has only been accentuated by the phenomena of secularisation and religious pluralism. We are not in a position in this context to consider in depth the question of secularisation. Suffice it to say that the claim made by radical secularists such as Sam Harris, Richard Dawkins, and Daniel Dennett[8]

124

that religion is simply a delusion which humanity has outgrown is at best one voice in a complex and diverse public arena in the context of which people must make autonomous and informed decisions. And physical, biological, and social scientists are in no better position to pronounce on properly philosophical questions such as the reasonableness of religious belief or the existence of God than a philosopher or theologian is to pronounce on the technical merits of a new proposal in string theory or statistical mechanics.

The Specific Role of Religious Studies in the Liberal Arts Core Curriculum

Historically, philosophy formed part of a rigorous and complete liberal education for precisely this reason. It was generally assumed, however, that religion was something one studied only in the context of one's own religious community. Religious colleges, therefore, often required courses in the scriptures or theology, depending on what they thought important; public institutions and most private liberal arts colleges and research universities generally did not. And this is very much the way things have remained even as religious studies has become accepted as an academic discipline or interdisciplinary field (which is a matter of much internal debate) outside of a confessional context.

This arrangement is problematic for three reasons. First, while philosophy forms the foundation for sapiential literacy, it is not by itself sufficient. Public discourse around fundamental questions of meaning and value has always involved appeals not only, or even primarily, to reason, but also to the sacred scriptures of various religious traditions, to insights gained from various meditative and contemplative practices, and to hybrid kinds of knowledge which involve both reason and these specifically religious forms. If students are to make their own, autonomous, rational determinations regarding the claims of humanity's religious traditions and to participate fully in public discourse regarding fundamental questions of meaning and value they must, therefore, master the disciplines relevant to evaluating these claims. This is true whether one accepts, with Thomas, that theology is the noblest of the sciences or believes, with Harris, Dawkins, and Dennett, that it is simply nonsense.

Second, quite apart from our engagement with religious questions themselves, and whether or not the claims of humanity's religious traditions have truth value, whether religion makes man or man makes religion, *religion is a social fact*, an integral dimension of human social existence historically and in the present period. It is thus quite impossible to understand human society apart from understanding religion. And religion understood as a social fact is not studied in courses in philosophy.

Third, an engagement with religious questions has, in fact, been central to the development not only of the traditional sapiential disciplines but also to the modern humanities and social sciences—so central, in fact, that it is quite impossible to understand these disciplines without understanding their engagement with religious questions. In the case of philosophy and theology, of course, this is obvious. Both emerged out of the axial age as traditional, commonly accepted meanings were contested and became the object of deliberate and argument. But, as we noted above, modern hermeneutics derive largely from the renewed engagement with scriptural texts which came out of the Reformation. And it is not too much to say that sociology *began* as the sociology of religion. How could one understand the evolution of Emile Durkheim's thought without tracing the line of development from *The Division of Labor*, in which he celebrates the liberation which secularisation has made possible, through *Suicide*, in which he bemoans the egoism and anomie which it has engendered, up to the *Elementary Forms*, which analyses religion in a very sympathetic (if also still very non-theological way)? How can one understand Weber apart from his comparative historical study of religion or his Protestant ethic thesis? Indeed, whatever one things of his larger theory of religion, Marx's claim is literally true: 'The criticism of religion is the *premise* of all criticism'.[9] This is true for the committed secularist, but it is also true for the religious philosopher or theology whose very disciplines were constituted by an older critique of religion— that mounted by the Sophists, Caravakas, and Legalists.

If we find ourselves unable to teach 'critical thinking' effectively (or even to explain clearly what we mean by it), perhaps that it is because what we teach and how we teach it has become cut off from this critical engagement with religious questions, which is foundational for our entire intellectual tradition.

Religion in the Core

What aspects of religious studies do students need to study as part of the liberal arts core curriculum? The first and most important, I would like to suggest, is the historical-critical method used in the scholarly study of the sacred scriptures. This method is, in its broad outlines, simply an application of standard humanistic and social scientific methods (which largely grew out of it) to religious texts. It involves:

- analysing the canonical text in order to break it down into the component sources out of which it was composed (source criticism),
- analysing these sources in order to identify the specific forms of discourse involved (form criticism),
- identifying the social locations (both the specific religious or ritual context and the broader economic, political, and cultural context) in which these forms emerged, and assessing the their impact on the larger social systems of which they were a part (sociological criticism),
- tracing out the process by which these component texts were assembled into the canonical text, and analysing the social basis and political-theological valence of each stage of the process (redaction criticism and tradition history, sociologically informed), and
- making an argument regarding the theological significance of the text in the present period (hermeneutics).

An introduction to historical criticism shades, more or less seamlessly, into a study of the history of religious institutions and ideas. Indeed, the line between these two is, from a purely scientific standpoint, quite arbitrary, being defined by what the tradition in question identifies as canonical texts. Students should, as part of their liberal arts education, learn the history of humanity's principal religious institutions and ideas, treated *both* as social facts *and* as claims regarding fundamental questions of meaning and value, across *all* of humanity's principal civilizational traditions. Some of this material may, to be sure, be properly philosophical (e.g. the principal texts of the Buddhist, Confucian, or Taoist traditions, which make no claims regarding the revealed nature of their wisdom). But such texts are rarely studied in courses in philosophy in western institutions, and many philosophers are not prepared to teach them.

What is true of history, furthermore, is also true of the present period. Students need to study the way in which religion functions socially *and* the competing claims made by the great religious thinkers of our time (and their critics from secular and atheistic traditions).

This brings us, finally, to the task of teaching students how to make independent decisions regarding religious claims. This is a broad area which crosses the boundaries between the philosophy of religion and what the west calls theological reflection. Students need to master the principal arguments for and against the possibility of supra-rational knowledge, for and against the existence of God, for and against the idea that humanity is ordered toward transcendental ends (as well as the arguments for and against the various ways of defining such ends), and the arguments for and against humanity's principal strategies for realising such ends—or for making sense of life without them. This will entail not only extended philosophical training, but also a real engagement with debates *with* the various religious traditions.

'Wisdom Across the Curriculum' or Dedicated Core Requirements

None of this, to be sure, necessarily implies that dedicated courses in religious studies need to be part of the core curriculum. It would, at least in principle, be possible to address most if not all of the concerns I have raised in the context of courses in the various disciplines of the humanities or in an interdisciplinary humanities and social science core. And there are powerful reasons for approaching the problem in this way. On the one hand, I would argue, 'religious studies' is not a *discipline* but rather an interdisciplinary field. There *is* a discipline which is devoted exclusively to the study of religious questions—i.e. theology—but it plays only a limited role in the engagement with religious questions which I am suggesting for the liberal arts core curriculum. It would, in other words, be *possible* to address all of the questions which I have identified by weaving the treatment of religion into other core courses. Second, as I noted above, engagement with religious questions was foundational to the development of certain disciplines which already form part of the core: philosophy, hermeneutics, and sociology, for example. Engagement with religious questions in the context of core courses in these disciplines would enhance the study of those disciplines themselves.

This said, there are reasons to opt for a dedicated core requirement, at the very least as a supplement for engaging religion in core courses in the disciplines of the humanities and social sciences. The most important of these is the fact that religion plays very little role in the way the principal disciplines of the humanities and social sciences are currently taught at most research universities. Most sociologists and literary theorists—and even some philosophers—therefore, are at best only vaguely aware of the role that engagement with religious questions or religious texts played in the development of their disciplines, and they are simply not prepared to engage religious questions in the classroom.

Second, the principal disciplines of the humanities and social sciences (with the exception of philosophy), precisely because they are disciplines (clusters of techniques) rather than fields, are not naturally ordered to engagement with fundamental questions of meaning and value. There is thus a danger that even if religious texts or practices were engaged, religious *questions* would not be.

Ultimately it is probably a question of what a particular university's faculty brings to the table. An institution with a faculty which is conscious of the roots of many of the disciplines of the humanities and social sciences in engagement with religious questions, with philosophers who are interested in religious questions, and with the flexibility to draw theologians into interdisciplinary courses could probably do most of what I have argued for by integrating the discussion of religious questions into the broader curriculum. The viability of this option would, furthermore, be strengthened if an institution took what I have called a question-centred approach to the liberal arts, organising the curriculum around fundamental questions rather than around disciplines or texts.[10] Ironically, however, it is institutions with a strong religious heritage which are most likely to have a faculty capable of engaging religious questions throughout the core and the flexibility to organise the core in a way which facilitates this. Most public institutions—and many private research institutions—will engage religious questions (if they engage them at all) only in the context of a dedicated core requirement.

OBJECTIONS

There are, broadly speaking, two principal objections which have been made to the arguments presented in this paper. There are, first of all, those who, like Steven Pinker, argue that religion is not sufficiently important to deserve special treatment within the core. I believe that this claim has been answered adequately in the main body of this paper.

The second argument which is often presented against including the treatment of religious questions in the core, especially at public institutions, is that it blurs the line between church and state. This argument is made most often by secularists, though one sometimes hears it as well from fundamentalists who are concerned that the non-confessional study of religion will expose students to critical perspectives which they would rather they not engage.

This argument fails on two grounds. First, much of the engagement with religious questions we are recommending is literary, historical, and sociological rather than philosophical or theological. And even where we are arguing for philosophical or theological engagement with religious questions, the engagement we are looking for is critical and non-confessional. This means that, even if individual professors advocate a particular doctrine (as one would expect philosophers or theologians to do), the *institution* does not, and the curriculum must be structured in a way that ensures that students are required to engage seriously a variety of perspectives (preferably, at least at the introductory level, in each course).

Second, unlike France or Mexico, for example, the United States is not a *secularist* state, but rather a *disestablishmentarian* state. This is an important distinction. Religion is not officially relegated to the private realm in favour of a common secular national identity. Rather, there is a constitutional prohibition on the establishment of any one religion (or, for that matter, of religion generally). The American public arena is thus one in which many different perspectives on fundamental questions (religious and secular) contend with each other, renouncing not the right to advance their own claims but only the right to hegemony. The same is true of public institutions such as public colleges and universities. Indeed, I would suggest that the genius of the (admittedly quite accidental) American church/state settlement is that it creates the possibility of an entirely new kind of public arena, one *constituted* by dialogue regarding fundamental questions of meaning and value. Our public colleges and universities, if they are to realise their fully promise, must lead the struggle to create such an arena and to guide it once it develops.

CONCLUSION

Including religion in the core presents some powerful challenges, both to the secularist consensus which is dominant in the academy and to those for whom the only possible discourse on religion is a confessional discourse, and would rather religion be discussed within the idiom of their own tradition or not at all. Ultimately, however, *both* the enlightenment ideals of rational autonomy and democratic citizenship *and* the claim on the part of particular religious traditions to engage a broader public beyond their own boundaries require such an engagement. Universities must rise to this challenge or else find that the education they offer is no longer truly liberal and no longer speaks to our deepest aspirations as human beings.

NOTES

[1] Thomas Aquinas, *Summa Theologiae* I:1 a1, a5. Chicago: Encyclopaedia Britannica.

[2] Karl Marx [1843] (1978), 'Contribution to the Critique of Hegel's Philosophy of Right: Introduction' in *Marx-Engels Reader*. New York: Norton.

[3] See Sam Harris (2005), *The End of Faith*. New York: Norton; Richard Dawkins (2006), *The God Delusion*. New York: Houghton-Mifflin; Daniel Dennett, (2007), *Breaking the Spell: Religion as a Natural Phenomenon*. New York: Penguin.

[4] Karl Jaspers (1953), *The Origin and Goal of History*. New Haven: Yale University Press.

[5] Jerry Bentley (1993), Old World Encounters: Cross Cultural Contacts and Exchanges in Pre-Modern Times. New York: Oxford University Press.

[6] Anthony Mansueto and Maggie Mansueto (2005), *Spirituality and Dialectics*. Lanham, MD: Lexington Books.

[7] Randall Collins (1998), *The Sociology of Philosophies*. Cambridge, Massachusetts: Belknap Press.

[8] Harris, *The End of Faith*; Dawkins, *The God Delusion*; Dennett, *Breaking the Spell: Religion as a Natural Phenomenon*.

[9] Marx, 'Contribution to the critique of Hegel's Philosophy of Right: Introduction', p. 53.

[10] Anthony Mansueto (2006), 'A question-centered approach to the liberal arts', *Liberal Education*, 92(4), pp. 48–53.

Anthony Mansueto
President and Senior Scholar
Seeking Wisdom
2334 West Buckingham Road #230-146, Garland, TX 75042

CONSOLIDATED BIBLIOGRAPHY

Akenson, D. (2004). *Intolerance, the Ecoli of the mind.* Canberra: Humanities Research Centre, Australian National University.

Alexander, K., & Alexander, M. D. (2005). *American public school law* (6th ed.). Belmont, CA: Thomson West.

Allport, G. W. (1954). *The nature of prejudice.* Cambridge, MA: Addison-Wesley Pub. Co.

Ammerman, N (1991). North American protestant fundamentalism. In E. M. Martin & R. S. Appleby (Eds.), *Fundamentalisms observed.* Chicago: University of Chicago Press.

Ammerman, N. (1999). 'Human like us: Some philosophical implications of naturalising fundamentalism. *Australian Religion Studies Review, 12*(1), 5–17.

Anderson, W. T. (1995). *The truth about the truth: De-confusing and re-constructing the postmodern World.* New York: Tarcher/Putnam.

Aquinas, T. ([1272]1952). *Summa theologiae.* Chicago: Encyclopaedia Britannica.

Baer, R. A. (1998). Why a functional definition of religion is necessary if justice is to be achieved in public education. In J. T. Sears & J. C. Carper (Eds.), *Curriculum, religion, and public education: Conversations for an enlarging public square* (pp. 105–115). New York: Teachers College Press.

Barcan, A. (1980). *A history of Australian education.* Melbourne: Oxford University Press.

Barker, M. (1981). *The new racism, conservatives and the ideology of the tribe.* London: Junction Books.

Bentley, J. (1993). *Old World encounters: Cross cultural contacts and exchanges in pre-modern times.* New York: Oxford University Press.

Berlin, I. (1969). Two concepts of liberty. In I. Berlin (Ed.), *Four essays on liberty.* London: Oxford University Press.

Bobo, L. & Hutchings, V. (1996). Perceptions of racial group competition, extending Blumer's theory of group position to a multiracial social context. *American Sociological Review, 61*(9), 51–72.

Botterill, L. C. (2006). Leaps of faith in the obesity debate: A cautionary note for policy-makers. *The Political Quarterly, 77*(4), 493–500.

de Botton, A. (2004). *Status anxiety.* London: Hamish Hamilton, Penguin.

Bourdieu, P., & Passeron, J-C. (1979). *The inheritors, french students and their relation to culture.* Chicago: University of Chicago Press.

Bourne, W. O. (1870). *History of the public school society of New York with portraits of the Presidents of the society.* New York: WM Wood & Company.

Bowers, C. A. (1995). *Educating for an ecologically sustainable culture.* Albany, NY: State University Press.

Brasted, H. (2001). Contested representations in historical perspective, images of Islam and the Australian press 1950–2000. In S. Akbarzadeh & A. Saeed (Eds.), *Muslim communities in Australia.* Sydney: UNSW Press.

Bullock, A. (1970). *The rise of Islam.* London: Marshall Cavendish Books.

Butterfield, H. (1977). Toleration in early modern times. *Journal of the History of Ideas. 38*, 573–574.

Bowers, C. A. (2001). *Educating for eco-justice and community.* Athens, GA: University of Georgia Press.

Bynner, J., Romney, D., & Emler, N. (2003). Dimensions of political and related facets of identity in late adolescence. *Journal of Youth Studies, 63*, 319–335.

Cam, P. (1995). *Thinking together: Philosophical enquiry for the classroom.* Alexandria, NSW: Hale & Iremonger.

Campbell, R. (1991). *Truth and historicity.* Oxford: Clarendon.

Caputo, J. (Ed.). (1997). *Deconstruction in a nutshell: A conversation with Jacques Derrida.* New York: Fordham University Press.

Carper, J. C. (1998). History, religion, and schooling: A context for conversation. In J. T. Sears & J. C. Carper (Eds.), *Curriculum, religion, and public education: Conversations for an enlarging public square* (pp. 11–24). New York: Teachers College Press.

Cassandro, V. J., & Simonton, D. K. (2002). Creativity and genius. In C. L. Keyes & J. Haidt (Eds.), *Flourishing: Positive psychology and the life well-lived*. Washington, DC: American Psychological Association.

Claxton, G. (1997). *Hare brain Tortoise mind*. New York: Eco Press.

Collins, R. (1998). *The sociology of philosophies*. Cambridge, MA: Belknap Press.

Chesterman, M. (1979). *Charities, trusts and social welfare*. London: Weidenfeld and Nicolson.

Cheung, F. (2006). *Multiculturalism & education: An evangelical Christian reflection on multiculturalism and its implications for intercultural education*. Box Hill: PTC Media.

Code, L. (1995). *Rhetorical spaces. Essays on gendered spaces*. New York: Routledge.

Cohn-Sherbok, D., Cohn-Sherbok, L., & Halstead, M. (1997). Teaching about Judaism and Islam. In L. J. Francis & W. K. Kay (Eds.), *Religion in education* (pp. 191–214). London: Gracewing.

Coleridge, S. T. (1825). *Aids to the formation of a manly character*. London: Taylor and Hessey.

Cox, H. (1988). *Many mansions: A Christian's encounter with other faiths*. Boston: Beacon Press.

Csikszentmihalyi, M (1990). *Flow: The psychology of optimal experience*. New York: Harper-Perennial.

Dalai Lama. (1996). *Beyond dogma: Dialogues and discourses*. Berkeley, CA: North Atlantic Books.

Dal Pont, G. (2000). *Charity law in Australia and New Zealand*. Melbourne: Oxford University Press.

Davis, R., & Stimson, R. (1998). Disillusionment and disenchantment at the fringe, explaining the geography of the one nation party vote at the Queensland election. *People and Place, 6*, 69–82.

Dawkins, R. (2006). *The God delusion*. New York: Houghton-Mifflin.

Dennett, D. (2007). *Breaking the spell: Religion as a natural phenomenon*. New York: Penguin.

Derrida, J. (1981). Violence and metaphysics. In *Writing and difference* (A. Bass, Trans.). Chicago: University of Chicago Press.

Dewey, J. (1938). *Logic: The theory of inquiry*. New York: Henry Holt and Company.

Dewey, J. (1966). *Democracy and education*. New York: The Free Press.

Dewey, J. (1991). *How we think*. New York: Prometheus Books.

DiNoia, J. (1993). 'Teaching Differences. *Journal of Education, 73*(1), 61–68.

Doll, W. E., & Gough, N. (2002). *Curriculum visions*. New York: Peter Lang.

Douglass, S., & Dunn, R. (2002). Interpreting Islam in American Schools. In D. Hastings (Ed.), *Interpreting Islam* (pp. 76–98). London: Sage.

Driel, B. V. (2004). *Confronting Islamophobia in educational practice*. Stoke-on-Trent: Trentham.

Dunn, K. (2005). Australian public knowledge of Islam. *Studia Islamika, Indonesian Journal for Islamic Studies, 12*(1), 1–32.

Dunscombe, R. (2004). *Heinemann media 1. Units 1 and 2*. Port Melbourne: Heinemann.

Edwards, J., Knott, A., & Riley, D. (1979). *Australian schools and the law*. Sydney: LBC Information Services.

Elliott, R. K. (1974). Education, love of one's subject and love of truth. *Proceedings of the Philosophy of Education Society of Great Britain, VII*(1), 135–153.

Elliott, R. K. (1982). Objectivity and education. *Journal of Philosophy of Education, 16*(1), 49–62.

Falzon, C. (1998). *Foucault and social dialogue: Beyond fragmentation*. London: Routledge.

Feinstein, L., Hammond, C., Woods, L., Preston, J., & Bynner, J. (2003). *The contribution of adult learning to health and social capital*, WBL Research Report No. 8. London: Centre for Research on the Wider Benefits of Learning.

Fishbein, M., & Ajzen, I. (1975). *Belief, attitude, intention and behaviour*. Reading, MA: Addison-Wesley.

Flaskerud, J., & Nyamathi, A. (1990). Effects of an AIDS education program on the knowledge, attitudes and practices of low income black and Latina Women. *Journal of Community Health, 15*(6), 343–355.

Ford, H. A. J., & Lee, W. A. (1990). *Principles of the law of trusts*. North Ryde, NSW: Law Book Co.

Foucault, M. (1972). *The archaeology of knowledge*. London: Tavistock Publications.

Foucault, M. (1977). *Discipline and punish, the birth of the prison*. London: Allen Lane.

Fowl, S. E., & Jones, G. L. (1991). *Reading in communion: Scripture and ethics in the Christian life*. Grand Rapids, MI: Eerdmans.

Fowler, R. B. (1985). *Religion and politics in America*. Metuchen, NJ: Scarecrow Press.

Fraser, J. W. (1999). *Between Church and State: Religion and public education in a multicultural America*. New York: St. Martins Press.

Freire, P. (1970). *Pedagogy of the oppressed*. New York: Herder and Herder.

Gallagher, S. (1992). *Hermeneutics and education*. New York: State University of New York Press.

Gardner, H. (1993). *Frames of mind: The theory of multiple intelligences* (2nd ed.). London: Fontana Press.

Goleman, D. (2006). *Social intelligence*. London: Hutchinson.

Goleman, D. (1996). *Emotional intelligence*. New York: Bloomsbury.

Griffin, L. C. (2007). *Law and religion: Cases and materials*. New York: Foundation Press.

Gunton, C. E. (1994). *The one, the three and the many: God, creation and the culture of modernity*. Cambridge: Cambridge University Press.

Guth, L., Hewitt-Gervais, C., Smith, S., & Fisher, M. (2000). Student attitudes toward AIDS and homosexuality, the effects of a speaker with HIV. *Journal of College Student Development, 41*(5), 1–10.

Hacking, I. (1996). The disunity of sciences. In P. Gallison & D. Stump (Eds.), *The disunity of science*. Stanford, CA: Stanford University Press.

Hage, G. (1998). *White Nation: Fantasies of white supremacy in a multicultural society*. Annandale, VA: Pluto.

Hamilton, M. (2005). *God vs. the Gavel: Religion and the rule of law*. New York: Cambridge University Press.

Haraway, D. (1998). Situated knowledges: The science question in feminism and the privilege of the partial perspective. *Feminist Studies, 14*(3), 575–599.

Hardy, D. (1989). Created and redeemed sociality. In C. E. Gunton & D. W. Hardy (Eds.), *Being the Church: Essays on the Christian community*. Edinburgh: T & T Clark.

Harris, S. (2005). *The end of faith*. New York: Norton.

Hart, C. (2003). *Doing a literature review*. London: Sage Publications.

Hart, T. (2004). Opening the contemplative mind in the classroom. *Journal of Transformative Education, 2*(1), 28–46.

Hastings, D. (2002). *Interpreting Islam*. London: Sage.

Hegel, G. W. F. (1984/5). *Lectures on the philosophy of religion* (P. C. Hodgson, Ed.). Berkeley, CA and Los Angeles: University of California Press.

Hegel, G. W. F. (1975). *Lectures on the Philosophy of World History: Introduction* (H. B. Nisbet, Trans). Cambridge: Cambridge University Press.

Hill, M., & Augoustinos, M. (2001). Stereotype change and prejudice reduction, Short- and Long-Term evaluation of a cross-ultural awareness programme. *Journal of Community and Applied Social Psychology, 11*(4), 243–262.

Huntington, S. P. (1996). *The clash of civilizations and the remaking of World order*. New York: Simon and Schuster.

Huxley, A. (1998). Doors on the wall. In H. Palmer (Ed.), *Inner knowing*. New York: Penguin Putnam.

Jacobs, M. (1988). *The cultural meaning of the scientific revolution*. New York: Alfred A. Knopf.

Jackson, R. (1995). Religious education's representation of 'Religions' and 'Cultures'. *British Journal of Educational Studies, 433*, 272–289.

James, W. [1890] (1950). *Principles of psychology*. New York: Dover.

Janoff-Bulman, R. (1992). *Shattered assumptions: Towards a new psychology of trauma*. New York: The Free Press.

Jaspers, K. (1953). *The origin and goal of history*. New Haven, CT: Yale University Press.

Kabat-Zinn, J. (1990). *Full catastrophe living*. New York: Delta.

Kabat-Zinn, J. (2005). *Coming to our senses*. New York: Piatkus.

Kant, I. (1963). Idea for a Universal history from a cosmopolitan point of view (L. W. Beck, Trans.). Indianapolis, IN: Bobbs-Merrill.

Krishnamurti, J. (1997). *Krishnamurti: Reflections on the self*. In R. Martin (Ed.), Chicago: Open Court.

Kierkegaard, S. (1944). *Concluding unscientific postscript* (D. F. Swenson, Trans.). Princeton, NJ: Princeton University Press.

CONSOLIDATED BIBLIOGRAPHY

Kharem, H. (2004). The great European denial, the misrepresentation of the moors in Western education. In J. L. Kincheloe & S. Steinberg (Eds.), *The miseducation of the West, how schools and the media distort our understanding of the Islamic World*. Westport, CT: Praeger Publishers.

Kincheloe, J. L., & Steinberg, S. (2004). *The miseducation of the West, how schools and the media distort our understanding of the Islamic World*. Westport, CT: Praeger Publishers.

Kukathas, C. (2003). *The liberal archipelago: A theory of diversity and freedom*. Oxford: Oxford University Press.

Lamb, W. W. H. (1998/9). The open heaven: Understanding other faiths in God's World. In V. Pfizner & H. Regan (Eds.), *The task of theology today: Doctrines and Dogmas*. Adelaide: ATF (1998) and Edinburgh: T & T Clark (1999).

Lamb, W. W. H. (1998). Facts that stay put: Protestant fundamentalism, epistemology and orthodoxy. *Sophia, 37*(2), 88–110.

Laura, R. S., & Cotton, M. (1999). *Emphatic education*. Philadelphia: Falmer Press.

Laura, R. S., & Marchant, T. (2007). *Don't let technology steal you soul*. New York: University of America Press.

Laura, R. S., & Marchant, T. (2000). *Surviving the high tech depersonalisation crisis*. Wellers Hill: Godbold Publishing.

Leominster, G., & Costain, B. E. (2005). *The really big beliefs project*. Asia Education Foundation, and Australia. Dept. of Education Science and Training, 2005. Curriculum Corporation, Carlton.

Locke, J. (1924). *An essay concerning human understanding*. In A. S. Pringle-Pattison (Ed.), (abridged). Oxford: Oxford University Press.

Locke, J. (1966). *On the conduct of the understanding*. (F. W. Garforth, Ed.), New York: Teachers College Press.

Locke, J. (1968). *Epistola de Tolerantia* (J. W. Gough, Trans.). Oxford: Oxford University Press.

Lorenzen, T. (1999). Towards a Christian theology of religions: Christianity in dialogue with other faiths. In G. Garrett & W. W. H. Lamb (Eds.), *Postmodernism and theology. Interface, II*(1), 39–55.

Lyotard, J. F. (1981). *The postmodern condition: A report on knowledge* (G. Bennington & G. Massumi, Trans.). Minneapolis, MN: University of Minnesota Press.

Macedo, S. (1995). Liberal civic education and religious fundamentalism: The case of God v. John Rawls. *Ethics, 105*(3), 468–496.

Machen, G. (1925). *What is faith?* New York: Macmillan.

MacIntyre, S., & Clark, A. (2004). *The history wars*. Melbourne: Melbourne University Press.

Mansueto, A. (2006). A question centered approach to the liberal arts. *Liberal Education, 92*(4), 48–53.

Mansueto, A., & Mansueto, M. (2005). *Spirituality and dialectics*. Lanham, MD: Lexington Books.

Marino, G. (2004). Before teaching ethics, stop kidding yourself. *The Chronicle Review, 50*(24), B5. Retrieved from http://chronicle.com

Marty, M. E. (1992). Fundamentalisms compared. In *The 1989 Charles strong memorial lectures*. Adelaide: Flinders University Press.

Martin, M. W. (2007). *Everyday morality*. Belmont, CA: Thompson/Wadsworth.

Marx, K. [1843] (1978). Contribution to the critique of Hegel's philosophy of right: Introduction. In R. Tucker (Ed.), *Marx-Engels reader*. New York: Norton.

Marx, K., & Engels, F. (1998). *The German ideology, including theses on Feuerbach and Introduction to the critique of political economy*. Amherst, NY: Prometheus Books.

Marsden, G. M. (1991). *Understanding fundamentalism and evangelicalism*. Grand Rapids, MI: Eerdmans.

McFague, S. (1997). *Super, natural Christians: How we should love nature*. Minneapolis, MN: Fortress Press.

McLeish, S. (1992). Making sense of religion and the constitution: A fresh start for section 116. *Monash University Law Review, 18*(2), 207–236.

McMillan, R. C. (1984). *Religion in the public schools: An introduction*. Macon, GA: Mercer University Press.

Mendus, S. (1989). *Toleration and the limits of liberalism*. Basingstoke: Macmillan.

Mill, J. (1971). *The principles of toleration*. New York: Burt Franklin.

Morris, D. (1996). *Schools: An education in charity law*. Aldershot: Dartmouth Publishing Company.

Moruzzi, N. C. (1994). A Problem about headscarves: Contemporary complexities of political and social identity. *Political Theory, 22*(4), 653–672.

Mouw, R. J., & Griffioen, S. (1993). *Pluralisms and horizons*. Grand Rapids, MI: Eerdmans.

Murdoch, I. (1970). *The sovereignty of good*. London: Routledge and Kegan Paul.

Neto, F. (2006). Changing intercultural attitudes over time. *Journal of Intercultural Communication, 12*.

Neuhaus, R. J. (1984). *Naked public square: Religion and democracy in America*. Grand Rapids, MI: Eerdmans.

Newbigin, L. (1991). *Truth to tell: The gospel as public truth*. Grand Rapids, MI: Eerdmans.

Nielsen, N. (1993). *Fundamentalism, mythos and World religions*. Albany, NY: State University Press.

Nussbaum, M. (2003, Winter). Compassion and terror. *Daedalus*, 10–26.

Peters, R. S. (1972). Reason & Passion. In R. F. Dearden, P. H. Hirst, & R. S. Peters (Eds.), *Education and the development of reason*. London: Routledge & Kegan Paul.

Pettigrew, T., Jackson, J., Ben Brika, J., Lemaine, G., Meertens, R., Wagner, U., et al. (1997). Outgroup prejudice in Western Europe. *European Review of Social Psychology, 8*, 241–273.

Plato. (1992). *The Republic*. London: J. M. Dent.

Poulter, S. (1997). Muslim headscarves in schools: Contrasting legal approaches in England and France. *Oxford Journal of Legal Studies, 17*(1), 43–74.

Poynting, S. (2002). Bin Laden in the suburbs, attacks on Arab and Muslim Australians before and after 11 September. *Current Issues in Criminal Justice, 14*(1), 43–64.

Puls, J. (1998). The wall of separation: Section 116, the first amendment and constitutional religious guarantees. *Federal Law Review, 26*(1), 139.

Ramsay, I. M., & Shorten, A. R. (1996). *Education and the law*. Sydney: Butterworths.

Rawls, J. (1993). *Political liberalism*. Columbia: University Press.

Rawls, J. (1999). The idea of an overlapping consensus. In S. Freeman (Ed.), *John Rawls: Collected papers*. Harvard: Harvard University Press.

Raz, J. (1986). *The morality of freedom*. Oxford: Clarendon Press.

Rifkin, J. (1985). *Declaration of a heretic*. New York: Routledge and Kegan Paul.

Riley-Taylor, E. (2002). *Ecology, spirituality, and education: Curriculum for relational knowing*. New York: Peter Lang.

Rilke, R. M. (2001). *Letters to a young poet* (M. Stephen, Trans.). New York: Modern Library.

Rogers, C. (1961). *On becoming a person*. New York: Houghton Mifflin.

Rorty, R. (1995). Ironists & Metaphysicians. In W. T. Anderson (Ed.), *The truth about the truth: De-confusing and re-constructing the postmodern World*. New York: Tarcher/Putnam.

Russo, C. J. (2006). Prayer and religious activities in American public schools. In J. L. Martinez Lopez-Muniz, J. De Groff, & G. Lauwers (Eds.), *Religious education in public schools: Study of comparative law*. Dordrecht, The Netherlands: Springer.

Said, E. (1981). *Covering Islam, how the media and the experts determine how we see the rest of the World*. New York: Pantheon Books.

Said, E. (1995). *Orientalism*. New York: Penguin.

Seligman, M. E. P. (1998). 'What is the "Good Life"?' President's column. *APA Monitor, 29*(10), 2.

Seligman, M. E. P., & Csikszentmihalyi, M. (2000). Positive psychology: An introduction. *American Psychologist, 55*, 5–14.

Shorten, A. (2005). Toleration and cultural controversies. *Res Publica, 11*, 275–299.

de Silva, P. (2006). The Tsunami and its aftermath in Sri Lanka: Explorations of a Buddhist perspective. *International Review of Psychiatry. 18*(3), 281–287.

de Silva, P. (2002). *Buddhism, ethics and society: The conflicts and dilemmas of our times*. Clayton: Monash Asia Institute.

Silverman, M. (1992). Deconstructing the nation: Immigration, racism and citizenship in modern France. London: Routledge.

Snyder, C. R., & Lopez, S. J. (2002). *The handbook of positive psychology*. New York: Oxford University Press.

CONSOLIDATED BIBLIOGRAPHY

Solomon, R. C. (2007). *True to our feelings*. Oxford: Oxford University Press.
Soskice, J. M. (1992). The truth looks different from here. In H. Regan & A. J. Torrance (Eds.), *Christ and context*. Edinburgh: T & T Clark.
Tannen, D. (1998). *The argument culture*. London: Virago Press.
Thomson, C., Currie, C., Todd, J., & Elton, R. (1999). Changes in HIV/AIDS education, knowledge and attitudes among Scottish 15–16 year olds, 1990–1994, findings from the WHO, health behaviour in school-aged children study HBSC. *Health Education Research, 14*(3), 357–370.
Troyna, B., & Griffiths, M. (1995). *Antiracism, culture and social justice in education*. British Educational Research Association. Stoke-on-Trent: Trentham Books.
Troyna, B., & Williams, J. (1986). *Racism, education, and the state*. London: Croom Helm.
Wegela-Kissel, K. (2002). Contemplative psychotherapy. *Ordinary mind, an Australian Buddhist review, 21*.
Westphal, M. (1996). *Becoming a self: A reading of Kierkegaard's concluding unscientific postscript*. West Lafayette, IN: Purdue University Press.
White, S. (1991). *Political theory and postmodernism*. Cambridge: Cambridge University Press.
Wittgenstein, L. (1953). *Philosophical investigations*. London: Blackwell.

CASES CITED

Ashfield Municipal Council v Joyce (1978). AC 122.
Attorney-General (Vic); ex rel Black v Commonwealth (1981). 146 CLR 559.
Board of Education of Central School District No 1 et al. v. Allen, Commissioner of Education of New York, et al. 392 U.S. 236 (1968).
Board of Education of the Westside Community Schools v. Mergens. 496 U.S. 226 (1990).
Brandon v. Board of Education of the Guilderland Central School District. 487 F. Supp. 1219 (1980).
Brown v. Gilmore. 533 U.S. 1301 (2001).
Carbery v Cox. (1852). 3 Ir Ch R 231.
Central Bayside General Practice Association Ltd v Commissioner of State Revenue. (2006). 228 CLR.
Cochran et al. v. Louisiana State Board of Education et al. 281 U.S. 370 (1930).
Commissioner of Education v. School Committee of Leyden, 358 Mass. 776 (1971).
Commissioners for Special Purposes of the Income Tax v Pemsel. (1891) AC 531.
Committee for Public Education & Religious Liberty, et al. v. Nyquist, Commissioner of Education of New York, et al. (1973).
Committee for Public Education & Religious Liberty, et al. v. Regan, Comptroller of New York, et al. 444 U.S. 646 (1980).
Doe v. School Board of Ouachita Parish. 274 F.3d 289 (2001).
Elk Grove Unified School District and David W. Gordon, Superintendent v. Michael A. Newdow et al. 542 U.S. 1 (2004).
Engel et al. v. Vitale et al. 370 U.S. 421 (1962).
Everson v. Board of Education of the Township of Ewing, et al. 330 U.S. 1 (1947).
Fountain Centre Christian School Incorporated v Harrington. (1990). 53 SASR 361.
Funnell v Stewart. (1996). 1 All ER 715.
Good News Club, et al. v. Milford Central School. 533 U.S. 98 (2001).
Grace Bible Church Inc v Reedman. (1984). 54 ALR 571.
Holden, J., et al. v. Board of Education of the City of Elizabeth, Union County. 46 N.J. 281 (1966).
Lee, R. E., individually and as Principal of Nathan Bishop Middle School, et al. v. Daniel Weisman etc. 505 U.S. 577 (1992).
Lemon v Kurtzmann. 403 US 602 (1971).
Lemon et al. v. Kurtzman, Superintendent of Public Instruction of Pennsylvania, et al. 411 U.S. 192 (1973).
Levitt, Comptroller of New York, et al. v. Committee for Public Education & Religious Liberty, et al. 413 U.S. 472 (1973).
McCollum, Illinois ex Rel. v. Board of Education of School District No. 71, Champaign County, Illinois, et al. 333 U.S. 203 (1948).

Minersville School District, Board of Education of Minersville School District, et al. v. Gobitis et al. 310 U.S. 586 (1940).

Mitchell v. Helms. 530 U.S. 793, (2000).

Mueller et al. v. Allen et al. 463 U.S. 388 (1983).

Oppenheim v Tobacco Securities Trust Co Ltd. (1951) AC 297.

Pierce, Governor of Oregon, et al. v. Society of Sisters: Pierce, Governor of Oregon et al. v. Hill Military Academy. 268 U.S. 510 (1925).

The Queen v Ligertwood. (1982). 30 SASR 328.

Re Compton. (1945). Ch 123.

Re Hawkins. (1906). 22 TLR 521.

Re Income Tax Acts (No 1). (1930). VLR 211.

Re Michel's Trusts. (1860). 28 Beav 39; 54 ER 280.

Santa Fe Independent School District v. Jane Doe, Individually and as next friend for her minor children, Jane and John Doe, et al. 530 U.S. 290 (2000).

School District of Abington Township, Pennsylvania, et al. v. Schempp et al., heard with Murray et al. v. Curlett et al. 374 U.S. 203 (1963).

State of Maryland et al. v. Lundquist etc, 262 Md. 534 (1971).

Verge v Somerville. (1924). AC 496.

Wallace v. Jaffree. 472 U.S. 38 (1985).

West Virginia State Board of Education et al. v. Barnette et al. 319 U.S. 624 (1943).

Widmar et al. v. Vincent et al. 454 U.S. 263 (1981).

Wolman et al. v. Walter et al. 433 U.S. 229 (1977).

Zelman v. Simmons-Harris. 536 U.S. 639 (2002).

Zorach et al. v. Clauson et al., Constituting the Board of Education of the City of New York, et al. 343 U.S. 306 (1952).

OTHER SOURCES

AAP. (2007, February 26). Hanson announces election bid. *Sydney Morning Herald.*

Albrechtsen, J. (2002, July 17). Blind spot allows barbarism to flourish. *The Australian.*

Australian Bureau of Statistics, Schools, Australia, 4221.0. (2006).

Australian Bureau of Statistics. (2006). *1301.0 —Year book Australia, religious affiliation.* Canberra: ABS.

Australian Government, Department of Education, Employment and Workplace Relations. (2003). *National framework for values education in Australian schools.* Retrieved September 2, 2009, from http://www.curriculum.edu.au/values/val_nine_values_for_australian_schooling,14515.html

Australia Institute. (2004). *The accountability of private schools to public values.* Discussion Paper Number 71.

Australian Taxation Office Tax Ruling. (2005). Income tax and fringe benefits tax: charities. TR 2005/21.

Community Relations Commission and Principles of Multiculturalism Act 2000 (NSW). (2000). Australian Government, Department of Education, Employment and Workplace Relations, Civics and Citizenship Education. Retrieved September 2, 2009, from http://www.civicsandcitizenship.edu.au/cce/default.asp?id=9500

Christian Democratic Party. (2007). *No more Muslims - Press release.* Retrieved September 30, 2007, from http,//www.cdp.org.au/fed/mr/0703010f.asp

Council for the Australian Federation. (2007). *Federalist paper 2, the future of schooling in Australia.* Melbourne: Council for the Australian Federation.

Daily Telegraph. (2007). Multiculturalism in Australia. *Daily telegraph.* [online]. Retrieved September 30, 2007, from http,//www.news.com.au/dailytelegraph/index/0,22045,5009120,00.html

Daily Telegraph. (2006). Muslims show no tolerance for the tolerant - Your comments. *Daily telegraph.* Retrieved September 30, 2007, from [online]. http,//blogs.news.com.au/dailytelegraph/piersakerman/index.php/dailytelegraph/comments/muslims_show_no_tolerance_for_the_tolerant/

CONSOLIDATED BIBLIOGRAPHY

Department of Education, Science and Training. (2007). *Values education for Australian schools.* Retrieved September 30, 2007, from http,//www.valueseducation.edu.au/values/values_homepage,8655.html

Department of Immigration and Citizenship. Retrieved from http://www.harmony.gov.au

Education (Accreditation of Non-State Schools) Act 2001 (Qld).

Education and Training Reform Act 2006 (Vic).

Education Act 1915 (SA).

Grimshaw, W. (2003). *Review of non-government schools in NSW: Report 1,* (the '*Grimshaw Report 1'*. New South Wales Government.

Income Tax Assessment Act 1997 (Cth) Division 50

Jackson, R. (2004). *Intercultural education and religious diversity, Interpretive and dialogical approaches from England.* Global Meeting on Teaching for Tolerance, Respect and Recognition in Relation with Religion or Belief, Oslo, 2–5 September.

Keskin, Z. (2007). *The voice of Turkish women in Australia today compared to yesterday, an analysis by a second generation Turkish woman,* presented at immigrants as citizens conference, University of Sydney, October 6–7.

Kleg, M. (1970). *Race, caste, and prejudice, the Influence of change in knowledge on change in attitude.* Unpublished PhD thesis, Athens, GA: University of Georgia.

Maiden, S. (2004, August 3). Doomsday cult wins federal cash. *The Australian.*

Maiden, S. (2004b, August 4). Cult's school investigated. *The Australian.*

Maiden, S. (2004c, August 7). Education grants keep the faith. *The Australian.*

Ministerial Council on Education, Employment, Training and Youth Affairs. (1999). *The adelaide declaration on national goals for schooling in the twenty-first century.* Adelaide: MCEETYA.

Ministerial Council on Education, Employment, Training and Youth Affairs. (2000). *National statement of principles and standards for more culturally inclusive schooling in the 21st century.* Canberra: MCEETYA.

Ministerial Council on Education, Employment, Training and Youth Affairs. (2000). *Model of culturally inclusive and educationally effective schools.* Canberra: MCEETYA.

Omar, W., Hughes, P. J., Allen, K., & Australian Bureau of Immigration Multicultural and Population Research. (1996). *The Muslims in Australia.* Canberra: Australia Govt. Pub. Service.

Pew Research Centre. (2006). *Conflicting views in a divided World.* Washington, DC: The Pew Global Attitudes Project.

Refshauge. A. (MP). (2004). Minster for Education and Training, NSW Parliamentary Papers (Hansard), Legislative Assembly, 18 February 2004. Education Amendment (Non-Government Schools Registration) Bill Second Reading. Hansard.

Rout, M. (2007, July 28). Questions about Steiner's classroom. *Sydney Morning Herald.*

Sautelle, C. J. (2005, August). Theory of knowledge. Essay addressing the question: Discuss the idea of values and the challenge of setting forth values for all Australian schools.

Sheppard, I., Fitzgerald, R., & Gonski, D. (2001). *Report of the inquiry into the definition of charities and related organisations.* Australian Commonwealth Government.

Teachers and Schools Registration Act 1905 (Vic).

UNESCO. (1995). *Declaration of principles on tolerance.*

Zimmerman, R., Langer, L., Starr, R., & Enzler, N. (1991). *Evaluation of theory-based high school AIDS education, impact of teacher vs. peer-led and active vs. passive education, and an HIV awareness campaign.* Paper presented at the International Conference on AIDS, June 16–21.

CONTRIBUTORS

Peter Balint is a lecturer in Politics at The University of New South Wales, The Australian Defence Force Academy, Canberra. He has published on the principles for diversity in liberal societies, in particular the concepts of respect and toleration, and the role of national identity in the maintenance and formation of social cohesion. In 2010 he was awarded a Fellowship to the Justitia Amplificata Centre for Advanced Studies, University of Frankfurt. He is a founding member of the Global Justice Network, and an editor of *Global Justice: theory practice rhetoric.*

Philip Cam is an associate professor and senior visiting fellow, School of History and Philosophy at the University of New South Wales. He is currently President of the Asia-Pacific Philosophy Education Network for Democracy, and has written several books related to philosophical inquiry for children, some of which have been widely translated. He has edited a series of books for UNESCO, including *Philosophy, Democracy and Education* (UNESCO, 2003). He has also published in philosophy of mind, with reference to the work of Dennett, Fodor, and Searle.

Amy K. Chapman is a teacher in the New South Wales Catholic Education System. She has completed a Bachelor of Arts and Bachelor of Teaching (Hon). She is also currently writing her doctoral thesis: 'A Critical Exploration of the Epistemological Foundations of Mental Health and their Implications for Reconceptualising the Importance of the Role of Teaching in the Enhancement of the Mental Health of Adolescents'.

Elizabeth Burns Coleman is a lecturer in Communications for the School of English, Communications and Performance Studies at Monash University. She was co-convener and co-editor, with Kevin White and Maria-Suzette Fernandes Dias, of the series conferences on Negotiating the Sacred, including *Blasphemy and Sacrilege in a Multicultural Society, Blasphemy and Sacrilege in the Arts Medicine, Religion and the Body,* and *Governing the Family.* She has published widely on ethics of archaeology and anthropology, cultural appropriation and indigenous arts. Her books include *Aboriginal Art, Identity and Appropriation,* (2005).

Winifred Wing Han Lamb teaches Philosophy and English at Narrabundah College in the Australian Capital Territory and is a visiting fellow in Philosophy at the Australian National University. She holds PhDs in Philosophy and Theology. She is author of *Living Truth and Truthful Living: Christian Faith and the Scalpel of Suspicion* (2004), and co-editor (with Marian de Souza) of *Children, Adolescents and Spirituality* (2007).

Ronald S. Laura is professor of Education at the University of Newcastle and a Perc Fellow of Harvard University. He has published over 200 scholarly articles and 30 books including: *Empathetic Education* (1999), *Surviving the High Tech*

Depersonalisation Crisis (2002) and *Integrating Eastern and Western Traditions in Health* (2004). He teaches in both the faculties of Education and Arts, offering subjects in the Philosophy of Education, Philosophy of Medicine and Public Health.

Anthony Mansueto is a scholar of religion with roots in social theory, philosophy, and theology. He holds a Ph.D. in Religion and Society from the Graduate Theological Union in Berkeley (1985) and is the author of *The Death of Secular Messianism: Religion and Politics in an Age of Civilizational Crisis* (Cascade 2010), *Spirituality and Dialectics* (with Maggie Mansueto, Lexington 2005), as well as four other books. His articles have appeared in leading scholarly journals such as the *Journal of Religion* and *Filosofskie Nauki*, as well as important journals of public opinion such as *Commonweal* and *Tikkun*. He is currently president and senior scholar at Seeking Wisdom, a non-profit, non-partisan, interfaith research, education, and organising institute. He teaches for the University of Mary, Central Michigan University, and Excelsior College.

Susan Mendus is professor of Political Philosophy, University of York.. She was Morrell Fellow in Toleration at York from 1985 to 1988, and from 1995 to 2000 she was Director of the Morrell Studies in Toleration Programme. She was elected a fellow of the British Academy in 2004. Her publications include: 'Innocent before God: Politics, Morality and the Case of Billy Budd' in *Philosophy* (2006); 'Choice, Chance and Multiculturalism', in Paul Kelly (ed.) *Multiculturalism Reconsidered*, Polity Press (2002); and 'Tolerance and Recognition: Education in a Multicultural Society', *Journal of Philosophy of Education* (1995). Professor Mendus delivered the 2007 Freilich Foundation lectures on the theme of "Religious Toleration in an Age of Terrorism".

James T. Richardson is director of the Judicial Studies Program, a faculty member of the Interdisciplinary Social Psychology Doctoral Program and professor of Sociology at the University of Nevada, Reno. His books include *Regulating Religion: Case Studies from Around the Globe* (Kluwer, 2004), and some of his most recent publications are 'The Sociology of Religious Freedom' (*Sociology of Religion,* 2006) and 'Religion, Constitutional Courts, and Democracy in Former Communist Countries' (*The Annals of the American Academy of Political and Social Science,* 2006). He also published on treatment of minority religions in Australia and New Zealand.

Pauline Ridge is a qualified barrister and solicitor in the ACT Supreme Court and a senior lecturer at the Australian National University College of Law. Her research interests include religion and law. She is author of *A Safe Place for Children – Care, Protection and Safety of Children in the Uniting Church in Australia*, Uniting Church Press, Melbourne (1999) Her articles include: 'The Financing of Religion: Guidelines for Legal Regulation', *Adelaide Law Review* (2009), 'The Legal Regulation of Religious Giving, (2006) *Law and Justice*, and 'Equitable Undue Influence and Wills' (2004) *Law Quarterly Review.*

Janice R. Russell is a doctoral student in Social Psychology, University of Nevada, Reno.

Padmasiri de Silva is a research associate of the School of Philosophical, Historical and International Studies and Center for Religion at Monash University. He was formerly professor and head of Philosophy and Psychology, Peradeniya University, Sri Lanka. He has held visiting positions at the University of Pittsburgh, the National University of Singapore and University of Waikato. His publications include, *Introduction to Buddhist Psychology*; *Environmental Philosophy and Ethics in Buddhism*; *Buddhism, Ethics and Society* and *Explorers of Inner Space.*

Kevin White is a reader in Sociology at the Australian National University. He has held appointments at Flinders University in South Australia, Wollongong University, and the Victoria University of Wellington, New Zealand. He was co-convener and co-editor, with Elizabeth Burns Coleman, of *Negotiating the Sacred I: Blasphemy and Sacrilege in a Multicultural Society* and *Negotiating the Sacred III: Medicine, Religion and the Body.* His other books include *An Introduction to the Sociology of Health and Illness,* (second revised edition 2009), *The Sage Dictionary of Health and Society* (2006), *The Early Sociology of Health and Illness* (2001) and, with A. Greig, F. Lewins, *Inequality in Australia* (2004).

Joel Windle is a lecturer in Education at Monash University. His publications include numerous book chapters and articles on equity and education including (co-authored with A. Ata) 'The Role of Australian Schools in Educating Students About Islam and Muslims: A National Survey', in Abe Ata (ed.) *Us and Them. Muslim-Christian Relations and Cultural Harmony in Australia,* (2009), 'Influences on the written expression of bilingual students: teacher beliefs and cultural dissonance' in J. Miller et. al., *Culturally and Linguistically Diverse Classrooms: New Dilemmas for Teachers* (2009).

INDEX

CPSIA information can be obtained at www.ICGtesting.com
Printed in the USA
BVOW031204080312

284675BV00002B/39/P